Translator Self-Training Portuguese

Practical Course in Technical Translation

Morry Sofer

Library of Congress Control Number: 2002105649
ISBN 1-887563-71-7

Printed in the U.S.A. by Schreiber Publishing, PO Box 4193, Rockville, Maryland 20849
www.schreiberpublishing.com

Preface

This practical course is for anyone who would like to pursue technical translation in Portuguese and English, in such areas as legal, medical, financial or other kinds of non-literary documents (literary translation is a different discipline from technical).

The course is based on the practical experience of a major translation company which has been translating—routinely and successfully—Portuguese-into-English and English-into-Portuguese documents in all technical areas for almost twenty years. The assignments in this book are taken from real-life documents which were translated by this company, with names and other information changed in some cases to protect proprietary information.

This book grew out of a correspondence course offered about ten years ago, which became a three-ring binder program for translator's self-training five years ago. During those five years, hundreds of translators have used this program each year, and many have offered unsolicited praise for this program, letting us know that it has improved their translation skills, and in more than a few cases helped the user pass accreditation or certification tests for such organizations as the American Translators Association (ATA).

Nothing sharpens translation skills more than the actual act of translating. But one needs an entry point, either into the technical translation field in general, or into new areas of translation, if one has already been doing one kind of technical translation, such as legal. This course provides the entry point.

We at Schreiber Publishing take a personal interest in translators in all languages and subjects, and are always happy to hear from you.

Enjoy the course!

Morry Sofer

Table of Contents

INTRODUCTION

Welcome to the **Translator Self-Training / Portuguese**. We are very pleased you selected this program, which has been in use since 1990. It has helped aspiring translators around the country get their start in this exciting field, while assisting practicing translators in improving their translation skills. Translation is one of the fastest growing professions in today's world, as different languages and cultures are coming closer together every day. Whether you wish to pursue translation full-time or as a sideline, you will find it to be a highly challenging and quite profitable occupation. The purpose of the following exercises is to help you improve your skills as a translator of Portuguese and English.

This program is designed to help you work at your own pace and gain experience through translation practice assignments. These assignments, excerpted from actual translation jobs, were selected to help you determine your own level of comfort and expertise, so that you may go on from there to choose the type of translation work you may like to pursue.

To derive the maximum benefit from these texts, you should carefully read the General Comments, the guidelines, and the specific notes which discuss each assignment. Every comment and every guideline represents years of experience in professional translation work. By carefully following this program, you will be able to achieve *in just a few days* what has taken others years to learn. You will be guided through many of the pitfalls of translation, taught how to avoid them, shown shortcuts in accomplishing a complex piece of translation work, and be given the benefit of comments designed to show you how to produce a translation acceptable to major clients such as government, industry, the legal world, and many more.

Before you read further, we strongly urge you to read Appendix A: Requisites for Professional Translators, and Appendix B: Translation Techniques.

The above-listed Appendices will give you a good overview on how translation work is to be approached and practiced, and how to position yourself in the translation market. Try to keep the contents of these two sections in mind as you translate the following assignments.

You are presented with four different texts, which, for most people, represent an increasing level of difficulty (although if you happen to be a lawyer, for example, it is possible that you will find the second assignment the easiest of the four). They are:

1. **General**
2. **Legal**
3. **Chemical/Medical**
4. **Business/Finance**

At a minimum, you may want to do the first and second assignments. Those two represent a vast body of material which is being translated in the United States on a regular basis, but which does not require a highly specialized vocabulary or technical background. The third assignment requires access to chemical and medical terminology, which can be managed by any intelligent translator. The fourth assignment should be approached with caution. Here one must have an understanding of the world of finance, which not all of us do. For your own self-assessment, you may want to try it (since we provide you with the translation, you can compare the results and see for yourself how you did). But if you find it too difficult, don't be discouraged. It is clearly not for everyone.

We hope you enjoy working with these texts, and we urge you to please be patient with yourself. One does not become an accomplished translator overnight. To learn, one must make mistakes. If your heart is in it, and if you love the challenge of working with two languages you happen to know well, then you are sure to get a great deal out of this program.

A Word about Portuguese Translation

Portuguese is a language spoken by close to 200,000,000 people around the world. The great majority of these people live in Brazil, while only some 10,000,000 live in Portugal itself. Most documents translated from Portuguese into English or vice versa originate in Brazil. Brazilian Portuguese differs from European Portuguese in several respects, including several sound changes and some differences in verb conjugation and syntax. Example: object pronouns occur before the verb in Brazilian Portuguese, but after the verb in European Portuguese. Brazilian Portuguese seems to be developing at a faster rate than its progenitor, and the gap between the two continues to grow. This impacts on the work of the translator, who has to be aware of the differences between the two.

The volume of Portuguese translation in the English-speaking world is not nearly as large as, say, German or Spanish. Nevertheless, Portuguese is one of the world's major languages, and the need for Portuguese translation is considerable. Certainly there is always a need for Portuguese freelancers, if only on a part-time basis, and there are indeed people who have successfully pursued full-time careers as Portuguese translators in places like England and the U.S. But clearly their numbers are not legion. As a general rule, if one happens to know Portuguese and has a flair for translation, it is certainly worthwhile to sharpen one's translation skills. If, on the other hand, one chooses to major in Portuguese in an American college or university with a view to making Portuguese translation a career, one should first examine the range of opportunities.

The following comments are offered with two purposes in mind: the immediate purpose is to help you with the assignments. The long-term purpose is to serve as reference material for actual translation work. Keep them for future use.

A reminder:

The "source language" is the language you translate from.

The "target language" is the language you translate into.

Every language has its own "personality," so to speak. When you translate, pretend you are two different persons - an "Portuguese Person" and an "English Person." The Portuguese Person reads the original Portuguese text, and becomes familiar with it. The Portuguese Person then turns to the English Person, and says to him/her, "Okay, now it's your turn to say the same thing your way." Now the English Person takes over, and starts writing the same text in English. You will be constantly switching back and forth between the Portuguese Person and the English Person, as the first checks the Portuguese word, phrase, sentence structure, and then the second thinks in English and comes up with the right equivalents. Here are some of the main language issues you will have to deal with:

Clarity

We each have our own personal style of expressing ourselves - in any language. Some people make their point clearly and succinctly, while others use more words than necessary, including esoteric words, to make their point. The same holds true in translation. You can translate the phrase,"*amigo-da-onça*" as "unreliable friend," or you could also translate it correctly as, "A friend you can never rely on." In the first instance, only two words were used; in the second, seven. Most of the time, the first type of translation is better, because it is simpler and more readily understandable. Make it your point to pursue simplicity whenever possible.

Consistency

Most of the time, if you start out translating the word "*casa*" as "house," stick to "house," and don't start suddenly shifting to "building," or vice versa. The reader may become confused, wondering why the word suddenly changed. Generally in English, building is bigger than house, and one may wonder whether the dimensions of that particular structure might have changed. If you are familiar with word-processing you know how easy it is to do a "global search and replace" throughout the text, so that if halfway into the document you decide that "building" is better than "house," then go back to the beginning and do a global change, replacing the word "house" with "building."

Sentence Structure

It is difficult, yet very important, to ensure that sentence structure is correct and makes sense, yet still retains the flavor of the original text, particularly if this is written in a flowery, elaborate, or otherwise unique style. This fine line is achieved mainly through practice, but it is definitely helpful to read the original several times before even beginning the translation process in order to gain a good idea of the author's style.

It is not necessary to follow the structure of a sentence literally. A run-on sentence which may make sense in one language may not make sense in the other, and therefore should be divided into two sentences (or more). The converse is also true. You should also avoid being too literal when it comes to word order, or your text will sound stilted, awkward, and artificial. You will need to rely on your own good writing skills in determining the most sensible word order and punctuation so that your translation flows smoothly.

Format

Format should be followed as closely as possible. Ideally, every page of translation should look exactly like the corresponding page of the original, except, of course, for the language. There is a very practical reason for this. It helps the reader, who may or may not know the source language, compare the two texts, make sure all the parts are there, and check a particular word or phrase in the source text. This, however, is not always possible, since a page of translation at times is longer than the same page in the source language. Nevertheless, every effort should be made to keep the format as similar as possible to the original.

Terminology

The use of the right terminology is critical in any translation, especially in any technical subject. Here the right kind of dictionaries and reference literature becomes very critical. Keep in mind, however, that dictionaries, no matter how good, are never complete, and do not provide all the answers. The other source of information is people who work in the field the particular translation covers. Their input is often more valuable than that of the dictionary, since they are the ones who work in the field and represent the potential readers of your translation.

The first thing to keep in mind about terminology - as was discussed before - is consistency. If you translate a word a certain way, do not change in the middle of the text to another synonym of the same word, even though it may be accurate. This will throw the reader off. The second thing is to make sure you are using the right terms, rather than trying to approximate them. Keep a list of those terms to maintain consistency throughout the document, and also for future use. If you continue to translate in the same technical field, these lists will become your most valuable translation tool.

Numbers

The use of commas and periods is reversed in numbers over 1000 (1,000 in English becomes 1.000 in Portuguese), and in decimals (0.5 in English, becomes 0,5 in Portuguese). This is one example of cultural differences which must be closely observed.

Punctuation

Quotation marks are appropriate in English, but this is not always so in Portuguese. Punctuation in general is not always used in the same places. These are just a few examples of how even a highly accurate translation will not always mirror its original text. You will often be called upon to be the judge, which involves a combination of excellent writing skills, knowledge of rules of grammar and punctuation, plus common sense.

Errors in the Source Text

Sometimes you will find that the original has errors, such as a misspelling where it is clear by the context that the author intended to say "*dom*" and not "*do*," or the sequence in a series of numbered clauses is wrong, or a name that has been in uppercase letters suddenly appears as lowercase, for no apparent reason. You can do a number of things in situations such as these. You can go ahead and make the correction and leave it at that. You can translate the text as is, and use the term [sic] after the error, to alert the reader. Or you can make a translator's note on a separate sheet of paper. Ultimately, the client will have to decide what to do with it.

Untranslatable Words or Terms

You may run into a word, a term or a phrase which cannot be translated, or which should be left in the original language (such as, for instance, "bossa nova"). If there is a need to explain it, it can be done in a footnote or in parentheses (or brackets, which makes it clearer that the bracketed text is not part of the original) following the word (bossa nova [popular Brazilian dance of the 1960s]). As a general rule, however, it is best not to burden your translation with footnotes or parenthetic or bracketed text.

In Conclusion

The above notes are by no means exhaustive. They do not cover all the issues facing a translator. Language is not mathematics. Keep this in mind, and do the best translation job you possibly can.

1. We are providing you with an Portuguese text and an English translation of that same text. Pretend you don't have the English translation. If you read it before you do the assignment, you will not be able to do an honest job, and you will not derive the benefit of learning from your own mistakes.

2. Read the Portuguese text once for general comprehension. Underline any difficult words or passages.

3. As you start the translation process by reading the text for the first time (see 2., above), keep track of time, so that when you finish you will know how long it took you to translate the text. This is very critical, because you want to increase your translation speed as you go along. The rule is simple: The more words you translate per hour, the more money you will make. A very low hourly word-count can earn you less than minimum wage, which is not at all desirable. (Note: The hours indicated at the top right hand corner for each assignment include two numbers. The first is for beginners while the second number is for an experienced translator. Therefore, an assignment that would take a beginner 5-7 hours to complete might take an experienced translator 2 hours. The timeframe includes research, draft, and final copy.)

4. Read it again. This time make a list of difficult words, and make any notes regarding things you need to clarify about the text (e.g., look up something in an encyclopedia to better understand some concept or piece of information).

5. Try to determine which dictionaries and reference books you need for this assignment, get hold of them, and keep them nearby.

6. Now you are ready to start translating. Preferably, you will be using a computer. If this is too intimidating, write it out the first time. It will take longer, but you will have more time to think. Remember, your objective is to translate on computer, not in longhand. These days, if you want to earn money translating, you have to submit text on disk. There are hardly any exceptions to this requirement.

7. Do a draft translation. Go over the draft. Do the best you can to make the English sound like good, clear, correct English, which does not sound like Portuguese, and does not retain any Portuguese forms in either style, format, or any technical points. Be sure you did not omit anything. Ask yourself if you succeeded in conveying the correct sense of every idea and every word in the source text. Be sure you are comfortable with every single word you chose in English, and that you have no doubts or hesitations. If, after all this, you do have some questions, do not worry. No one expects you to do perfect work the first time around. You will do better next time.

8. Now that you have accomplished your translation, figure out the time it took you to reach your final version (including all the previous steps - namely, first reading, research, draft, and final copy).

9. Make a list of the words, passages, and concepts in the text where you encountered difficulty, and keep for future reference. This kind of record keeping will help you improve your performance, and serve as a reminder not to repeat the same mistake twice.

10. Print out your corrected and edited text.

1. Turn to the English translation in Section 3, and compare it to yours. Next read the notes concerning the pitfalls and salient points of this text very carefully, and see how they compare to your own experience with the text. They may not necessarily coincide with everything you experienced personally, but they do provide you with some tips on the do's and don'ts of technical translation.

2. The most important thing for you to keep in mind as you compare your translation to the one in Section 3, is that there is no one absolutely correct way of translating a text. Many words can be translated in more than one way. Many sentences can be structured in more than one way. Many ideas can be conveyed in different words. In fact, your translation may turn out to be just as good, and in some spots even better than the one in the book.

3. Keep track of the shortcomings of your translation. The areas you are interested in are the following:

    Omissions - did you fail to translate any particular word or phrase, or even paragraph?

    Format - does your format follow the original (breaking into paragraphs, for instance)?

    Mistranslations - did you mistranslate any particular word?

    Unknown words - were there any words you were not able to translate?

    Meaning - did you miss the meaning of any particular phrase or sentence?

    Spelling - did you misspell a word?

    Grammar - did you make any grammatical mistakes?

    Punctuation - did you mispunctuate or miss any punctuation marks?

    Clarity - did you fail to clearly convey the meaning of any particular part of the text?

    Consistency - did you call something by one name, and then by another without good reason?

Cognates - were you "tripped" by a word in the source text, whereby you mistranslated it because it looked the same, though it changes meaning in the target language (for instance, the word "actual" exists in both English and Portuguese, but means two different things)?

Style - are you satisfied with the way your translation reflects the style of the original (for example, the original is written in a clear, direct style, while the translation sounds more complex and indirect)?

These are some of the questions you have to ask yourself. As you go on to translate other texts, always keep these questions in mind as you self-assess your translation. By improving your performance in the above areas, you are on your way to becoming an accomplished translator.

Part One

Translation: Portuguese into English

Custos e administração num hospital brasileiro

O Instituto Materno-infantil de Pernambuco (IMIP) é um hospital particular sem fins lucrativos, criado em 1960 para atender à área metropolitana do Recife. Em 1992, foi o primeiro hospital brasileiro a receber o prêmio do UNICEF, em reconhecimento ao tratamento que dispensa às crianças, sobretudo promovendo o aleitamento materno. Noventa e cinco por cento da receita do IMIP provêm de contratos com o Instituto Nacional de Assistência Médica e Previdência Social (INAMPS), órgão do Ministério da Saúde do Brasil. A despesa anual gira em torno de US$6 milhões.

Desde 1989, o sistema contábil adotado pelo IMIP divide os serviços entre 11 "centros de custo", tendo em vista o resultado final. Nesse resultado final são computados serviços de apoio como administração, lavanderia, alimentação, raios-X, laboratório, transporte e outros. O cômputo é proporcional à utilização medida ou estimada.

Os custos médios do IMIP têm de equiparar-se às suas reitas médias, determinadas pelo esquema de preços do INAMPS, que visa mais a tratamento de grupos que ao atendimento individual. Se algum "centro de custo" for deficitário, o superávit de outro compensará o déficit. Chegam ao hospital crianças gravemente doentes, transferidas de todo o Nordeste do Brasil. Registram-se por dia três óbitos infantis. No intuito de reduzir a mortalidade, o IMIP criou uma unidade de tratamento pediátrico intensivo. No entanto, o custo dos tratamentos é muito superior ao que o INAMPS poderia pagar. E não houve redução de mortalidade. Mesmo sem terem sido feitos cáculos de eficácia em termos de custo, era evidente que um número maior de crianças se salvaria se a unidade de terapia intensiva fosse desativada (exceto para recém-nascidos) e outros serviços recebessem mais atenção. Morriam no hospital crianças que já chegavam muito doentes e quase sempre com desnutrição grave. Por isso, talvez fosse mais eficaz em termos de custo tentar identificar primeiro os casos mais graves e tratá-los mais cedo. Adotou-se então a estratégia de ampliar a rede de pequenos postos de saúe comunitários nas favelas da periferia do Recife. O primeiro desses postos começou a funcionar em 1983; em 1986, a mortalidade infantil nessas áreas já caíra de 147 para 101 óbitos por mil nascimentos.

A experiênca do IMIP oferece três lições acerca da prestação de atendimento básico de um modo eficaz em termos de custos. A primeira é a possibilidade de maior eficiência de alocação, mesmo sem e dispor de informações completas; os médicos conhecem bem os resultados e não raro só precisam conhecer melhor os custos. A segunda é que tais mudanças ficam mais fáceis se houver autonomia: considerando-se que os serviços particulares costumam ter bem mais autonomia que os públicos, pode-se pleitear com boa base que a iniciativa privada financie mais serviços públicos, ou então que os sistemas públicos sejam descentralizados. A terceira lição é que se pode decidir sobre que tipo de atendimento prestar, mesmo quando os preços não se baseiam em critérios de eficácia em termos de custo. Para o governo, é mais conveniente estabelecer os preços corretos do que tentar fazer todas as opções de alocação de verbas.

Reforma do sistema russo de saúde

Antes dos distúrbos politicos de 1990/91 que provocaram a desintegração da URSS, os 3-4% do PNB que a república russa gastava com o atendimento médico dos seus quase 150 milhões de habitantes eram financiados pela receita do governo geral, sendo esse atendimento prestado por uma vasta rede de serviços, programas e funcionários públicos. Esse sistema, altamente centralizxado e burocrático, produziu um número excessivo de médicos e hospitais. pouco incentivava a eficiência ou a prestação de atendimento de boa qualidade, e descuidava das medidas preventivas necessárias ao combate dos mais graves problemas ambientais e de comportamento do país: poluição industrial, dependêcia em relação a bebidas alcoólicas e fumo, e má nutrição. Conseqüentemente, as condições de saúde do povo russo estagnaram durante as décadas de 70 e 80. Em 1990, a expectativa entre os cidadãos do sexo masculino era de apenas 64 anos, 10 anos menos que na Europa ocidental, e a taxa de mortalidade infantil, de 22 para cada mil nativivos, era o dobro da média da Europa ocidental.

O novo governo russo vem promovendo várias reformas fundamentais no velho sistema soviético de saúde. O financiamento e a administração da área da saúde estão sendo descentralizados e entregues a 88 regiões. Grande parte da prática médica está sendo privatizada, enquanto uma lei recente sobre seguro de saúde introduz e regulamenta novas formas de seguro. Nos termos dessa lei e das emendas propostas, cada região terá um findo de seguro social, enquanto um fundo nacional garantirá a igualdade de recursos entre regiões. Esses fundos de seguro receberão um misto de deduções compulsórias em folha de pagamento e transferências de verbas do governo a partir da receita pública geral. Assinarão contratos de atendimento de saúde com fornecedores públicos e privados. Os cidadãos poderão adquirir voluntariamente um seguro privado complementar para cobertura de serviços adicionais de saúde.

A legislação do seguro de saúde está em vigor desde o final de 1991, mas sua implementação tem sido lenta. Certos aspectos importantes do projeto do sistema ainda não estão resolvidos - entre eles o papel e o grau de concorrência entre seguradoras públicas e privadas; a questão de se os riscos devem ser classificados em base individual ou entre grupos maiores de indivíduos; e como os fundos de seguro pagarão os fornecedores, ou seja, em uma base de taxa por serviço prestado, capitação, ou pro algum outro método ou combinação de métodos.

Os obstáculos práticos à implementação do novo sistema são enormes, em parte devido à incerteza reinante no contexto administrativo e econômico. Os governos regionais não dispõem capacidade de administrar e regulamentar o sistema de saúde que estão herdando. A economia e o orçamento do governo estão submetidos a graves pressões. Os salários reais caíram drasticmente nos últimos anos. Os custos de medicamentos e equipamentos aumentaram acima da inflação, causando grave escassez. Os ijmpostos sobre folhas de pagamento, destinados a cobrir benefícios de empregados, já absorvem 38% dos salários, tornando difícil finciar um pacote razpáve; de servoços de saúde através do sistema de seguridade social. Para ajudar a resolver tais problemas, vários órgãos internacionais, inclusive o Banco Mundial, vêm trabalhando em íntima cooperacão com as

autoridades russas no projeto e implantação de reformas na política de saúde.

word count: 1060

Advogados
Henri Yutaka Yamagata
Raimundo Rodrigues Fonseca

Procuração "Ad-Judicia"

palo presente instrumento de procuração, nomeia_____e constitui_____ seus bastante procuradores os advogados Dr. Henri Yutaka Yamagata, OAB/SP 83.624 - CIC/MF 135.819. 968/04, e Dr. Raimundo Rodrigues Fonseca, OAB/SP 28.625 - CIC/MF 058.540.248/53, com escritório à Rua Vilalobos, 123 - Vila Caterina - CEP 05433 fones

555-5955 e 555-5588, a quem confere amplos poderes para a fôro em geral, com cláusula ad-judicia, em qualquer juizo, instância ou Tribunal, podendo propor contra de direito as ações competentes a defendé-nas contrárias, seguindo umas e outras, até final decisão, usando os recursos legals acompanhando-os, conferindo-lhes, ainda, poderes especiais para conferir, desistir, transigir, firmar compromissos ou accordos, promover abertura de sucessão, assinar compromissos de inventariante, impugnar inventariantes, aceitar ou não avaliações, prestar contas, requerer sobrepartilha, receber e dar quitações, agindo em conjunto ou separadamente, podendo ainda substabelecer esta em outrem com ou sem reservas de iguais poderes, dando tudo por bom, firme e valioso.

São Paulo,   de   de 19

Contrato de Prestação de Serviços

Contratante: Chiu Mei Shiang ou mei Shiang Chi espolio representada pala Inventariante Chi Kow Mei RS. 3.877.552CIC636.922.958.C4 brasileire, separada, funcionária pública, residente nasta capital à Rua Vasco da Gama, 456 fone 555-4629

Contratados: Dr. Raimundo Rodrigues Fonseca, inscrito na OAB/SP 28 625 CIC/MF 058.540.248/53 e Dr. Henri Yutaka Yamagata, inscrito na OAB/SP 83624 CIC/MF 135.819.968/04, brasileiros, casados, advogados, com escritório à Rua Vilalobos, 123 - Vila Caterina SP, CEP 05433 - Fones 555-5955 e 555-5586, contrata como contratado tem para prestar serviços juridicos no que couber, sob as cláusulas e condiçoes segintes:

1.ª)   Pelos serviços prestados na área juridica o(s) contratante(s) compromete-se a pagar aos contratados a quantia de Cr$ 5.000,00 (cinco mil reeis) paçavel ⅓ am 30.11.95 e o saldo em contra entrego de Formal de Partilha a titulo de honorários advocaticios, mais as despesas de custas, taxas, locomoção, seja de taxi ou veiculo próprio a que vale dizer gasolina, estacionamento, etc., bem como refeição e hospedagem paara problemas fora da Capital de S.P.

2.ª)   Nos casos em que ocorrer sucumbência, estas se reverterão em beneficios dos contratados nos têrmos do artigo 99 § 1.ª da lei 4.215/63.

3.ª)   Este contrato é celebrado por prazo indeterminado, tendo início em 17/11/95, contudo, se uma das partes desejar rescindi-lo, deverá comunicar por escrito a outra, com um prazo minimo de trinta dias do recebimento da comunicação.

4.ª)   Se a rescisão partir da Contratante, os honorários serão devidos integralmente independente do estado em que se encontra o processo.

5.ª)   Em havendo necessidade dos contratados ingressarem em juizo para fazer valer seus direitos, a ação competente será Execução contra devedor solvente, embassada no item II do artigo 585 CPC, sendo este instrumento titulo de divida.

6.ª)   Se os contratados, substabelecerem a procuração ad-judicia por ordem dos contratante(s), estes se responsabilizarão pelos honorários contratados.

7.ª)   Os valores contratados, sofrerão sempre juros de mora de 1% ao mês mais correção monetária nos termos da lei 6.899/81, se não forem pagos no prazo estabelecido.

8.ª)   As partes elegem o foro da Capital de S. Paulo Regional de Pinheiros, para dirimir qualquer pendências oriundas deste instrumento, dispensando qualquer outro.

9.ª)   Considerando, que o desempenho da advocacia é de maios, não de resultado. Assim, os honorários serão devidos no caso de êxito, ou não, da demanda ou do desfecho do assunto tratado.

        E por estarem justos e contratados, as partes assinam o presente instrumento em duas vias de igual teor, perante as testemunhas abaixo.

São Paulo, 22 de novembro de 1995

_____[signature]

Contratante

_____[signature]

Contratado

Testemunhas

_____

_____

word count: 622

ANÁLISE E ESPECIFICAÇÃO DOS CIRCUITOS DO TOKAMAK ETE

O Plasma

•Introdução a Fisica de Plasmas

O termo Plasma na fisica foi utilizado pela primeira vez por dois fisicos americanos, *Langmuir* e *Tonks* no ano de 1923, quando estudavam oscilações de cargas no espaço, e deram o nome deste estudo de oscilações de plasmas.

A palavra plasma vem da medicina onde e utilizada para apontar perturbação ou estado não distinguivel. Denominou-se plasma a parte coagulavel do sangue, onde não se sabia exatamente o que era.

O Plasma é um conjunto de particulas carregadas e neutras que satisfazem determinados critérios, e são chamados de conjunto quasi-neutro de particulas. Os elétrons e ions constituem o plasma e são produzidos através de ionização de átomos e moléculas, a recombinação dos elétrons e ions, faz com que o plasma emita radiação, que pode wr visivel ou não. Se a radiação for no espectro visivel, a cor da luz emitida pelo plasma vai depender do tipo de gás utilizado, po exemplo o hidrogènio a cor do plasma e azul.

O Plasma só se forma em condições especiais, aqui na superficie da Terra, não é possivel obter plasma sem que este esteja confinado, isto é possivel em càmaras de vácuo, muito utilizado em laboratórios de estudos de plasma. Devido a força gravitacional da terra ser fraca para reter o plasma, não é possivel mantè-lo continada por longos periodos como acontece no sol, o so, assim como todas estrelas que emitem luz e o centro do planeta Terra se encontram no quarto estado da matéria. Na ionosfera terrestre, temos o surgimento da Aurora Boreal, que é um plasma natural, assim como fogo.

O objetivo da fisica de plasma é o estudo de sistemas gasosos ionizados e macroscopicamente neutro. São sistemas compostos de por um grande número de particulas carregadas, distribuidas dentro de um volume (macroscópio) onde haja a mesma quantidade de cargas positivas e negativas.

Este meio recebe o nome de *Plasma*, e foi chamado pelo fisico inglès *W. Clux* de o quarto estado fundamental da metéria, por conter propriedades diferentes do estado gasoso, liquido e sólido. Esta relação acontece da sequinte forma: ao adicionarmos calor ao sólido este se transforma em liquido, se adicionarmos mais calor, este se transforma em gás e se aquecermos este gás a altas temperaturas, obtemos o plasma. Sendo assim se colocarmos em ordem crescente conforme a quantidade de energia que a matéria possui teremos:

SOLIDO - LIQUIDO - GASOSO - PLASMA

•**Conclusão**

A maior dificuldade encontrada foi devido a alta potência a ser utilizada no Tokamak. Ficou impraticável a utilização de chaves de fabricação nacional, devido ao elevado I^2t nas chaves, que dependem dos bancos de capacitores, e é mas problemático no banco lento que no rápido. Desta forma, utilazamos equipamentos importados, como ignitrons para o circuito do transformador ôhmico e tiristores e diodos de potência para o circuito da bobina de campo toroidal. Todos os bancos de aspscitores até agora específicados, são eletroliticos e de fabricação nacional.

A mesma análise não pode ser feita para circuito ôhmico devido a um efeito fisico não esperado. Pois o disparo do banco C2, enviava correnta para a chave S1, isto dificulta a abertura da chave. no circuito deve ser considerado a utilização de outros edispositivos que ajude na abertura desta chave, podendo ser utilizado um indutor saturado, capacitor de abertura ou um vacum break.

Para a compreensão fisica dos circuitos foi necessário o entendimento do funcionamento do Tokamak bem como as caracteristicas fisicas do plasma. O trabalho realizado foi acompanhado pelo meu orientador, Dr. Edson Del Bosco e pelo eng. eletricista Osvaldo Rossi. Ambos deram bases e conceitos para que o trabalho fosse realizado da forma prevista.

DESCRIÇÃO DO FUNCIONAMENTO DO SISTEMA DE ENERGIZAÇÃO DO CECI

1   INTRODUÇÃO

CECI é um dispositivo de geometria toroidal no qual se estuda o confinamento magnético de plasma. Um conjunto de bobinas toroidal, poloidal e vertical é utilizado para geração deste campo de confinamento.

Aqui descreveremos os circuitos eletrônicos envolvidos nas construções dos aparatos necessários para a acionamento destas bobinas. na parte final do relatório descrever-se-á também o circuito de pré-ionização do plasma.

O diagrama de blocos da Fig. 1.1 mostra todas as partes constituintes do sistema de energização no CECI.

O campo toroidal é gerado por corrente DC, portanto, constante com o tempo. uma fonte de 30V/600A fornece corrente contínua à bobina toroidal que é refrigerada para se evita superaqueciemtno.

Os campos poloidal e vertical são pulsados, necessitando de bancos de capacitores que, após serem carregdos, são descarregados nas respectivas bobinas, por um circuito de gatilhamento.

6   COMENTÁRIOS E CONCLUSÕES

O sistema de energização do dispositivo CECI é constituiído por circuitos de construção simples.

Quase na sua totalidade, exceto fonte DC 30V/600A, construído no próprio LAP (Laboratório Associado de Plasma) a baixíssimo custo.

Em se tratando de um sistema pulsado, a circuitaria envolvida é de pequeno porte, o que constitui grande vantagem em termos de custo e manutenção.

Todo o aparato eletrônico descrito é necessário para realização de descargas indutivas no CECI, dispositivo de confinamento magnético com geometria toroidal, que possibilita a obtenção de configurações Tokamak, RFP (Reversed Field Pinch) e Ultra Low Q (das quais as duas últimas são possíveis alternativas para fusão nuclear frente aos Tokamaks).

word count: 874

-REDUÇÃO DE SUBSÍDIOS PARA GRUPOS MAIS ABASTADOS. Os governos devem reduzir e finalmente eliminar os subsídios públicos oferecidos a grupos relativamente afluentes. Isso ode ser feito cobrando-se preços que cubram interiamente os custos, no caso de pessoas seguradas que usem hospitais do governo e recorram a clínicas para obtenção de serviços não incluídos no pacote nacional de serviços essenciais, e reduzindo-se as deduções de ipostos referentes a contribuições de seguro. Na África do Sul e no Zimbábue, indivíduos cobertos por seguro privado pagam menos que o custo total dos serviços que recebem na rede pública de saúde. Além disso, podem deduzir da renda bruta uma parte ou o total de seus gastos com tratamento de saúde. Também os empregadores podem deduzir suas contribuições ao seguro de saúde. Todos esses métodos reduzem as quantias disponíveis para financiamento de serviços essenciais. Na África do Sul, calcula-se que as deduções de impostos de pessoa física em 1990 equivaleram a 18% dos gastos do governo na área da saúde. Em recente esforço no sentido de revrter situação semelhante, o Zimbábue limitou fortemente as deduções de impostos referentes a tratamento a seguro de saúde, aumentou as taxas cobradas e intensificou a cobrança de taxas de pacientes com seguro privado. Os hospitais do governo sabem que, quase sempre, podem identificar pacientes segurados oferecendo-lhes comodidades não-médicas extras, tais como quartos particulares e, caso aceitem, fazer através deles uma agressiva recuperação de custos.

Em paises nos quais o seguro social cobre apenas parte da população, o governo pode ampliar o autofinanciamento dos serviços de saúde eliminando os subsídios públicos ao seguro social. Esses subsísidios, muito freqüentes na América Latina, beneficiam principalmente as classes médias e são, portanto, regressivos. Sua eliminação liberaria recursos que poderiam ser usados em serviços de saúde para os pobres. Além disso, a eliminação de tais subsídios imporia maior disciplina financeira aos órgãos de seguridade social, os quais freqüentemente registram déficits que, mais tarde, são cobertos por transferências de outros programas de seguro social ou do orçamento do governo geral. Na Venezuela, por exemplo, o governo subsidia contribuições ao fundo de assistência médica do órgão parestatal de seguridade social. Em 1990, apesar desse subsídio, o fundo registrava um déficit equivalente a 37% do total de seus gastos com a saúde.

AMPLIAÇÃO DO SEGURO. Nos casos em que o groso do contingente de mão-de-obra já está empregado, qualquer medida tomada pelo governo para ampliar a cobertura do seguro de modo a estendê-lo ao resto da pupulação - inclusive autônomos, idosos e pobres - contribui para corrigir as desigualdades inerentes aos sistemas de saúde que fazem distinção entre classes e para expandir o conteúdo do pacote de assistência oferecido a todos. Quando a cobertura do seguro se torna universal, como na Coréia e na Costa Rica, os subsídios terminam beneficiando os pobres e são, portanto, progressivos. Mas somente alguns países de renda média que dispõem dos recursos financeiros, da vontade política e da capacidade administrativa necessários poderão atingir essa cobertura universal de seguro. A ousada iniciativa coreana, de criar do nada um sistema nacional de seguro de saúde entre 1978 e 1989, bem como os esforços empreendidos pela Costa Rica, nos anos 80, no sentido de universalizar um sistema que, até então, cobria somente o contingente de mão-de-obra industrial demonstram que esse ojetivo é difícil porém viável. Seria mais fácil realizar a cobertura univerasal se o governo limitasse o pacote essencial àqueles serviços segurados que fossem altamente eficazes do ponto de vista de custos.

OPÇÃO PARA O CONSUMIDOR. A concorrência entre fornecedores de um pacote de serviços de saúde, claramente especificados e previamente pagos, contriguiria para melhorar a qualidade e aumentar a eficência. E mesmo quando existe pouca ou nenhuma concorrência direta entre as seguradoras, como no Japão e na Coréia, pode ainda ser melhor ter várias instituições de seguro semi-independentes do que apenas um único grande órgão parestatal. Fundos de seguro locais, como existem na Alemanha, geridos por uma diretoria composta de representantes de empregados, empregadores e governo local, costumam ser mais responsáveis perante os segurados. Em vários países latino-americanos, os gigantescos "institutos" de seguridade social já estão bastante desacreditados em virtude da ineficiência e da corrupção demonstradas no passado. Dois dos principais objetivos da reforma do seguro social que vem sendo proposta na Argentina são maior concorrência e maior responsabilidade.

CONTENÇÃO DE CUSTOS. A cotização de certos serviços entre os segurados pode contribuir para limitar o uso dos mesmos, mas não costuma ser um método muito eficaz de contenção de custos. Na Coréia, esse sistema de cotização chega a responder por uma média de 40% do total das despesas, mas pouco tem ajudado a reduzir a taxa de aumento dos gastos com a saúde, que cresceram de 3,7% para 6,6% do PNB nos anos 80. Da mesma forma, a prática, introduzida por seguradoras privadas norte-americanas, de analisar retrospectivamente a utilização da assistência médica aparentemente produz apenas uma modesta economia esporádica de despesas com a saúde, mas não tem efeitos duradouros sobre a taxa de aumento das mesmas.

Em contraposição, o pagamento antecipado dos prestadores de assistência médica é um método promissor de contenção de despesas com a saúde. Os governos podem ajudar a promover tais esquemas eliminando os obstáculos jurídicos que, em muitos países, impedem que a mesma instituição seja, al mesmo tempo, seguradora e prestadora. Recentemente, o governo da África do Sul decidiu permitir a criação de organizações de manutenção de saúde (ORMS), principalmente como forma de conter os gastos com a saúde. Mais de 20 dessas organizações, criadas em poucos anos, introduziram a capitação e o sistema de taxas negociadas - dois meios mais eficazes de limitar os custos que o sistema de pagamento em aberto por serviço prestado, tradicionalmente empregado na África do Sul.

Há muitas medidas que os governos podem tomar para melhorar o sistema de incentivos criado pelo seguro social. Quando os segurados utilizam prestadores de serviços privados, os esquemas de taxa por serviços prestado devem ser substituídos por uma alternativa - capitação ou taxas uniformes, negociadas anualmente, para médicos e hospitais (com base em tipos de procedimentos para determinados diagnósticos, por exemplo), ou orçamentos preestabelecidos para os hospitais. Quando o seguro social cobre serviços prestados por hospitais do governo, a concorrência com o setor privado pode contribuir para melhorar o desempenho. Outros métodos promissores são permitir que os hospitais do governo concorram entre si como empresas semi-autônomas, como vem acontecendo no Reino Unido nos últimos anos, e oferecer aos administradores dos hospitais incentivos financeiros e de carreira para o cumprimento de metas de desempenho, como no Chile.

O caso do Chile (Box 7.2) é um exemplo dos benefícios e riscos da reforma do setor de saúde em um país de renda média. O Chile conseguiu aumentar a eficiência, melhorar a qualidade da assistência e criar opções para o consumidor, mas as reformas criaram também novos problemas de administração, financiamento e eqüidade.

word count: 1152

Cost information and management decisions in a Brazilian hospital

The Instituto Materno-Infantil de Pernambuco (IMIP) is a private, nonprofit hospital founded in 1960 to serve the metropolitan area of Recife. In 1992 it received the first UNICEF award to a "child-friendly" hospital in Brazil in recognition of its work, particularly in the promotion of breastfeeding. IMIP depends for 95 percent of its revenue on contracts from the Instituto Nacional de Assistência Médica e Previdência Social (INAMPS) of Brazil's Ministry of Health. Annual spending runs about $6 million.

Starting in 1989, IMIP organized an accounting system that divides services according to eleven cost centers for final output. Administrative, laundry, food, radiology, laboratory, transport, and other nonfinal services were assigned to these final outputs in proportion to their measured or estimated use.

IMIP must match its average costs to average revenues determined by the price schedule of INAMPS, which is organized by treatment groups rather than by individual services. Losses in any cost center must be offset by surpluses elsewhere. Gravely ill children are referred to the hospital from all over northeast Brazil, and there are three infant deaths per day among them. To reduce mortality, IMIP created a pediatric intensive care unit. The treatments provided, however, cost much more than INAMPS would pay. And mortality did not decline. Even without cost-effectiveness calculations, it was evident that closing the intensive care unit (except for newborns) and strengthening other services would save a greater number of children's lives. In particular, since the children who died in the hospital typically arrived very sick and often severely malnourished, it appeared more cost-effective to try to find high-risk children and treat them earlier. The strategy used was to expand the network of small community health posts in the slum neighborhoods of Recife. IMIP opened the first such posts in 1983; by 1986 infant mortality in those neighborhoods had fallen from 147 to 101 per 1,000 births.

The experience of IMIP illustrates three lessons about cost-effective delivery of essential care. One is that allocative efficiency can be improved without complete information: medical professionals know much about outcomes and often need only to know more about costs. A second lesson is that autonomy facilitates such changes: since private facilities generally have much more autonomy than public ones, this is an argument for more public finance of private provision or for decentralization of public systems. The third lesson is that even prices that are not based on cost-effectiveness criteria can guide decisions about what care to provide. It is more useful for government to set those prices correctly than to try to make all the allocative choices.

Reform of the Russian health system

Before the political upheavals of 1990-91 that led to the breakup of the Soviet Union, the 3 to 4 percent of GNP that the Russian republic spent on health care for its nearly 150 million inhabitants was financed from general government revenues and delivered through a vast network of public facilities, programs, and employees. This highly centralized and bureaucratic system led to excessive numbers of doctors and hospitals. It gave few incentives for efficiency or for providing quality care, and it neglected the preventive measures needed to combat the country's most serious environmental and behavioral problems: industrial pollution, alcohol and tobacco dependency, and poor nutrition. Consequently, the health status of Russians stagnated during the 1970s and 1980s. In 1990 life expectancy for Russian men was just sixty-four years, a full ten years less than in Western Europe, and the infant mortality rate, at twenty-two per 1,000 live births, was twice the Western European average.

The new Russian government has pursued several fundamental reforms of the old Soviet health system. Health financing and management are being decentralized to eighty-eight regions. Much medical practice is being privatized, and a recent health insurance law provides for the introduction and regulation of new forms of insurance. Under the law and its proposed amendments, each region is to have a social insurance fund, and a national fund will equalize resources across regions. These insurance funds will receive a combination of compulsory payroll deductions and budget transfers from general government revenues. They will sign contracts for care with public and private providers. Individuals can then voluntarily purchase supplementary private insurance to cover additional health services.

The health insurance legislation has been in effect since late 1991, but progress in implementing it has been slow. Some important issues in the design of the system still need to be resolved. These include the role and extent of competition among public and private insurers; whether risks are to be rated on an individual basis or across larger pools of individuals; and how the insurance funds will pay providers - on a fee-for-service basis, through capitation, or by some other method or combination of methods.

The practical obstacles to the implementation o the new system are formidable, partly because of the unsettled administrative and economic environment. The regional governments lack the capacity to manage and regulate the health system they are inheriting. The economy and the government budget are under severe strain. Real wages have fallen dramatically in the past few years. The costs of drugs and equipment have increased faster than inflation, leading to serious shortages. payroll taxes to cover employee benefits already absorb 38 percent of wages, making it difficult to finance an affordable package of health services through the social insurance system. To help overcome these problems, a number of international agencies, including the World Bank, are working closely with Russian health officials on designing and carrying out health policy reforms.

Instituto Materno-Infantil de Pernambuco (IMIP) (line 6) - The name of an established organization and its acronym (IMIP) often remain untranslated. One could also include an English translation of the entire name, but the acronym in any case should not be translated, unless so indicated. The same rule applies to INAMPS (line 10).

Criado em 1960 (line 6) - It was translated as "founded in 1960." If criado had been translated as "created" it could be taken to mean "originated" or "generated." "Founded," however, is better in this case, meaning "established" or "instituted."

UNICEF (line 8) - UNICEF is well-known throughout the world and does not have to be translated. The Portuguese translation for UNICEF is *Fundo das Nações Unidas para a Infância.*

Nesse resultado final ...estimada (lines 13-15) - This is an example of changing the order within the sentence and combining the two sentences so that they will sound better in English. As long as one does not change any of the meaning of the sentence and does not omit any of the text, one should not hesitate to rearrange sentences to make them sound better.

mil nascimentos (line 28) - In English large numbers are routinely rendered in figures, not words. Also, be aware of the use of the comma in English for numbers 1,000 or higher, as opposed to the use of the period for the same numbers in Portuguese.

Oferece (line 29) - It should be translated as illustrates because it actually means to explain or to make clear rather than to offer.

1990/91 (page 2, line 2) - In English the hyphen replaces the slash.

3-4% (line 2) - In English the word "percent" is spelled out. Usually, you have the option of using the percent symbol or the word ("percent" or "per cent"). Whichever one you use, stick to it, and don't change it later in the text for no good reason.

ocidental (line 11) - "Western" is the appropriate translation for *ocidental*. In Portuguese, the West is referred to as "o ocidente" and the East as "o oriente." They do not have to be capitalized.

A legislação do seguro de saúde está em vigor desde o final de 1991 (line 22) - In English, we use the present perfect tense instead of the present tense that is correctly used in Portuguese.

Attorneys at Law
Henri Yutaka Yamagata
Raimundo Rodrigues Fonseca

Power of Attorney "Ad-Judicia"

By the present instrument conferring power of attorney, he nominates_____and appoints his powers of attorney, with extensive powers, the attorneys at law Drs. Henri Yutaka Yamagata, OAB/SP 83.624-CIC/MF 135.819.968/04, and Raimundo Rodrigues Fonseca, OAB/SP 28.625-CIC/MF 058.540.248/53, with office at Rua Vilalobos, 123 - Vila Caterina - CEP 05433, telephones 555-5955 and 555-5586, on whom he confers extensive powers before the courts in general, with ad-judicial clause, in any court, jurisdiction or tribunal, they being empowered to contest in law all competent actions and defend them when contested, following one or the other until a final decision, employing legal remedies, accompanying them, and also delegating to them special powers to verify, renounce, compromise, sign contracts or agreements, promote the introduction of substitutes, sign administration agreements, reject administrators, accept or reject assessments, render accounts, plead for new distributions of assets, accept or provide acquittances, acting jointly or separately, being also empowered to delegate equal powers to others with or without reserve, giving all for good, firm and valid.

São Paulo   19

Contract for the extension of services

Party to the contract: Chiu Mei Shiang or mei Shiang Chi, estate represented by the administrator, Chi Kow Mei RS.3.877.552 CIC 636.922.958-C4, Brazilian, separated, public employee, resident in this capital at Rua Vasco da Gama, 456; telephone 555-4629

Those contracted: Dr. Raimundo Rodrigues Fonseca, registered in OAB/SP 83624 CIC/MF 058.540.248/53 and Dr. Henri Yutaka Yamagata, registered in OAB/SP 83624 CIC/MF 135.819.968/04, Brazilian, married, attorneys at law, with offices at Rua Vilalobos, 123 - Vila Caterina SP, CEP 05433, telephones 555-5955 and 555-5586 agree to provide legal services under the following clauses and conditions:

1)   For services extended in the legal area the party(ies) to the contract undertake to pay those contracted the sum of Cr$ 5,000.00 (five thousand reis) one third of which payable on 11/30/95 and the balance against delivery of the deed of distribution

as legal retainer, plus costs, fees, transportation expenses, whether by taxi or own vehicle, that is to say, gasoline, parking, etc., as well as meals and lodging expenses incurred when attending to problems outside the capital of São Paulo.

2)   In cases involving the payment of the prevailing party's legal fees and costs, these will revert to the benefit of the contracted parties under the terms of article 99 § 1 of law 4.215/63.

3)   This contract is of indefinite duration, commencing on 11/17/95; however, if one of the parties should wish to rescind it, he must communicate his intention to the other in writing, with a minimum of thirty days from receipt of communication.

4)   If rescission is initiated by the party to the contract, fees shall be due in full, regardless of the stage that proceedings have reached.

5)   In the event of the contracted parties' needing to enter suit to uphold their rights, the competent action shall be an execution against a solvent debtor, based on item II of article 585 CPC, this document being an acknowledgement of debt.

6)   If the contracted parties should substitute an ad-judicia power of attorney by order of the party(ies) to the contract, the fees agreed on shall be for the account of the latter.

7)   Amounts contracted shall always be subject to late interest at the rate of 1% per month, plus monetary correction under the terms of law 6.809/81, if unpaid within the stipulated term.

8)   The parties choose the court of the capital of S. Paulo Regional de Pinheiros to settle any claims arising from this document, dispensing with any other.

9)   Whereas the exercise of advocacy is that of means, not of results, consequently, fees shall be due whether the lawsuit on, or the outcome of, the matter dealt with is successful or not.

And being righteous persons and under contract, the parties sign the present instrument in two copies, of equal content, before the witnesses below.

São Paulo, 22 November, 1995

_____ [signature]
Party to the contract

_____ [signature]
Party contracted

Witnesses

_____

_____

General Comments:

Format:

This being a *legal text, notice how the format of the translation follows closely that of the original. This includes capitalization of proper names and item numbers, spelling out numbers, and, in general, making the page closely resemble the original page.*

Also, the original being one long paragraph with long sentences, great care was taken to make the English sentences sound clear and logical.

Text:

Sometimes Portuguese legal translations are more relaxed and informal. When translating legal documents into English, make sure that the text reflects a more formal legal terminology. A good Portuguese-English legal dictionary is essential for this type of legal translation. You may also find samples of Portuguese and English power of attorney texts and contracts of much use.

"Ad-Judicia" (line 6) - This is a Latin legal term and should be left untranslated.

palo presente instrumento de procuração ... (line 10) - The word "conferring" was added because it explains better what the text is trying to convey.

nomeia (line 10) - Notice that there is no pronoun before *nomeia*. It is essential, however, to have it in English as the subject of the sentence.

OAB/SP 83.624 etc. (line 11) - Be sure to carefully check all such numbers and designators, since legal documents are expected to be letter-perfect.

Rua Vilalobos (line 12) - The address is left in Portuguese, since it can be used for mailing purposes, and there is no point in translating it.

seus bastante procuradores (lines 10-11) - In English, it was translated as his powers of attorney, with extensive powers. The Portuguese, in this particular case, was very concise and the translator had to add a few more words to make it more consistent with the English language.

Cr$ 5.000.00 (page 2, line 10) - Be sure to replace the period with a comma in English, after the number 5.

Capital de S.P. (line 14) - São Paulo is spelled out in English for the sake of clarity.
17/11/95 (line 17) - Month and day always reversed in American English.

Closing note: Legal documents often end with signatures, seals, stamps, etc. Be sure to translate every last item on the last page, not omitting anything. If you cannot decipher a signature or any text in a stamp, add the word [illegible] in brackets. A legal translation has to be done "verbatim," which means complete, fully accurate, and usable in a court of law.

TOKAMAK ETE CIRCUITS:
ANALYSIS AND SPECIFICATIONS

Plasma

•Introduction to the Physics of Plasma

The term *plasma* was used in physics for the first time in 1923 by two American Physicists, *Langmuir* and *Tonks*, during their studies on how charges oscillate in space. They called this study Oscillations of Plasma.

Plasma is a term used in medicine to denote a disturbance or an undistinguishable state. The coagulated part of blood was called plasma, referring to the blood's unknown component.

Plasma is a set of neutral and charged particles that satisfies given criteria and is called a quasi-neutral set of particles. Plasma consists of electrons and ions produced through the ionization of atoms and molecules. The recombination of electrons and ions causes the plasma to emit radiation. This radiation may or may not be visible. If the radiation occurs within the visible spectrum, the light's color will depend upon the kind of gas used. For instance, if hydrogen is used, the plasma's color will be blue.

Plasma takes form only under special conditions. On the earth's surface it is only possible to obtain plasma through confinement, which can be achieved by using vacuum chambers - a highly utilized method in laboratories for the study of plasma. The earth's gravitational force hinders the retention of plasma, making it impossible to confine plasma for longer periods than occurs, for example, with the sun. The sun and all stars that emit light, as well as the center of the earth, are all in the fourth state of matter. Fire and the Aurora Borealis, which emerges in the earth's ionosphere, are natural plasmas.

The objective of the physics of plasma is the study of ionized and macroscopically neutral gaseous systems. These are systems composed of a large number of charged particles, distributed inside a (macroscopic volume where the same amount of positive and negative charges exists.

This environment has been named *plasma*. The English physicist *W. Clux* called it the fundamental fourth state matter because it has different properties than the other three states of matter: gas, liquid and solid. This relationship occurs as follows: a solid material is transformed into a liquid when heat is applied to it. When more heat is added, the liquid is transformed into a gas. And finally, when this gas is heated at high temperatures, it is transformed into plasma. Therefore, when these four states are arranged in increasing order according to the amount of energy found in matter, one has:

•**Conclusion**

The greatest problem encountered was due to the necessarily high power utilized in the Tokamak device. The Brazilian-made switches were not suited to function normally under high I^2t. These switches rely upon capacitor banks, where more problems had arisen in the slower banks than in the faster ones. Consequently, imported equipment was used, including ignitrons for the circuit of the ohmic transformer, and thyristors and power diodes for the circuit of the toroidal field coil. All capacitor banks that have been mentioned so far are electrolytic and Brazilian-made.

The same analysis could not be carried out for the ohmic circuit because of an unexpected physical effect. The trigger of bank C2 had been sending a current to switch S1, affecting the switch opening. The utilization of other devices, such as a saturated inductor, an open-capacitor or a vacuum break, should be considered to assist in this switch opening.

For a better understanding of how the circuits operate, it was first necessary to comprehend how the Tokamak device works and what the physical characteristics of plasma are. Dr. Edson Del Bosco, my mentor, and electrical engineer Osvaldo Rossi have closely followed this research, and both have contributed to this field of knowledge so that the work could be realized as anticipated.

DESCRIPTION OF THE CECI's
ENERGIZED SYSTEM FUNCTIONING

1.   INTRODUCTION

CECI is a mechanism of toroidal geometry in which the plasma's magnetic confinement is studied. A set of toroidal, poloidal, and vertical coils are used to generate this confinement field.

Herein we will describe the electronic circuits used to construct the devices needed to activate those coils. The final part of this report will also describe the plasma's pre-ionization circuit.

The diagram in Fig. 1.1 shows all parts that form the CECI's energized system.

The toroidal field is generated by direct current, and therefore it is constant with time. A 30V/600A source provides direct current to the toroidal coil which is refrigerated to avoid superheating.

The poloidal and vertical fields are pulsated. They need capacitor banks which, after being charged, are discharged by a trigger circuit into their respective coils.

6. COMMENTS AND CONCLUSIONS

The energized system of the CECI mechanism consists of circuits of plain construction.

It is built almost completely, excepting source DC 30V/600A, in the LAP (Associated Plasma Laboratory) at a very low cost.

Because it is a pulsated system, the circuit set to be used is a small one. This is quite advantageous in terms of cost and maintenance.

In order to produce inductive discharges into the CECI, it is necessary to use the complete electronic device described herein. CECI is a magnetic confinement mechanism with toroidal geometry, which makes it possible to attain Tokamak configurations, RFP (Reverse Field Pinch) and Ultra Low Q. (The last two are possible alternatives to nuclear fusion opposing the Tokamaks).

General Comments:

A good technical dictionary should have most if not all of the technical terms in these two texts. If, after a thorough consultation with such sources you still have an unknown term, the next best thing to do is to call someone with a technical background.

Also, bear in mind that technical texts have well defined vocabularies. Repeated work in any particular area will find you handling the same terms over and over again.

Análise e Especificações ... (line 1) - This sentence sounds better in English if it is split up into two parts.

TOKAMAK ETE (line 2) - This is an example of an acronym which remains the same in both texts, because it pertains to a system of classification recognized as such in Portuguese and in English.

Plasma (line 5) - In Portuguese plasma can be used in the singular or plural (plasmas). In English, only in the singular.

O termo Plasma na física... (line 5) - Notice the long paragraph in Portuguese. In English it was split into two sentences for a better translation.

O Plasma é um conjunto de partículas ...(line 10) - Again this is a long paragraph split up into three sentences. In English, it was split up into five sentences to be more consistent with the English language.

CECI (page 2, line 21) - This is an example of an acronym which remains the same in both texts, because it pertains to a system of classification recognized as such in both Portuguese and in English.

Os campos poloidal e vertical são pulsados...(line 29) - Again a long sentence was split up into two sentences to be more consistent with the English language.

LAP (Laboratório Associado de Plasma) (page 3, line 4) - The acronym is left the same, while the name of the entity is translated for information purposes.

Closing note: If you are not familiar with this field of science, some good scientific references, such as the McGraw-Hill *Dictionary of Scientific and Technical Terms* (Fifth Edition), or a science encyclopedia may be quite useful.

-REDUCTION OF SUBSIDIES TO BETTER-OFF GROUPS. Governments should reduce and eventually eliminate public subsidies to relatively affluent groups. This can be done by charging full-cost fees to insured persons who use government hospitals and clinics for services not included in the national essential clinical package and by cutting tax deductions for insurance contributions. In South Africa and Zimbabwe privately insured individuals have been charged less than the full cost of the services they receive in government health facilities. In addition, they have been allowed to deduct from taxable income part or all of their out-of-pocket payments for health care, as well as their health insurance premiums. Employers can also deduct their insurance contributions. These measures reduce the amounts available for financing essential services. In South Africa individual tax deductions were estimated to be equivalent to 18 percent of total public sector health expenditures in 1990. In a recent effort to reverse a similar situation, Zimbabwe has sharply limited tax deductions for health care and insurance, raised fees, and intensified efforts to collect fees from privately insured patients. Government hospitals have learned that they can often identify insured patients by offering them extra nonmedical amenities, such as private hospital rooms, and can then target them for aggressive cost recovery if they accept.

In countries where social insurance covers only a fraction of the population, governments can increase the extent to which health services are self-financing by eliminating public subsidies to social insurance. These subsidies, which are widespread in Latin America, mostly benefit the middle classes and are therefore regressive. Elimination of the subsidies would free resources for health services for the poor. Eliminating subsidies also imposes more financial discipline on the social insurance agencies, which are often allowed to run deficits that are later covered by transfers from other social security programs or from the general government budget. In Venezuela, for example, the government subsidizes contributions to the medical assistance fund within the parastatal social security agency. Despite this subsidy, in 1990 the fund ran a deficit equivalent to 37 percent of its health expenditures.

EXTENSION OF INSURANCE. Where the bulk of the labor force is already employed, government policies that extend insurance coverage to the rest of the population - including the self-employed, the elderly, and the poor - remove the inequities inherent in multitiered systems of health financing and expand the content of the universally available package of care. When insurance coverage becomes universal, as in Costa Rica and Korea, subsidies actually end up targeting the poor and are thus progressive. But only a few middle-income countries that have adequate financial resources, political resolve, and administrative capacity will be able to achieve such universal insurance coverage. Korea's bold initiative to create a national health insurance system from scratch between 1978 and 1989 and Costa Rica's efforts in the 1980s to universalize a system that had previously covered only the industrial labor force show that this is a difficult but achievable goal. Attaining universal coverage would be more feasible if governments limited the essential package of insured services to those with high cost-effectiveness.

CONSUMER CHOICE. Competition among suppliers of a clearly specified prepaid package of health services would improve quality and encourage efficiency. And even where there is little or no direct competition among insurance funds, as in Japan and Korea, multiple semi-independent insurance institutions may still have advantages over a single large parastatal agency. Local insurance funds managed by boards composed of representatives of workers, employers, and local government, as in Germany, tend to be more accountable to their members. In a number of Latin American countries monolithic social security "institutes" are already heavily discredited because of their past inefficiencies and corruption. Greater competition and accountability are two of the main objectives of current proposals for reforming social insurance in Argentina.

COST CONTAINMENT. Copayment by insured individuals for some services can help to restrain their use of the services but is unlikely to be a very powerful cost-containment method. Copayments amounting to an average 40 percent of expenditures in Korea have done little to slow the rate of increase in health spending, which grew from 3.7 to 6.6 percent of GNP during the 1980s. Similarly, the practice, introduced by private U.S. insurers of retrospective reviews of utilization of medical care appears to lead to a modest one-time savings in health spending but does not have long-lasting effects on the rate of growth of expenditures.

By contrast, prepayment of health care providers is a promising approach to containing health expenditures. Governments could help to promote such schemes by removing legal barriers that in many countries prevent the same institution from acting as both insurer and provider. In South Africa the government recently decided to allow the creation of health maintenance organizations (HMOs), mainly as a way of containing health costs. More than twenty such organizations have been established in just a few years. They have introduced capitation and negotiated fees, which limit costs more effectively than did the open-ended fee-for-service payment arrangements historically used in South Africa.

Governments can do much to improve the incentives created by social insurance. Where the insured use private providers, fee-for-service payment schemes need to be replaced with an alternative - capitation or annually negotiated uniform fees for doctors and hospitals (based on diagnostic-related groups of procedures, for example) or preset overall budgets for hospitals. Where social insurance covers services by government hospitals, competition with the private sector can improve performance. Other promising approaches ar to allow government hospitals to compete with one another as semiautonomous enterprises, as in the United Kingdom in recent years, and to give hospital managers financial and career incentives to meet performance targets, as in Chile.

The example of Chile (Box 7.2) illustrates the benefits and perils of health sector reform in a middle-income country. Chile has been able to improve efficiency, quality of care, and consumer choice, but the reforms have also created new problems regarding administration, financing, and equity.

General comments:

a. Financial Translation

In translation, there is a basic difference between translating financial subjects and other technical subjects, such as legal or medical. While it is relatively easy to master the methodology of working with most technical vocabularies, even if one does not have the technical or professional background of the particular field in which one translates, in financial subjects it is necessary to have at least a general knowledge of the subject. This may be due to the fact that financial terminology and concepts are not always as readily translatable as other technical subjects. The upshot of all this is that one should not be hasty to accept a financial assignment if one does not work in this field on a regular basis.

b. Style

This particular assignment consists of a text derived from the field of insurance. It represents the work of an international organization involved in assistance to economies in developing countries. As with most majr organizations, this corporation has its own "corporate style," which affects the way this material is translated. Normally, an organization of this magnitude employs its own translators, or uses outside translators on a regular basis, to acquaint them with its style. If called upon to translate this kind of text, be sure to familiarize yourself with the organization's style.

Preços (line 5) - Even though it means costs and charges, it was translated as fees because it is the term more often used in the United States.

pagam menos que o custo total dos serviços (line 8) - It was translated as "have been charged less than the full cost of the services" rather than "pay less than the full cost of the services to avoid being too literal and it also explains better what the author is trying to convey.

total de seus gastos com tratamentos de saúde (line 9-10) - It should be translated as "all of their out-of-pocket payments for health care." Out-of-pocket is a common expression which frequently appears in the business and insurance industries throughout the United States.

Dois dos principais objetivos (page 2, lines 8-9) - The sentence order was changed, however, the translation remains true to the original.

3,7% (line 14) - Remember to replace the comma with a period in English, and be consistent in either using the percent symbol or spelling it out.

Mais de 20 dessas organizações (line 22-23) - Notice that in the English version it was split up into two sentences for a better sounding English.

Outros métodos promissores (line 31-32) - "Approaches" was used rather than methods because it explains better to the English ear what the translator is trying to convey.

O caso do Chile...é um exemplo (line 35) - *Caso* and *exemplo* are synonyms in Portuguese. Therefore, when translating the sentence into English one of the words was eliminated and the verb "illustrate" was added for a better translation style.

Observation: Notice that the sentences are more concise in the English version. The Portuguese author uses quite a few more words to express his ideas and meanings.

Part Two

Translation: English into Portuguese

Evaluating caesarean sections in Brazil

Operations research can examine variations in medical practice with a view to identifying areas in which changes in practice are needed, as well as possible instruments for modifying provider practice. In the early 1980s, Brazil was estimated to have the highest overall caesarean section rate in the world - 31 percent of all hospital births in 1981. Although caesarean sections are a life-saving procedure in certain circumstances, their unnecessary use raises costs and poses medical risks for the mother and the newborn. The financial cost of unnecessary publicly financed caesareans in Brazil was estimated at about $60 million annually in the late 1980s. Medical risks stem from incorrect estimation of the length of gestation (leading to premature deliveries), infection from surgery, and the use of general anesthesia. Among the many factors responsible for the rising rate of caesareans in Brazil are the financial and administrative incentives for hospitals and doctors to perform caesarean deliveries, the desire to use a caesarean delivery as a vehicle for obtaining a sterilization, and the widespread view that caesarean section is the preferred, "modern" way to deliver.

Brazilian studies of caesarean section rates illustrate systematic variations by region, type of hospital, socioeconomic status of the woman, and reimbursement patterns. Rates in 1981 were higher in the more prosperous Southeast (38 percent) and lowest in the poor Northeast (20 percent). In every region the incidence of caesarean section increased with family income. A 1986 survey showed that rates were highest for women with a university education (61 percent) and for births in private hospitals (57 percent), Other studies showed that rates were lowest among women with no insurance. Women covered under the social security system had higher rates of caesarean section, and women with private insurance had the highest.

The country's social security institute changed its reimbursement policies in the early 1980s to remove some of the financial incentives for caesarean sections, and education campaigns for physicians were initiated. But it is clear that even stronger policies are needed *to* reverse these trends, as caesarean section rates have continued at high levels. A large sample of births in the state of São Paulo in 1991, for example, indicated a caesarean section rate of 47 percent.

The Tamil Nadu Integrated Nutrition Project: making supplementary feeding work

In the late 1970s the government of the state of Tamil Nadu in south India was operating twenty-five different supplementary feeding programs. Evaluation showed these programs to be ineffective and identified several reasons. The programs were not directed toward malnourished children; they provided food that was often not suitable for small children and was eaten by other family members; they replaced rather than supplemented home consumption of food; they did not educate mothers; and they failed to provide needed nutrition-related health care. The Tamil Nadu Integrated Nutrition Project, the first phase of which ran from 1980 to 1989, was accordingly designed to target services more effectively, to improve family nutrition and health practices, and to improve maternal and child health services.

Children ages 6-36 months were weighed each month. Of every 100 children selected for feeding, 44 were normal in weight but faltering in growth, 34 were moderately malnourished and faltering, and 22 were severely malnourished. Supplementary feeding was provided immediately to those who were severely malnourished, and feeding for children with faltering growth was provided after one month (for children ages 6-12 months) or three months (for children ages 12-35 months). The children selected were fed for at least ninety days. If they failed to gain at least 500 grams in weight, they were referred to health care, and feeding was continued for up to 180 days. Intensive nutrition education was directed at mothers of at-risk children. Food supplementation was also offered to women whose children were being fed, to those who had numerous children, and to those who were nursing while pregnant.

The project cut severe malnutrition in half and prevented many at-risk children from becoming malnourished. Of those receiving food supplementation, 67 percent gained enough weight to graduate in ninety days; all except the severely malnourished graduated within 150 days. Because participants were fed only when required, food was only 13 percent of the project's total cost, much less than is typical in supplementation programs. (The initial share dropped during the course of the project as the number of children who needed feeding declined.) When the program began in 1980, 45 to 50 percent of the children required feeding; by 1988 the project had brought the share down to 24 percent. Selective, limited-duration supplementary feeding worked in Tamil Nadu because the community nutrition workers were well trained and highly motivated and because mothers came to understand the importance of feeding for healthy growth and were pleased when their children grew well. The experience of Tamil Nadu suggests that appropriate supplementary, feeding is both an inexpensive and an effective form of nutrition education.

word count: 827

AGREEMENT

BETWEEN: NOVA INVESTMENTS, INC.

AND: MANAGEMENT LIMITED

ARTICLE I
INTRODUCTION

1.1.   Date and parties to the agreement. This AGREEMENT, dated 12 May 1994,
has been reached between Nova Investments, Inc. (THE CUSTOMER) a Brazilian company, and Management Limited (ML), a Brazilian corporation.

1.2.   Goal of the agreement. This AGREEMENT establishes the terms and conditions under which the Customer has retained the services of ML to manage and operate the Food Service for the clientele: the employees, visitors, and tenants of the Customer in the facilities (premises) of the Customer located at 5 Recife Street, São Paulo. The term "Food Service" as used in this AGREEMENT describes the operation of conventional facilities to provide food, beverages and other products that the Customer might authorize.

1.3.   Duration of the agreement. The initial duration of the AGREEMENT is for two (2) years, beginning 1 June 1994 and is renewable on an annual basis, until one of the parties terminates it according to the conditions provided below.

ARTICLE 4
MANAGEMENT AND PERSONNEL

4.1   The employees of ML. ML must provide a sufficient number of employees who are qualified at the management level and staff for good operation of the Food Service. These employees will be supervised by the support and management staff of ML. All personnel hired by ML must at all times and in all duties be in the exclusive employment of ML. The initial understandings pertaining to salary negotiations and other conditions will be the understandings which are reached between the two parties. ML will directly pay its employees.

4.2   Hiring policy agreement.

a) ML undertakes to recruit, train, manage, guide, discipline and if necessary dismiss personnel working in the Food Service.

b) The Customer may not hire, enter into agreements or allow the hiring for its own food services, any management personnel of the ML Food Service before one (1) year passes following termination of his employment with ML or before one (1) year following termination of this AGREEMENT.

c) The Customer will have the right to inspect management personnel.

ARTICLE 8
GENERAL TERMS AND CONDITIONS

8.1   Taxes. ML will collect all taxes which are applied and will remit these taxes to the pertinent agencies. The water bill and business taxes will be paid for by ML.

8.2   Legal provisions. ML must adhere to the applicable laws, ordinances, regulations and rules of the federal, state, municipal and local government bodies, offices and administrations in charge of sanitation, safety and health of the Food Service and must procure and maintain all necessary licenses and permits. The Customer will provide all necessary assistance to ML in its efforts to procure and obtain this conformity.

8.3   Responsibility for general insurance. ML must obtain and keep in force during the time period of this AGREEMENT general insurance against bodily injury and property damage for the combined limit of not less than one million U.S. dollars ($1,000,000) including, but not limited to, responsibility for all bodily injury, contractual responsibility and responsibility for losses of produce, covering only the operations and activities of ML which are stipulated in the present AGREEMENT. ML will provide to the Customer the certificates indicating the insurance policies which cover operation under this AGREEMENT. The insurance policy must include a clause of the issuing company to the effect that the policy will not be canceled unless a written notification is given to the Customer at least thirty (30) days in advance.

8.4.   Recovery waiver. Each of the parties to this AGREEMENT renounces according to mutual agreement all their rights as well as rights of their branches and affiliates to obtain compensation from the other party for losses or damages to buildings, improvements or other property caused by fire, explosion or by any other cause normally included in a standard insurance policy or a policy covering fire, bodily injury, or civil responsibility. The Customer will protect his building including the Food Service area, its contents and other insured properties against losses or damage from fire, explosion and damages of that kind.

OPERATING AGREEMENT
Between
EMBRATEL-BRASIL
and
U.S.TELEPHONE

FOR THE PROVISION OF DIGITAL PRIVATE LINE TELECOMMUNICATIONS SERVICES

1.   EMBRATEL-BRASIL and U.S. TELEPHONE hereby agree to interconnect operating facilities in order to provide customers with digital private line services via SATELLCOM WBS. These services will be developed in accordance with existing C.C.I.T.T. recommendations and the appropriate SATELLCOM WESS documentation.

2.   Agreement for any equipment to be provided directly to EMBRATEL-BRASIL by U.S. TELEPHONE will be via attachment to this agreement.

3.   Under this agreement, each of the parties will be responsible for providing the segment of the communications link from the customer's premise in its respective   country to the Atlantic region midpoint; that is, in the U.S.A., U.S. TELEPHONE will be responsible for the telecommunications segment between the customer's premises and the satellite; in Brazil, EMBRATEL-BRASIL will be responsible for the telecommunications link between operationally compatible with each other in order to provide the desired services.

4.   EMBRATEL-BRASIL and U.S. TELEPHONE will make separate and independent arrangements with the customer, and each will establish the rates and conditions under which its portion of the service will be provided. However, TELECOM-BRAZIL and U.S. Telephone will enact One-Stop Shopping and Single End Billing arrangements at the request of and on behalf of individual customers. Where appropriate, other arrangements may also be used by mutual agreement of the parties. In the event of a service interruption, there will be nonfinancial obligation between EMBRATEL-BRASIL and U.S.TELEPHONE. However, each of the parties will give interruption allowances to the customer for the period of time when the service is unavailable in accordance with the terms and conditions of their respective tariffs applicable to the particular service. Operating Agreement, p.2.

5.   Points of contact in both EMBRATEL-BRASIL and U.S.TELEPHONE will be designated; names of these persons will be exchanged to ensure the operational integrity of the services offered.

6.   Other terms and conditions may be added to the agreement from time to time as they may be mutually agreed upon by EMBRATEL-BRASIL and U.S.TELEPHONE.

Signed for and on behalf of

U.S.TELEPHONE	EMBRATEL-BRASIL
Signature: _____	Signature: _____
Name: _____	Name: _____
Title: _____	Title: _____

word count: 1020

Controlling river blindness

Onchocerciasis, or river blindness as it is more commonly known, is caused by a parasitic worm which produces millions of larvae that move through the body, causing intense itching, debilitation, and eventually blindness. The disease is spread by a small, fiercely biting blackfly that transmits the larvae from infected to uninfected people.

The goals of the Onchocerciasis Control Programme (OCP), set up in 1974 and covering eleven Sahelian countries, are to control the blackfly by destroying its larvae with insecticides sprayed from the air. The environmental impact of the insecticides is continuously monitored by an independent ecological committee, in cooperation with the national governments. The committee has full authority to screen insecticides and to approve or reject their use. The program has also collaborated with the pharmaceutical industry to develop for human us a drug, ivermectin, that safely and effectively kills the larvae in the body. Ivermectin, however has little impact on the adult worm and so must be supplemented with vector control by aerial spraying. The producer of ivermectin, Merck & Co., has committed itself to provide the drug free of charge as long as it is needed to combat river blindness.

The OCP's four sponsoring agencies - the Food and Agriculture Organization, the United Nations Development Programme (UNDP), the World Bank, and WHO - through a steering committee chaired by the World Bank, make broad policy decisions and oversee operations. WHO has executive responsibility through a team of entomologists, epidemiologists, field staff, and pilots; 97 percent of the staff are nationals of the participating countries. The World Bank organizes the finances and manages them through a trust fund. It also supports socioeconomic development in the areas affected by the disease.

The program is widely regarded as a great success. It protects from river blindness about 30 million people, including more than 9 million children born since the OCP began, at an annual cost of less the $1 per person. More than 1.5 million people who were once seriously infected have completely recovered. It is estimated that the program will have prevented at least 500,000 cases of blindness by the time it is wound up around the end of the century. And it is already freeing approximately 25 million hectares of previously blighted land for resettlement and cultivation, boosting agricultural production.

The estimated cost of the OCP during the whole of its existence, from 1974 to 2000, is about $570 million. Its estimated internal rate of return is in the range of 16 to 28 percent (depending on the pace at which the newly available land is settled, the incremental output added by the new land, the income level of the OCP area, and the productivity growth rate that is projected). These estimated benefits do not include the program's favorable effects on income distribution; its main beneficiaries are subsistence farmers whose incomes are well below average.

It is easy to determine which health problems among children under age 5 deserve priority. As Appendix table B.6 shows, nine diseases each account for more than 1 percent of the total disease burden in this age group. These diseases range from acute respiratory infections (more than 17 percent in both boys and girls) to iodine deficiency (1.2 to 1.3 percent). Of these problems, which cause fully 80 percent of young children's ill health, eight can be addressed by interventions costing less than $100 per DALY saved. The only exception is congenital problems, which are responsible for more than 6 percent of the disease burden but for which no cost-effective interventions are known.

The situation is much more complicated for adults (Appendix table B.7). For example, cerebrovascular disease is the leading cause of healthy life years lost in both sexes after age 60 and in women ages 45-59, but interventions to deal with it cost $1,000 or more per DALY saved. Ischemic heart disease is the second or third leading cause of ill health in both sexes after age 45, but the cost per DALY of dealing with it is $250 to $1,000. Among the ten principal noncommunicable causes of ill health in this age group, interventions costing less than $100 per DALY saved exist only for cataracts, anemia, and cancers of the respiratory system (through reduction of smoking) and the cervix. These problems account for only 7.9 percent of the disease burden in women ages 45-59 and for smaller shares in other age and sex groups. Among communicable diseases tuberculosis, AIDS, and respiratory infections deserve priority, but they cause less than 10 percent of all ill health after age 45 and only 20.1 percent in men ages 15-44.

Large disease burdens and cost-effective interventions coincide for only one group of adults, women ages 15-44. Six of the ten main sources of ill health can be prevented or treated for less than $100 per DALY. These range from maternal health problems (18.0 percent of the burden) to respiratory infections and anemia (2.5 percent of the burden each) and account in total for 44 percent of ill health among women of reproductive age. Two other problems - depression and self-inflicted injury - each cause at least 3 percent of the disease burden, but dealing with them is much more problematic.

These calculations illustrate the chief problem a health care system faces as the population ages: the marginal cost of a year of healthy life gained rises sharply, leading to difficult choices between increased health problems of the elderly that cannot be fully resolved may be palliated at low cost. And much can be done at earlier ages to improve the health of future generations of old people.

word count: 980

ASSIGNMENT 4: BUSINESS/ECONOMICS

Public and private finance of clinical services

Around the world, clinical services are financed through four main channels. Two— out-of-pocket payments and voluntary insurance— are private. The other two are public; compulsory insurance (sometimes known as social insurance) that is either publicly managed or heavily regulated by governments, and funding from general government revenues.

In the poorest countries total health expenditure may be as low as $2 per person a year, and more than half of this comes from private sources, mainly in the form of out-of-pocket payments. insurance mechanisms in those countries are weak, and the amount of government revenues devoted to health is low. As incomes increase, so do both the percentage of income spent on health (as shown in the upper panel of Figure 5.1) and the share of health spending that comes from public sources (illustrated in the lower panel). in the formerly socialist economies and the established market economies (excluding the United States) public spending accounts for a full three-quarters of total health expenditure.

In addition to the four sources of health financing, there are three ways of organizing clinical health services: public, private nonprofit, and private for-profit. All national health systems use at least two of the twelve possible combinations of financing method and health service organization, and sometimes the different combinations serve sharply differentiated populations. Even so, it is possible to group countries according to income level and the predominant system of providing health care. A principal distinction is whether insurance pays for much care and, if so, what is the dominant type of insurance (Table 5.2).

In *low-income countries* private out-of-pocket payments account for more than half of the mere $2 to $40 per person spent each year for health care. Most of this sum goes for doctors' fees, payments to traditional healers, and drugs. NGOs, particularly those related to religious institutions, make important contributions to the provision of health services in many low-income countries. In Tanzania and Haiti NGOs operate nearly half of the hospitals, and in Cameroon and Uganda they manage 40 percent of health facilities. in Ghana and Nigeria about a third of all hospital beds are located in mission hospitals. Government spending from general tax revenues generally amounts to less than half of the 2 to 7 percent of GNP allocated to health services. There is little or no insurance.

Until recently, China was an important exception among low-income countries. There, between 1960 and 1980, state enterprises provided health care directly to their workers or contracted with government hospitals to do so. Rural communes were required to earmark a portion of their financial resources for health services for all their members. By the late 1970s insurance covered virtually all the urban population and 85 percent of the rural population - a unique achievement for a low-income developing country. Since the elimination of communal agriculture and the liberalization of industry in the early 1980s, however, these forms of health insurance and service delivery have weakened considerably. The rural population increasingly relies on a system of government-provided health care financed in part out of general revenues, but with substantial cost recovery through user charges, not unlike systems prevailing in other low-income countries.

In the *middle-income countries* there are two major types of health systems, distinguished by whether the government or the private sector provides health insurance. Health spending, at $20 to $400 per capita, is higher than in low-income countries, and both public and private managerial capacity is stronger. in countries with private insurance, such as South Africa and Zimbabwe, the government uses general revenues to pay for health care for middle- and low-income groups, while upper-income households (less than 20 percent of the population) use private insurance to pay for private physicians and hospitals or for private rooms in government hospitals.

In countries with social insurance, mandatory contributions from employees and employers, and sometimes government funds, finance insurance for part of the population, including most middle-class workers. Health care for the poor is financed from general revenues. This is the system that prevails in Korea, Turkey, and most of Latin America.

In the *formerly socialist economies* of Eastern Europe and the Soviet Union, general revenue financing with government provision of health services was until recently the only officially recognized form of health care. public spending on health now accounts for 3 to 6 percent of GNP in theses countries, or $30 to $200 per capita. Prior to the period of political and economic liberalization in the late 1980s, private payments were frequently made for "public" health services (for example, gratuities were given physicians in government hospitals), and drugs often leaked from the public sector into private markets. Since the political and economic reforms that swept across these countries in the late 1980s, the health systems there have been in crisis. Dwindling public funding and deteriorating government services have created strong pressures for new forms of public and private insurance.

The *established market economies,* with the exception of the United States, rely on one of the two types of public financing for more than three-quarters of their health expenditures, which range from $400 to $2,500 per person per year. Norway, Sweden, and the United Kingdom use general tax revenues to pay for health services that are provided directly by the government. In France, Germany, and Japan, among others, social insurance is the dominant mode of financing. The United States, with annual health spending of about $2,800 per capita, has a bewildering combination of systems, including voluntary private employment-based insurance, compulsory insurance for federal workers with each employee having a choice of alternative insurers and packages, and full public finance and provision for veterans. A single-payer approach financed from general revenue is used at the federal level for health care for the elderly (Medicare) and at the state level for the poor (Medicaid).

word count: 994

Avaliação de cesarianas no Brasil

A pesquisa operacional permite examinar variações de prática médica com o fito de identificar as áreas onde há necessidade de mudanças, bem como possiveis instrumentos para modificar os métodos dos prestadores de serviéos de saúde. Em começos da década de 80, verificouse que o Brasil tinha a maior taxa global de cesarianas do mundo - 31% de todos os partos realizados em hospital em 1981. Embora a cesariana seja um procedimento capaz de salvar vidas em certas circunstâcias, o seu uso desnecessário eleva os custos e acarreta riscos para a mãe e para o recém-nascido. O custo financeiro de cesarianas calculado em cerca de US$60 milhões por ano em fins da década de 80. Os siscos médicos resultam da estimativa incorreta da duração da gestação (o que leva a partos prematuros), de infecções cirúrgicas e do uso de anestesia geral. entre os muitos fatores responsáveis pela taxa crescente de cesarianas no Brasil estão os incentivos financeiros e administrativos oferecidos a hospitais e médicos que realizam cesarianas, o desejo de aproveitar a cesariana para esterilizar a mulher, e a opinião generalizada de que a cesariana é o método "moderno" preferido de realizar um parto.

Os estudos brasileiros da taxa de cesariana mostram variações sistemáticas por região, tipo de hospital, posição sóio-econômica da mulher e sistemas de reembolso. Em 1981, a proporção de cesarianas era mais alta na região mais próspera, o Sudeste (38%), e mais baixa na região pobre, o Nordeste (20%). Em todas as regiões, a freqüência de cesarianas aumentava na razão direta da renda familiar. Um levantamento feito em 1986 mostrou que a proporção mais elevada ocorria entre mulheres com instrução universitátia (61%) e no caso de partos realizados em hospitais privados (57%). Outros estudos demonstraram que a proporção era menor entre mulheres sem qualquer cobertura de seguro. As maiores taxas de cesariana ocorriam entre mulheres cobertas pelo sistema de seguridade social, sendo que as taxas mais elevadas de todas ocorriam entre mulheres cobertas por seguro privado.

O instituto de seguridade social do pais mudou suas normas de reembolso em começos da década de 80, de modo a eliminar alguns dos incentivos financeiros à intervenção cesariana, e lançou campanhas de esclarecimento para médicos. Mas, evedentemente há necessidade de medidas ainda mais severas para reverter tais tendècias, pois a proporção de cesarianas continua elevada. uma grande amostra de partos no estado de São Paulo em 1991, por exemplo, indicou uma taxa de cesariana de 47%.

O Projeto Integrado de Nutrição de Tamil Nadu: a alimentação suplementar funciona

Em fins dos anos 70 o governo do estado de Tamil Nadu, no sul da India, conduzia 25 programas diferentes de alimentação suplementar. A avaliação desses programas revelou serem eles ineficazes, or vários motivos. Os programas não se destinavam ás crianças desnutridas; forneciam alimentos que nem sempre convinham a crianças pequenas e eram consumidos pelos outros membros da família; substituíam, em vez de suplementar, o consumo familiar de alimentos; não instruíam as mães; e não conseguiam prestar atendimento sanitário no campo da nutrição. Conseqüentemente, o Projeto Integrado de Nutrição de Tamil Nadu, cuja primeira fase foi de 1980 a 1989, destinava-se a direcionar os serviços com mais eficácia, para melhorar os hábitos familiares de nutrição e higiene, bem como os serviços de atendimento médico a mães e filhos.

As crianças com idade de seis a 36 meses eram pesadas mensalmente. De cada 100 crianças selecionadas para serem alimentadas, 44 tinham peso normal mas sofriam de alguma deficiência de cerscimento, 34 eram moderadmente desnutridas e debilitadas, e 22 estavam gravemente desnutridas. A alimentação suplementar foi fornecida de imediato às que se encontravam gravemente desnutridas, e a alimentação para as crianças com problemas de crescimento foi fornecida após um mês (às crianças entre seis e 12 meses) ou três meses (às crianças entre 12-35 meses). As crianças selecionadas foram alimentadas pelo menos durante 90 dias. Se não conseguissem ganhar as menos 500 gramas de peso, eram encaminhadas para tratamento médico e continuavam recebendo alimentação por mais 180 dias. As mães das crianças em risco foram instruídas acerca de nutrição. Também foi fornecida suplementação alimentar às mães cujos filhos estavam sendo alimentados, às que tinham prole numerosa, e às que estavam amamentando durante a gravidez.

O projeto reduziu à metade a desnutrição grave e evitou que muitas crianças em risco se tornassem desnutridas. Das que receberam suplementação alimentar, 67% engordaram o suficiente e chegaram ao peso normal em 90 dias; todas, à exceção das gravemente desnutridas, chegaram ao peso normal em 150 dias. como os participantes foram alimentados qpenas quando necessário, os alimentos corresponderam a apenas 13% do custo total do projeto, muito menos que o usual nos programas de suplementação. (A percentagem inicial diminuiu durante o projeto, à mededa que caía o número de crianças que necessitavam de alimentação suplementar.) Quando o programa começou, em 1980, 45-50% das crianças precisavam de alimentação suplementar; em 1988, graças ao projeto, essa proporção caíra para 24%. A alimentação suplementar seletiva, de duração limitada, funcionou em Tamil Nadu porque os nutricionistas comunitários estavam bem treinados e altamente motivados, e porque as mães compreenderam a importância da alimentação para o crescimento saudável e gostaram de ver seus filhos crescerem bem. A experiência de Tamil Nadu sugere que a suplementação alimentar adequada é uma forma eficaz e barata de educação nutricional.

General Comments:

Subject Matter:

While these two texts discuss health and nutrition topics, they are written in general terms, with little if any truly technical terminology. They require a general, well-rounded education and knowledge on the part of the translator, rather than in-depth knowledge of either medicine or nutrition. As such, they are a good test for your translation ability, and a way to check on your overall skills as a translator.

Style:

These texts represent the work of a major international organization, and as such are written in a formal style typical of major organizations. Usually this material is handled by in-house translators in the organization, who are used to writing in such a style. In general, when you approach a text, you need to ask yourself whether the style is formal, casual, "off the cuff," etc. Part of the translation process is to remain faithful to the style of the original text.

In general, Brazilian Portuguese is a less formal language than English (although British English is often more formal than American English), and this must be taken in consideration when translating from and into those two languages.

$60 million (line 10) - Since the U.S. dollar sign is also used for currencies in Latin America, it is necessary in the Portuguese translation to specify "US$60."

insurance (line 21) - Translated in Portuguese as *cobertura de seguro*, or "insurance coverage," to make the point clearer for the Portuguese-language reader.

Women covered under... (lines 21) - This is an example of an English sentence that had to be rearranged in Portuguese to make it sound better. Rearranging sentences is part of good translation, which takes into account the differing character of each language, making it necessary to say the same thing in a different way. Needless to say, rearranging for rearranging's sake does not make much sense; it does not accomplish much. But when it is called for, then by all means do it.

47 percent (line 27) - Notice how both the English original and the Portuguese translation are consistent in how they render percentages. The English uses the word "percent" throughout, while the Portuguese uses the percent symbol. Consistency is one of the basic principles of translation.

CONTRATO

ENTRE: NOVA INVESTMENTS, INC.

E   :   MANAGEMENT LIMITED

ARTIGO I
INTRUDUÇÃO

1.1   Data e partes integrantes do contrato. Em 12 de maio de 1994, um CONTRATO foi assinado entre a Nova Investments, Inc. (O CLIENTE), uma companhia brasileira, e a Management Limited (ML), uma corporação brasileira.

1.2   Objeto do contrato. Este contrato estabelece os termos e condições pelos quais o Cliente contratou os serviços da ML para administrar e poerar o Serviço de Comidas e Bebidas para a clientela; os emprogados, visitantes e inquilinos do Cliente nas instalações (prédio) do Cliente situadas à Rua Recife nº 5, São Paulo. O termo "Serviço de Comidas e Bebidas" usado neste CONTRATO descreve a operação de fornecer comida, bebidas e outros produtos em instalações convencionais que o Cliente possa autorizar.

1.3   Prazo deste contrato. O prazo inicial deste CONTRATO é de dois (2) anos, com início em 01 de junho de 1994 e é renovável anualmente, até que uma das partes o termine de acordo com as condições que se seguem.

ARTIGO 4
ADMINISTRAÇÃO E PESSOAL

4.1   Os empregados da ML. A ML deverá fornecer um número suficiente de empregados qualificados para administrar e uma equipe para o bom funcionamento do Serviço de Comidas e Bebidas. Estes empregados serão supervisionados pela pessoal contratado pela ML deverá trabalhar entendimentos iniciais pertinentes à discussão dos termos salariais e outras condições serão os entendimentos a serem resolvidos entre as duas partes. A ML pagará a seus empregados diretamente.

4.2   Normas contratuais.

a) A ML compromete-se a contratar, treinar, administrar, orientar, disciplianr e, se necessário, despedir pessoal que trabalha para o Serviço de Comidas e Bebidas.

b) O Cliente poderá contratar, iniciar contratos ou permitir a contratação para o seu próprio Serviço Comidas e Bebidas, de qualquer pessoal da gerência do Serviço de Comidas e Bebidas um (1) ano após o término do seu emprego com a ML ou após um (1) ano do término deste contrato.

c) O Cliente terá o direito de inspecionar a sua equipe de gerentes.

ARTIGO 8
TERMOS E CONDIÇÕES GERAIS

8.1   Impostos.   A ML arrecadará todos os impostos exigidos e remeterá estes impostos às agências pertinentes. A conta da água e os impostos comerciais serão pagos pela ML.

8.2   Provisões legais.   A ML deverá seguir as leis, decretos, regulamentos e regras aplicáveis das entidades, dos departamentos e das administrações do governo federal, de estada, municipal e local, encarregados da higiene, segurança e saúde do Serviço de Comidas e Bebidas e deverá obter e manter todas as licenças e autorizações necessárias. O Cliente deverá fornecer a ML toda a assistência necessária para que possa satisfazer esta exigência.

8.3   Responsabilidade em obter um seguro geral. A ML deverá obter e manter em vigor durante o prazo deste contrato um seguro geral contra lesões fíicas e danos de propriedade, no limite mínimo combinado de um milhão de (US) dólares ($1.000.000.00) incluindo, porém não limitado a, responsabilidade contratual e responsabilidade por perdas de produtos, cobrindo somente as operações e atividades da ML que estão incluir uma cláusula da companhia emissora, especificando que a apólice não será cancelada a menos que o Cliente receba uma notificação por escrito com pelo menos trinta (301) dias de antecedência.

8.4   Desistência do direito de recuperação. Cada uma das partes deste contrato renuncia de comum acordo não só a todos os seus direitos como também aos direitos de suas filiais e associações edifícios, reformas ou outra qualquer propriedade causados por incêndio, explosão ou por qualquer outra causa normalmente incluída numa apólice de seguro padrão ou numa apólice cobrindo incêndio, lesões físicas ou responsabilidade civil. O Cliente protegerá seu edifício inclusive a área de Serviço de Comidas e Bebidas, os materiais nela contidos e todas as demais propriedades seguradas contra perdas ou danos causados por incêndio, explosão e danos daquele tipo.

CONTRATO OPERACIONAL
entre
a EMBRATEL - BRASIL
e
a U.S. TELEPHONE

PARA O FORNECIMENTO DE SERVIÇOS DIGITAIS DE TELECOMUNICAÇÕES
PARA LINHAS PARTICULARES

1.   A EMBRATEL-BRASIL e a U.S. TELEPHONE, pelo presente documento, comprometem-se a conectar instalações operacionais a fim de fornecer aos clientes serviços digitais para linhas particulares via SATELLCOM WBS. Estes serviços serão desenvolvidos de acordo com as recomendações exestentes da C.C.I.T.T. e da documentação apropriada da SATELLCOM WESS.

2.   O contrato para que qualquer equipamento seja fornecido diretamente a EMBRATEL-BRASIL pela U.S. TELEPHONE será feito por meio de um anexo a este contrato.

3.   De acordo com este contrato, cada uma das partes terá que fornecer o segmento para   a conexão das comunicações do prédio do cliente, no seu país respectivo, até o ponto central da região atlântica; isto é, nos Estados Unidos. A U.S.TELEPHONE será responsável pelo segmento de comunicações entre o prédio do cliente e o satélite; na Brasil, a EMBRATEL-BRASIL será responsável pela conexão das telecomunicações entre o préedio do cliente e o satélite. Entretanto, estes segmentos serão tecnicamente e operacionalmente compatíveis entre si para que possam proporcionar os serviços desejados.

4.   A EMBRATEL-BRASIL e a U.S. TELEPHONE criarão planos separados e independentes para o cliente, e cada uma estabelecerá as tarifas e as condições de acordo com a porção do serviço a ser fornecido. Entretanto, a EMBRATEL-BRASIL e a U.S. TELEPHONE farão uma permuta de tarifas e de outras   informações de marketing. A EMBRATEL-BRASIL e a U.S. TELEPHONE aprovarão planos para "Compras numa só parada" e "Contas Unilaterais" a pedido e em nome dos clientes. Onde for apropriado e, quando houver um comum acordo   entre as partes, outros planos também poderão ser usados. No caso de interrupção de serviço, não haverá uma obrigação financeira entre a EMBRATEL-BRASIL e a U.S. TELEPHONE. Não obstante, cada uma das partes dará ao Cliente uma compensação pelas interrupções durante o período em que o serviço não estava disponível de acordo com os termos e condições das respectivas tarifas aplicáveis ao serviço em questão. Contrato operacional, p.2.

5.   Os pontos de contato para a EMBRATEL-BRASIL e a U.S. TELEPHONE serão designados; os nomes destas pessoas serão intercambiados para garantir a integridade operacional dos serviços oferecidos.

6.   Outros termos e condições poderão ser anexados ao contrato de tempos em tempos desde que a EMBRATEL-BRASIL e a U.S. TELEPHONE estejam de comum acordo.

Assinado por e em nome da

U.S.TELEPHONE

Assinatura:_____

Nome:_____

Cargo:_____

Data:_____

EMBRATEL-BRASIL

Assinatura:_____

Nome:_____

Cargo:_____

Data:_____

General Comments:

a. Subject matter:

These texts represent a specific area of law, namely, business law as it applies to business agreements. With this in mind, one should be sensitive to the fact that these original English texts, which relate to international agreements, reflect the legal terminology of the respective countries. The translation is obviously intended for use in Brazil, and therefore should reflect Brazilian legal usage. Here a good Brazilian Portuguese legal dictionary, as well as basic Brazilian dictionaries, can be very useful.

b. Format:

We draw your attention to the fact that the original text is typed in a legal text format, following established form. Therefore, the Portuguese translation was formatted to look like the original, and each page of translation corresponds exactly to each page of the original. This was done for several good reasons: (a) an end-user of a translation would often need to compare the two texts, and this exact replication makes it very easy to compare, and also to make sure nothing is missing; (b) it helps the translator to check his/ her own work, making sure nothing was left out; and (c) it conveys the sense of orderliness and accuracy which is critical in legal documents.

AGREEMENT (line 3) - The heading of the document was translated into Portuguese as *Contrato,* which in effect conveys the legal sense of the word "agreement" in English.

NOVA INVESTMENTS, INC. (line 4) - The names of companies remain the same in Portuguese, since they are legal entities. Sometimes it may be necessary to provide a translation of a company's name, for informational purposes or other reasons, but the general practice is to leave the name in the original form.

AGREEMENT (line 8) - In legal documents certain words are capitalized, because of legal implications. It is important to follow this capitalization format (*CONTRATO)* in the text of target languages.

"Food Service" (line 14) - Translated into Portuguese as *"Serviço de Comidas e Bebidas,"* literally "food and drink service," to clarify the full meaning of the term, although one could argue that "food" also covers drinks.

($1,000,000) (page 2, line 16) - In Portuguese the commas become periods.

One-Stop Shopping (page 3, line 21) - This is a colloquial American expression, which is hard to translate into another language. You may have a better suggestion.

Additional Observations:

Since legal documents such as business agreements contain a fairly standard text, you may want to get hold of one or more texts of such Portuguese-language agreements, to familiarize yourself with their style and terminology. Clearly, one does not always have the time and means to obtain this kind of information, but if this is a subject you expect to translate fairly regularly, it is worth the effort.

Also, it is important to know the purpose of a particular translation, although a translator is not always given this information by the client. If it is to be used as a legally binding agreement, it has to be accurate to the point of being accepted as a legal contract. On the other hand, if it is only for informational purposes - say, the end-user in this case does not read English - then you need not spend nearly as much time and effort to make sure every single word is the best possible equivalent of the original.

Controle da cegueira dos rios

A oncocercose ou cegueira dos rios, como é mais comumente chamada, é causada por um verme parasítico que produz milhões de larvas que circulam pelo corpo, provocando prurido intenso, debilitação e por fim cegueira. A doença é propagada por um mosquito borrachudo que transmite as larvas das pessoas contaminadas para as não-contaminadas.

O objetivo do Programa de Controle da Oncocercose (PCO) - estabelecido em 1974 e abrangendo 12 países do Sahel - é controlar os borrachudos destruindo suas larvas mediante pulverização aérea de inseticidas. O impacto ambiental dos inseticidas é constantemente monitorado por uma comissão ecológica independente, em cooperação com os governos nacionais. A comissão tem plena autoridade para examinar os inseticidas e aprovar ou condenar sua utilização. O programa colaborou também com a indústria farmacêutica para criar uma droga para uso humano, ivermectin, que extermina as larvas instaladas no corpo. A droga, porém tem pouco efeito sobre o verme adulto, e seu uso deve ser complementado pelo control do vetor mediante pulverização aérea. O fabricante do ivemectin, a Merck & Co., comprometeu-se a fornecer o remédio gratuitamente enquanto ele for necessário para combater a cegueira dos rios.

As quatro agências patrocinadoras do PCO - a Organização para Alimentação e Agricultura, o Programa das Nações Unidas para o Desenvolvimento, o Banco Mundial e a OMS - , através de uma comissão coordenadora presidida pelo Banco Mundial, decidem sobre as políticas e fiscalizam as atividades. A OMS tem responsabilidade executiva, através de uma equipe de entomologistas, epidemiologistas, pessoal de campo e pilotos; 97% do pessoal são naturais dos países participantes. O Banco Mundial os organiza, financia e administra mediante um fundo fiduciário. Além disso, apóia o desenvolvimento sócio-econômico das áreas atingidas pela doença.

O programa é considerado um grande sucesso. Protégé contra a cegueira dos rios cerca de 30 milhões de pessoas, incluindo as mais de 9 milhões de crianças nascidas desde que o PCO foi criado, a um custo anual de manos de US$1 *per capita*. Mais de 1,5 milhão de pessoas que estavam contaminadas restabelecerm-se completamente. Estimase que o Programa terá evitado pelo menos 500 mil casos de cegueira até estar concluído por volta do final do século. E presentemente já está liberando para reassentamento e cultivo cerca de 25 milhões de hectares de terras anteriormente infestadas, fomentando assim a produção agrícola.

O custo estimado do PPCO em toda a sua duração , de 1974 a 1000, é approximadamente US$570 milhões. Sua taxa interna de retorna estimada varia entre 16 e 28% (dependendo do ritmo de ocupação das áreas recuperadas, da produção incremental das novas áreas, do nível de renda da região coberta pelo PCO e da taxa projetada de aumento da produtividade). Tais beneficios estimados não incluem os efeitos positivos do programa na distribuição de renda; os principais beneficiados são os agricultores de subsistência cuja renda é bem inferior à média.

Problemas prioritários na saúde: grandes impactos da doença e intervenções eficazes em função dos custos

Entre os problemas de saúde que afetam crianças menores de cinco anos, é fácil determinar os prioritários. Como se vê na Tabela B.6 do Apêndice, nove doenças respondem por mais de 1% do impacto total da doença nesse segmento etário. São moléstias que vão desde infecções respiratórias agudas (mais de 17% no caso de meninos e meninas) até carência de iodo (de 1,2 a 1,3%). Oíto desses problemas responsáveis por 80% dos óbitos de crianças pequenas, podem ser tratados com intervenções que custam menos de US$100 por AVAI ganho. Constituem exceção apenas problems congênitos, responsáveis por mais de 6% do impacto da doença, e para os quais não se conhecem intervenções eficazes em função dos custos.

No caso de adultos, a situação é muito mais complicada (Tabela B.7 do Apêndice). A principal causa de perda de anos de vida saudável são doenças vasculares-cerebrais em homens com mais de 60 anos e em mulheres entre 45 e 59 anos. No caso dessas doenças, as intervenções custam US$1.000, ou mais, por AVAI ganho. A isquemia cardiaca fica em segundo ou terceiro lugar entre as doenças que atacam homens e mulheres com mais de 45 anos, e seu tratamento custa entre US$250 e US$1.000 por AVAI. Dentre as 10 principais doenças não-contagiosas que afetam esse grupo etário, apenas a catarata, a anemia, o câncer do aparelho respirotóro (mediante redução do fumo) e o câncer do colo do útero podem ser tratados a um custo inferior a US$100 por AVAI. Esses problemas respondem por apenas 7,9% do impacto de doença sobre mulheres entre 45 e 59 anos, e por percentuais ainda menores em outras faixas etárias e outros grupos sexuais. No tocante a doenças contagiosas, merecem prioridade a tuberculose, a AIDS e as infecções respiratórias, embora causem menos de 10% dos problemas de saúde após 45 anos e apenas 20,1% dos problemas em homens entre 15 e 44 anos.

Um maior impacto da doença e intervenções eficazes em termos de custo só coincidem em um grupo de adultos, que são as mulheres entre 15 e 44 anos. Das 10 maiores causes de doença, seis podem ser tratadas gastando-se menos de US$100 por AVAi. São doenças ligadas a gestação e parto (18% do impacto), infecções respiratórias e anemia (2,5% do impacto, cada uma), que respondem por 44% dos problemas de saúde de mulheres em idade fértil. Dois outros problemas - a depressão e lesões provocadas pelo próprio paciente - causam no mínimo, cada um, 3% do impacto da doença. Seu tratamento, porém, é muito mais problemático.

Percebe-se por esses cáculos o maior problema com que se defronta um sistema de atendimento médico á medida que a população envelhece: verifica-se acentuado aumento no custo marginal de um ano de vida saudável ganho, o que dificulta a opção entre maiores gastos e menos ganhos em termos de saúde. No entanto, se não há solução completa para muitas doenças de idosos, pode haver pliativos de baixo custo. Além disso, pode-se fazer muito em grupos mais jovens a fim de que no futuro os idosos gozem de melhor saúde.

General Comments:

In general, medical and other life science topics (one may also want to include most areas of chemistry), do not require formal training to be able to translate them from one language into another. These disciplines invariably produce explicit texts that can be followed quite easily with the aid of good references, particularly good dictionaries. In effect, the vocabulary of any given topic in those areas is well defined and quite repetitive, and after working with it a few times, one begins to see the same technical terms appearing over and over again. This is certainly true of the present texts, which discuss river blindness and health cost. They do not present any technical challenge beyond the general scope of translation.

Onchocerciasis (line 2) - This is certainly not the kind of word most of us run into every day, so if you are not absolutely sure of its spelling, look it up.

Onchocerciasis Control Programme (OCP) (line 6) - The decision whether to keep the original acronym or to change it to conform with the translated name is not always clear. In this case, one could have done it either way. In the next line, the acronym UNDP was not rendered in Portuguese at all, which may simply be an omission, and WHO (World Health Organization) was given its Portuguese equivalent, OMS. Acronyms are one of the most difficult aspects of translation, and require special attention and frequent clarification.

$1 (line 22) - In Brazilian Portuguese this is rendered as US$1, since the dollar sign is also used in Latin America for local currencies, and one has to specify that it is a U.S. dollar.

1.5 million (line 23) - In Portuguese the period becomes a comma in denoting decimals.

DALY (page 2, line 6) - This acronym is not expanded in this text, and you may not know what it means (it means Disability Adjusted Life Years). In this case, you may just leave it as it is, or you may add in brackets following this acronym the words [expansion unknown].

cost-effective (line 19) - This is a typical American business term, translated into Portuguese as *eficazes em termos de custo*. Romance languages do not have the flexibility of the English language, which can turn nouns into verbs without batting an eyelash, or combine nouns and adjectives into new words. To say *custo eficaz* in Portuguese simply won't do.

Financiamento público e privado de serviços clínicos

Em todo o mundo, há quatro canais principais para o financiamento de serviços clínicos. Dois deles são de caráter privado - o pagamento do próprio bolso e o seguro voluntário. Os dois réstantes são de caráter público: o seguro compulsório (também chamado de previdência social), que os governos administram ou regulamentam estritamente, e o custeio mediante as receitas do governo geral.

Nos países mais pobres, a despesa total com saúde talvez nem chegue a US$2 anuais por pessoa, e mais de metade desse montante provém de fontes privadas, sobretudo pagamentos do próprio bolso. Nesses países, o seguro funciona de modo precário e é pequena a receita governamental destinada à saúde. À medida que as rendas se elevam, elevam-se também os percentuais de renda gastos com saúde (como se vê no quadro superior da Figura 5.1) e a parcela de despesa com saúde proveniente de fontes públicas (como se vê no quadro inferior). Tanto nas ex-economias socialistas quanto nas economias de mercado consolidadas (com exceção dos EUA) os gastos públicos representam três quartos da despesa total com saúde.

Além das quatro fontes de financiamento da saúde, há outras três maneiras de organizar os serviços clínicos: custeio público, custeio privado sem fins lucrativos e custeil privado com fins lucrativos. São 12 as combinações diferentes podem atender a populações extremamente diferentes. Todos os sistemas nacionais de saúde utilizam pelo menos duas dessas combinações. Mesmo assim os países podem ser agrupados segundo o nivel de renda e o sistema predominante de prestação de atendimento médico. É muito importante verificar sse o seguro cobre muitos serviços e, em caso afirmativo, saber qul é o tipo predominante de seguro (Tabela 5.2).

Nos *países de baixa renda*, os pagamentos do próprio bolso correspondem a mais da metade do que cada pessoa gasta por ano com assistência médica - ou seja, de US$2 a US$40. Esse dinheiro paga principalmente honorários médicos, curandeiros tradicionais e medicamentos. As ONG, em especial aquelas ligadas a instituições religiosas, contribuem muito para a prestação de serviços de saúde em vários países de baixa renda. Na Tanzânia e no Haiti, cerca de metade dos hospitais é administrada por ONG; nos Camarões e em Uganda, as ONG administram 40% dos serviços médicos. Em Gana e na Nigéria, cerca de um terço dos leitos hospitalares fica em hospitais missionários. A despesa governamental, custeda com as receitas tributárias gerais, geralmente não é nem metade dos 2 a 7% do PNB alocados a serviços de saúde. Não existem seguros, ou existem poucos.

Alé pouco tempo atrás, a China constituía exceção entre os países de baixa renda. Entre 1960 e 1980, as empresas estatais prestavam assistência médica direta a seus empregados, ou contratavam hospitais públicos para a prestação dessa assistência. As comunas rurais tinham de destinar parte de seus recursos financeiros à prestação de atendimento médico a todos os seus membros. Em fins dos anos 70, praticamente toda a população urbana e 85% da população rural eram cobertas por seguro - feito jamais conseguido por qualquer outro país em desenvolvimento de baixa renda. No início dos anos 80, porém, quando a agricultura comunal deixou de existir e a indústria foi liberalizada, tais tipos de seturo de saúde e prestação de serviços foram bastante prejudicados. A população rural depende cada vez mais da assistência médica prestada pelo governo e custeada em parte pelas receitas gerais; mas a cobrança de taxas aos usuários permite uma significativa recuperação de custos, à semelhança do que ocorre em outros países de baixa renda.

Nos *países de renda média* os sistemas de saúde são principalmente de dois tipos: ou o seguro de saúde é fornecido pelo governo, ou é fornecido pelo setor privado. Os gastos com saúde, entre US$20 e US$400 *per capita*, são mais altos que nos países de baixa renda, e também há mais capacidade administrativa, nos setores público e privado. Em países onde existe seguro privado, como África do Sul e Zimbábue, o governo utiliza as receitas gerais para pagar assistência médica a grupos de renda média e baixa; já as famílias de renda alta (menos de 20% da população) utilizam seguros privados para pagarem médicos e hospitais particulares ou quartos particulares nos hospitais do governo.

Nos países onde há seguro social, o seguro que cobre a maior parte da população, inclusive a maioria dos empregados de classe média, provém de contribuições obrigatórias de empregadores e empregados e às vezes de recursos governamentais. A assistência médica prestada aos pobres é financiada com as receitas gerais. Este sistema prevalece na Coréia, na Turquia e na maioria dos países latino-americanos.

Nas *ex-economias socialistas* do Leste europeu e da URSS, a única forma de atendimento médico oficialmente reconhecida, até pouco tempo atrás, era a prestação desse atendimento pelo governo, mediante a receita geral. Hoje, os gastos públicos com saúde montam a 3-6% do PNB desses países, ou seja, de US$30 a US$200 *per capita*. No final dos anos 80, antes do período de liberalização politica e econômica, eram freqüentes o pagamento particular por serviços de saúde "pública" (por exemplo, dar gratificações aos médicos que trabalhavam em hospitais públicos) e o desvio de medicamentos do setor público para mercados privados. Após as reformas políticas e econômicas empreendidas nesses países no final dos anos 80, os sistemas de sa3de entraram em crise. Passou a haver pressões fortes por novas formas de seguro público e privado, em função da deficiência de recursos públicos e da deteriorção dos serviços governamentais.

Nas *economias de mercado consolidadas*, com a exceção dos EUA, mais de três quartos dos gastos com saúde - que vão de US$400 a US$2.500 por pessoa, anualmente - dependem de dois tipos de financiamento público. Na Noruega, no Reino Unido e na Suécis, as receitas tributárias gerais são usadas para pagar serviços de saúde prestados diretamente pelo governo. Na Alemanha, na França e no Japão, assim como em outros países, o seguro social é a principal forma de financiamento. Nos EUA, onde a despesa anual com saúde é de aproximadamente US$2.800 *per capita*, a combinação de sistemas é surpreendente - há seguros privados voluntários vinculados ao emprego, há seguros compulsórios para funcionários públicos federais, podendo cada funconário optar por outros seguros e outros pacotes, e há também serviços para veteranos, inteiramente financiados e prestados pelo setor público. O sistema de pagador único, financiado pela receita geral, é usado no nível federal para assistência médica aos idosos (Medicare) e no nível estadual para assistência médica aos pobres (Medicaid).

General comments:

a. Financial Translation

In translation, there is a basic difference between translating financial subjects and other technical subjects, such as legal or medical. While it is relatively easy to master the methodology of working with most technical vocabularies, even if one does not have the technical or professional background of the particular field in which one translates, in financial subjects it is necessary to have at least a general knowledge of the subject. This may be due to the fact that financial terminology and concepts are not always as readily translatable as other technical subjects. The upshot of all this is that one should not be hasty to accept a financial assignment if one does not work in this field on a regular basis.

b. Style

This particular assignment consists of a text derived from the field of health services economics. It represents the work of an international organization involved in assistance to economies in developing countries. As with most major organizations, this corporation has its own "corporate style," which affects the way this material is translated. Normally, an organization of this magnitude employs its own translators, or uses outside translators on a regular basis, to acquaint them with its style. If called upon to translate this kind of text, be sure to familiarize yourself with the organization's style.

Out-of-pocket (line 4) - This is yet another example of American business coinage which can give a translator in a Romance language a headache. Translated into Portuguese as *pagamento do própio bolso,* it can certainly be translated in other ways as well.

$2 (line 8) - See above, Assignment 3: Notes.

NGO (line 23) - This acronym means Nongovernmental Organizations. If you are not familiar with it, leave it as it is, or add [expansion unknown] after it.

GNP (line 27) - This is a very common business term, meaning Gross National Product, or PNB in Portuguese.

$400 (page 2, line 24) - For note on U.S. dollars, see note above.

$2,500 (line 24) - For note on use of comma in numbers, see note above.

After you have completed all the assignments, or at least those you have chosen to do, you have to make a major decision. If you have never translated for profit before, you have to ask yourself if you are ready to try your hand at soliciting for-profit translation work. If the answer is yes, contact one or two of the enclosed work sources (Appendix E) and apply for a test or a short assignment. If you have translated for profit before in a specific area, such as legal documents, and you feel you are now ready to venture into another area, such as medical translation, first try out some short assignments in that field, until you become comfortable with it. it is important that you develop a relationship with one or more translation companies in your own geographical area. There is absolutely no reason in this day and age for a translator, say, in Wisconsin, not to develop a profitable relationship with a translation company in Florida, and in time you may indeed find out that a certain company on the other side of the continent is your best source of work. But as a beginner, there are many advantages to interfacing personally with the staff of a translation company close to home. They can give you a great deal of practical advice, help you with the hardware and the software, and share other kinds of experience with you. There is an old saying: "A good neighbor is better than a distant relative."

If, on the other hand, you feel you are not ready to take the plunge, you may want to consider a translation course or study program. Refer to Appendix 4 in the book, and see if there is a program close to home you can sign up for. Or you may decide to continue practicing on your own.

Whatever you decide to do, don't give up too easily. If you do enjoy the challenge of translation, continue to improve you skills. Remember: Translation can be a full-time career or a very fulfilling and profitable sideline. It is definitely the kind of expertise worth having, no matter what else you choose to do with your time.

APPENDICES

APPENDIX A: REQUISITES FOR PROFESSIONAL TRANSLATORS

Any person who knows more than one language has the ability to explain a word or a sentence in what translators call "the source language" (the language you translate from) by using an equivalent word or sentence in what they call "the target language" (the language you translate into). This, in effect, is the beginning of translation. But it is only the beginning. It does not automatically turn a person into an accomplished translator. Along with the knowledge of the source and the target language, a translator must have an aptitude for translation. Some people are endowed with a talent for translation. It is not an acquired skill, like riding a bicycle. It is rather a talent, like playing the violin. Some people have it and some don't. It is not necessarily an indication of a lower or higher IQ. Nor is it an indication of how linguistically gifted one is. It is an inborn skill that enables a person to change a text from one language into another quickly and accurately, or, if you will, think in more than one language at the same time. If you possess this skill, then it behooves you to develop it and make use of it, because there is never an overabundance of good translators, and it is almost axiomatic that the good ones can always find either full-time or part-time work.

The **first** requisite for the working translator is a thorough knowledge of both the source and the target languages. There is no point in billing oneself as a translator if one is not fully familiar with both languages, or does not possess a vocabulary in both equal to that of a speaker of those languages who has a university education or its equivalent.

The **second** requisite is thorough "at-homeness" in both cultures. A language is a living phenomenon. It does not exist apart from the culture where it is spoken and written. It communicates not only the names of objects and different kinds of action, but also feelings, attitudes, beliefs, and so on. To be fully familiar with a language, one must also be familiar with the culture in which the language is used, indeed, with the people who use it, their ways, manners, beliefs and all that goes into making a culture.

Third, one must keep up with the growth and change of the language, and be up-to-date in all of its nuances and neologisms. Languages are in a constant state of flux, and words change meaning from year to year. A pejorative term can become laudatory, and a neutral term can become loaded with meaning. Thirty years ago the English word "gay" simply meant "joyous." Now it is used to define an entire segment of society. We once spoke of the "almighty dollar." Now as we travel abroad we may find out the dollar is not necessarily everyone's preferred currency.

Fourth, a distinction must be made between the languages one translates from and into. Generally speaking, one translates from another language into one's own native language. This is because one is usually intimately familiar with one's own language, while even years of study and experience do not necessarily enable one to be completely at home with an acquired language. The exceptions to this rule are usually those people who have lived in more than one culture, and have spoken more than one language on a regular basis. Those may be able to translate in both directions. There are also rare gifted individuals who have mastered another language to such a degree that they can go both ways. They are indeed extremely rare. Given all of this, one should allow for the fact that while the ability of the accomplished translator to write and speak in the target language (i.e., one's native tongue) may be flawless, that person may not necessarily be able to write excellent prose or give great speeches in the source language (i.e., the language from which one translates). Then again, it is not necessary to be able to write and speak well in the language one translates from, while it is to be expected that a good translator is also a good writer and speaker in his or her native language.

Fifth, a professional translator has to be able to translate in more than one area of knowledge. Most professional translators are called upon to translate in a variety of fields. It is not uncommon for a translator to cover as many as twenty or thirty fields of knowledge in one year, including such areas as political subjects, economics, law, medicine, communications and so on. Obviously, it would be hard to find a translator who is an economist, a lawyer, a medical doctor, and an engineer all wrapped into one. In fact, such a person probably does not exist. One does not have to be a lawyer to translate legal documents. Many a professional translator has been able to gain enough knowledge and acquire a vocabulary in a variety of technical fields to be able to produce perfectly accurate and well-written translations in those fields. This is not nearly as difficult as it may seem, since most technical fields utilize a well-defined number of terms which keep repeating themselves, and as one keeps translating the same subject, they become more and more familiar to the translator. One must, however, have a natural curiosity about many different areas of human knowledge and activity, and an interest in increasing one's vocabulary in a variety of related as well as unrelated fields.

Sixth, an effective translator must have a facility for writing or speaking (depending on whether the method used is writing, speaking, or dictation), and the ability to articulate quickly and accurately, either orally or in writing. Like a reporter, a translator must be able to transmit ideas in real time, and in good understandable language. Translation is a form of writing and speech-making, and a translator is, in a sense, a writer and an orator.

Seventh, a professional translator must develop a good speed of translation. There are two reasons for this: First, most clients wait until the last minute to assign a translation job. As a result, they turn to a translator or a translation service with what is perhaps the most typical question in this business: "How soon can you have this job ready for me?" The professional translator has to be prepared to accept that long job with the short turnaround time, or there will be no repeat business from that particular client or from most other clients, for that matter. Secondly, translation is generally paid by the word. The more words one can translate per hour, the more income one will generate. Translating 50 words per hour can land a translator in the poorhouse. Serious translation starts at 250 words per hour, and can reach as high as 1000 words per hour using word processing, and close to 3000 words per hour using dictation (the author actually knows such a translator). High volume translators are the ones who will be the most successful.

Eighth, a translator must develop research skills, and be able to acquire reference sources which are essential for producing high quality translation. Without such sources even the best of translators cannot hope to be able to handle a large variety of subjects in many unrelated fields. Dedicated translators are the ones who are always on the lookout for new reference sources, and over time develop a data bank which can be used in their work.

Ninth, today's translator cannot be a stranger to hardware, software, fax, modem, the Internet, and the latest developments in all those media. Translation has become completely dependent on electronic tools. Gone are the days of handwriting, the typewriter, and all the other "prehistoric" means of communication. The more one becomes involved in translation, the more one finds oneself caught up in the latest high-tech developments.

Tenth, a translator who wishes to be busy on a fairly regular basis doing translation work must carefully consider the fact that certain languages are in high demand, say, in Washington or in Los Angeles, while others are not. Thus, for example, there is high demand for Japanese, German, Spanish, French, Chinese, Italian, Russian and Italian in both Washington and Los Angeles, but not nearly as much for Bulgarian, Farsi, Czech, or Afrikaans. If your language falls within the second group, it is extremely advisable to also have language expertise in one of the languages of the first group, or to seriously consider whether your particular language has enough of a demand to warrant a major investment of time and effort on your part. One should always check and see what kind of a potential one's language specialty has in a given geographic area.

The above ten points are the essential criteria for developing a translation career. There are many other considerations, but none as important as these. If you feel that you can meet all of the above criteria, then you should continue reading this handbook and putting it to good use.

The Well-Rounded Translator

The main division in the translation field is between literary and technical translation. Literary translation, which covers such areas as fiction, poetry, drama, and the humanities in general, is often done by writers of the same genre who actually author works of the same kind in the target language, or at least by translators with the required literary aptitude. For practical reasons, this handbook will not cover literary translation, but will instead focus on the other major area of translation, namely, technical translation. High quality literary translation has always been the domain of the few, and is hardly lucrative (don't even think of doing literary translation if your motive is money), while technical translation is done by a much greater number of practitioners, and is an ever-growing and expanding field with excellent earning opportunities. This chapter discusses the characteristics of the well-rounded technical translator.

The term "technical" is extremely broad. In the translation business it covers much more than technical subjects in the narrow sense of the word. In fact, there is an overlap between literary and technical translation when it comes to such areas as social sciences, political subjects, and many others.

One way of defining technical translation is by asking the question, does the subject being translated require a specialized vocabulary, or is the language non-specialized? If the text being translated includes specialized terms in a given field, then the translation is technical.

The more areas (and languages) a translator can cover, the greater the opportunity for developing a successful translation career. Furthermore, as one becomes proficient in several areas, it becomes easier to add more. Besides, many technical areas are interrelated, and proficiency in one increases proficiency in another. In addition, every area breaks down into many subareas, each with its own vocabulary and its own linguistic idiosyncrasies. Thus, for example, translating in Italian does not make one an expert in all spoken Italian dialects, yet a knowledge of several of those dialects is very beneficial for the professional Italian translator.

How does one become a well-rounded translator? The answer can be summed up in one word—experience. The key to effective translation is practice. Since human knowledge grows day by day, and since language keeps growing and changing, the well-rounded translator must keep in touch with knowledge and language on a regular basis. The worst thing that can happen to a translator is to be out of touch with the source language for more than a couple of years. What the rusty translator may find out is that new words, new concepts and new ways of using those words and applying those concepts have come into being during that period of "hibernation," and one's old expertise is no longer reliable.

Translation, therefore, is a commitment one makes not for a limited period of time, but rather long-term. It is to be assumed that anyone who becomes a translator is the kind of person who loves words and loves the challenge of using words effectively and correctly. Such a person will not become an occasional translator, but will make translation a lifelong practice.

Good and Bad Translation Habits

The accomplished translator can develop good as well as bad habits. Starting with the bad, we have already pointed out one—losing touch with the source language for long periods of time. Another bad habit is taking illegitimate shortcuts while translating. There are several types of such shortcuts. The most typical is failing to look up a word one is really not sure how to translate. Being ninety percent sure of a word's meaning is not good enough in professional translation. If one is not sure of a word's meaning, even after all available means have been exhausted, then one must put in a translator's note to that effect, or make it known in some other way that there is a problem with translating that particular word. Anything less would be deceptive.

Another illegitimate shortcut is summarizing a paragraph instead of providing a *full* translation. There is such a thing as summary translation of a paragraph or a document. If a summary is called for, then this is precisely what the translator is expected to provide. But the most common form of translation is what's known in the business as a verbatim translation, which is a full and complete rendition of the source text. When verbatim translation is ordered, anything less than a full translation is an illegitimate shortcut. Unfortunately, some translators tend to overlook this from time to time, especially when they undertake more work than they can accomplish by a given deadline, and decide to summarize rather than miss that deadline.

Perhaps the worst habit for a translator is to decide at a certain point in time that his or her knowledge of either the source or the target language is so good that it cannot possibly stand any improvement. The moment one stops growing linguistically, one is no longer on the cutting edge of one's profession. The good translator is a perennial language student, always eager and willing to learn more and to keep up with the latest.

As for good habits, the most important, perhaps, are the ones we obtain by reversing the above-mentioned bad habits. But there are many more. One excellent habit is to read professional literature in the field one will be called upon to translate in with reasonable frequency. One good example is *Scientific American*, which can help anyone who translates subjects of science and technology to learn the style or styles used in scientific writing. People who work in the field of translating business documents should definitely read business periodicals, not the least of which is *The Wall Street Journal*. One does not have to be a scientist to translate scientific articles, or have a business degree to translate business documents, but a general understanding of the subject goes a long way towards providing an accurate translation of the subject.

Another excellent habit is to translate not only for profit but also for enjoyment and experience. Most people, unfortunately, are not so taken with their daily work that they would want to continue doing it after hours for fun or practice. But an accomplished translator is someone who will on occasion translate simply for the sake of sharpening his or her skill, or accept a very small fee because of personal commitment to the subject matter, or because of a personal interest. This writer, for example, enjoys translating poetry because of the challenge of doing what is perhaps the most difficult type of translation, and, quite simply, because of the enjoyment of poetry.

Yet another good habit is always to be on the lookout for dictionaries. Many dictionaries are hard to find, and are available in few places. This writer in all his travels across the United States and abroad always stops in bookstores to look for dictionaries. One can also order dictionaries from bookstores and from publishers, but then one has to know what to order and from whom.

The last good habit I would like to mention is the practice of compiling word lists and building a reference library. Dictionaries do not have all the words and terms a translator needs, nor do they contain all the information which specialized references may have. There are aids for translators put out by certain organizations, and there is professional literature in every field. In recent years there has been a growing awareness of the need for terminology management, and with the constant advances in computer technology databases have been proliferating, making the work of the translator much easier than ever before. Good references are worth their weight in gold when they are needed for a specific translation, and over time the experienced translator develops an extensive library of glossaries which become essential for any translation assignment.

APPENDIX B: TRANSLATION TECHNIQUES

Preliminary Considerations

You are given a text to translate. Before you commit yourself to doing any work on it, you must ask yourself a few preliminary questions. They are:

1. Is the text legible?
2. Am I familiar enough with the subject to tackle it?
3. Do I have the linguistic resources (dictionaries, human contacts) to decipher unfamiliar words?
4. Is the text complete, or are there any missing parts?
5. Can I do it within the requested timeframe?
6. Do I have a good reason for doing it (doing it as a learning experience, or because you enjoy it, or to help a friend, or because you are properly compensated for doing it)?

Once you have answered all the above questions to your own satisfaction, you are ready to proceed with the translation.

Effective Approaches

There is no single effective approach to translation, and over time translators develop personal techniques which enhance the quality and the speed of their translation. No one set of rules applies equally to everyone, but there are certain methods and means of translation which can help almost any translator achieve greater accuracy and output. The following is a review of some of the key techniques which are becoming almost universal among professional translators.

The first and foremost question a translator must deal with today is what kind of equipment to use in the process of translating. In the days of the pen and the typewriter this question was much less crucial. Today, however, translation has become almost totally dependent on computers, for several good reasons: (a) Word processing allows far greater flexibility in producing text than any other contemporary means. The output of most translators has been tripled and quadrupled through the use of computers; (b) Computers allow text to be stored on a disk and reprinted or modified later on, a function which is invaluable in the translation field; (c) Clients nowadays are getting used to asking for translation on disk, since it allows them to edit, reprint, modify and enhance the physical appearance of a document; (d) If more than one translator is involved in a given translation project, the text from the various translators can be entered by an editor on one disk and equalized or manipulated as necessary, without having to redo any particular portion thereof.

In addition, it is becoming more common every day to use electronic means such as a modem, fax or e-mail to transmit and receive text. These tools are no longer a luxury. Their cost has been coming down, and more and more translators are acquiring them. Many people today are saying they cannot imagine how translators were ever able to manage without them. The answer is very simple: manage we did, but it took us ten days to two weeks to do what we can now receive, translate and deliver in two or three days.

The next question when approaching a translation assignment is: Am I qualified to do this particular translation? Only an honest answer will do. If one is not sure, then chances are one should not tackle that particular task. One must feel confident about a particular assignment if the results are to be satisfactory. The exception to this rule is a case where a client cannot find anyone else to do that particular job, and for some good reason is either willing to take a chance or to receive less than a complete and fully accurate rendition. In such a case it should be made clear between translator and client that the translation is not legally binding.

Once the commitment is made to proceed with the job, the translator will spend some time going over the entire document even if it is book-length and do a realistic assessment of the following points:

a. How long will it take to translate the document?

b. What reference tools are needed to get it done?

c. What kind of preliminary steps are needed prior to the actual work of translating?

d. What special problems are related to the document, such as legibility of blurred or poorly copied text or difficult handwriting?

e. Does the document contain text in a language or languages other than the main source language, and, if so, can the translator handle that language?

Regarding the question of time, one can do a quick estimate of the length of the document by averaging words per line, times lines per page, times number of pages. An experienced translator has a pretty good idea of the number of words per hour he or she can translate. This is an essential feature of undertaking a professional translation job, since most clients have tight deadlines and tend to give repeat business to those translators known for keeping to their deadlines.

As for reference tools, if, for example, one is given a document about telecommunications, one should make use of one=s own resources in that field and/or borrow from other sources whatever one needs to accomplish the task.

Preliminary steps prior to actual translation can include a consultation with an expert in a specialized technical field regarding a difficult term, phrase, paragraph or concept which the translator does not feel comfortable with. Having access to such experts is one of the translator=s most cherished assets. It can make all the difference in the world between a correct and effective translation and one that misses the main point of the entire text. Another preliminary step is a trip to the local, regional or even specialized library to do some research on the subject.

The problem of legibility should be identified *before* one begins the task, not after. Sometimes the problem may start in the middle of the document and be so severe as to render the translation of the first part useless. In that case, the translator may have wasted a great deal of time. Sometimes the problem is minor, and does not affect the overall outcome of the translation. In other cases, the client may decide to proceed with the translation and simply put the designation [illegible] (between brackets rather than parentheses) wherever a word or part of the text cannot be deciphered.

Unbeknownst to client and translator, when a translation job is first assigned, there may be portions of text inside the source document in a language other than the main language of the document. This can happen in commercial, scientific and scholarly documents. It even happens in Tolstoy=s novel *War and Peace,* when the author starts using French instead of Russian. This too should be detected prior to commencing the translation work, and a decision has to be made as to: (a) Does that text need to be translated? (b) Can the translator handle it? (c) Is it necessary to assign it to another translator?

Once all this preliminary work has been done, one is ready to proceed with the actual translation work.

Depending on the particular text, one should either start translating at this point, or, in the case of a text containing highly specialized terminology which may send the translator on frequent trips to the dictionary, one should first go through the document and make a list of as many unknown or uncertain terms as possible, and then spend some time looking them up and making a word list. This technique saves a great deal of time, since

once a list is completed it is much easier to sail through the text, and the time spent initially on making the list is very short compared to the time wasted on repeated interruptions to look up words. Moreover, by first mastering the more difficult terminology of the text, one gains a much better understanding of the subject and is certain to produce a better translation. From the very start, make it a habit to compile word lists and glossaries of subjectspecific terminologies, and keep it in a computer database program for future reference. In time, these lists will become your most valuable translation tool.

One should also follow good work habits. Some translators, particularly those engaged in freelance work, tend to overdo it, especially during their Abusy season,@ when they can generate a large income during a relatively short period of time. They will go for twelve or more hours a day, and before they know it they will start complaining of stiffness in the neck and shoulders, blurred vision, and fatigue. One should not translate more than eight hours a day. Six is ideal. Eight is tolerable, provided one takes a few short ten to fifteen minute breaks. Ten is pushing it. Over ten is definitely hazardous to your health.

Before you get ready to submit your translation go over it again, using the following checklist:

Omissions– did you fail to translate any particular word or phrase, or even paragraph?

Format– does your format follow the original (breaking into paragraphs, for instance)?

Mistranslations– did you mistranslate any particular word?

Unknown words Cwere there words you were not able to translate which you would like to explore further?

Meaning– did you miss the meaning of any phrase or sentence?

Spelling– did you misspell any word which the spell-check function on your computer did not catch?

Grammar– did you make any grammatical mistakes?

Punctuation– did you mispunctuate or miss any punctuation marks?

Clarity– did you fail to clearly convey the meaning of any particular part of the text?

Consistency– did you call something by one name and then by another without any good reason?

Sound-alike words– did you mistranslate a word because it looks or sounds like the word in your target language but in reality has a different meaning?

Style– are you satisfied with the way your translation reflects the style of the original text (for example, the original is written in a clear, direct style, while the translation sounds more complex and indirect?)

This checklist is by no means exhaustive, but it does cover the main areas a translator must pay attention to.

As was already explained, your personal computer is your best friend when it comes to translating, editing, and producing a final copy. One can learn a few basic commands, say, in WordPerfect or Microsoft Word, and start using the computer. But there is much more to software than entering, deleting and inserting text. The better acquainted with software you become, the more it will help you with translation. Learn how to do columns and tables, how to use special technical and scientific symbols, do graphic functions, use the spell-check and the thesaurus, create data bases for glossaries and for your own administrative records, and you will tackle a great variety of technical text in many fields at a speed that will amaze you. Remember: speed in translation is the most important thing next to language proficiency. Without it you will not be profitable, and you will be overrun by the competition. With an established record of fast accurate translation you can write your own ticket.

After a few years of using the computer you may want to consider dictation. Personally, I prefer a mix of PC and dictation. When I have an unusually long job and not enough time to do it in, I may revert to dictation. Otherwise, I prefer word-processing. One could argue that by dictating one gets more done and earns more, but there are other things to consider, such as the cost of transcription, the need to edit transcription, and the better control one has over writing than speaking. Some of us are natural speakers; others are writers.

One continues to develop translation techniques over time. One of the most wonderful things about translation, in my opinion, is the fact that your mind is never idle, never in a rut, but rather always being challenged by new tasks, new subjects, new knowledge, and the need to keep up with new developments in language, with different fields of human knowledge, and with the events of the world. As a translator in the Washington area since the late seventies, I have found myself in the middle of world events, beginning with the peace treaty between Egypt and Israel in 1979, when I met Begin, Sadat and Carter, and, more recently, in my daily dealings with events in post-Cold War Eastern Europe, with a strife-torn Middle East, the famine in Somalia, the new North American Free Trade Agreement (NAFTA) between the United States, Canada and Mexico, and the growing involvement of the U.S. space program with the space programs of other nations. Very few people cover as broad an area as a translator. Every day we in the translation business find new challenges, and have to solve new problems. As a result, we are always developing new techniques and finding new answers.

APPENDIX C: TRANSLATOR'S SELF-EVALUATION

The following criteria were developed some years ago by a U.S. Government agency for determining the skill level of a potential translator whom that agency might have liked to hire. You may want to read this chapter carefully to try to make an honest determination as to where on this scale you find yourself at this time. If you are below Level 2+, you need to keep practicing. If you are at Level 3 or higher, you can start doing some professional translating. After Level 4 you are ready for some serious translating, and at Level 5 you can start making a living as a translator.

Translator Skill Levels

Level 0

No functional ability to translate the language. Consistently misunderstanding or cannot comprehend at all.

Level 0+

Can translate all or some place names (i.e., street or city designations), corporate names, numbers and isolated words and phrases,
often translating these inaccurately.

In rendering translations, writes using only memorized material and set expressions. Spelling and representation of symbols (letters, syllables, characters) are frequently incorrect.

Level 1

Sufficient skill to translate the simplest connected written material in a form equivalent to usual printing or typescript. Can translate either representations of familiar formulaic verbal exchanges or simple language containing only the highest-frequency grammatical patterns and vocabulary items, including cognates when appropriate. Translated texts include simple narratives of routine behavior; concrete descriptions of persons, places and things; and explanations of geography and government such as those simplified for tourists. Mistranslations common.

In rendering translations, writes in simple sentences (or clauses), making continual errors in spelling, grammar and punctuation, but translation can be read and understood by a native reader used to dealing with foreigners attempting to translate his/her language.

Level 1+

Sufficient skill to translate simple discourse for informative social purposes in printed form. Can translate material such as announcements or public events, popular advertising notes containing biographical information or narration of events and straightforward newspaper headlines. Has some difficulty with the cohesive factors in discourse, such as matching pronouns with referents.

In rendering translations, writing shows good control of elementary vocabulary and some control of basic syntactic patterns, but major errors still occur when expressing more complex thoughts. Dictionary usage may still yield incorrect vocabulary of forms, although can use a dictionary to advantage to translate simple ideas. Translations, though faulty, are comprehensible to native readers used to dealing with foreigners.

Level 2

Sufficient skill to translate simple authentic written material in a form equivalent to usual printing. Can translate uncomplicated, but authentic prose on familiar subjects that are normally present in a predictable sequence, which aids the translator in his/her work. Texts may include description and narration in context, such as news items describing frequently occurring events, simple biographical information, social notices, formatted business letters and simple technical material written for the general reader. The prose is predominantly in familiar sentence patterns. Some mistranslations.

In rendering translations, has written vocabulary sufficient to perform simple translations with some circumlocutions. Still makes common errors in spelling and punctuation, but shows some control of the most common formats and punctuation conventions. Good control of morphology of language (in inflected languages) and of the most frequently used syntactic structures. Elementary constructions are usually handled quite accurately, and translations are understandable to a native reader *not* used to reading the translations of foreigners.

Level 2+

Sufficient skill to translate most factual material in nontechnical prose as well as some discussions on concrete topics related to special professional interests. Has begun to make sensible guesses about unfamiliar words by using linguistic context and prior knowledge. May react personally to material, but does not yet detect subjective attitudes, values or judgments in the material to be translated.

In rendering translations, often shows surprising fluency and ease of expression, but under time constraints and pressure language may be inaccurate and/or incomprehensible. Generally strong in either grammar or vocabulary, but not in both. Weaknesses or unevenness in one of the foregoing or in spelling results in occasional mistranslations. Areas of weakness range from simple constructions, such as plurals, articles, prepositions and negatives, to more complex structures, word order and relative clauses. Normally controls general vocabulary, with some misuse of everyday vocabulary still evident. Shows a limited ability to use circumlocutions. Uses dictionary to advantage to supply unknown words. Translations are understandable to native readers not used to dealing with foreigner's attempts to translate the language, though style is obviously foreign.

Level 3

Able to translate authentic prose on unfamiliar subjects. Translating ability is not dependent on subject matter knowledge. Texts will include news stories similar to wire service reports, routine correspondence, general reports and technical material in his/her professional field, all of which include hypothesis, argumentation and supported opinions. Such texts typically include grammatical patterns and vocabulary ordinarily encountered in professional reading. Mistranslations rare. Almost always able to correctly translate material, relate ideas and make inferences. Rarely has to pause over or reread general vocabulary. However, may experience some difficulty with unusually complex structures and low-frequency idioms.

In preparing translations, control of structure, spelling, and general vocabulary is adequate to convey his/her message accurately, but style may be obviously foreign. Errors virtually never interfere with comprehension and rarely disturb the native reader. Punctuation generally controlled. Employs a full range of structures. Control of grammar good, with only sporadic errors in basic structures, occasional errors in the most complex frequent structures and somewhat more frequent errors in low-frequency complex structures. Consistent control of compound and complex sentences. Relationship of ideas presented in original material is consistently clear.

Level 3+

Increased ability to translate a variety of styles and forms of language pertinent to professional needs. Rarely mistranslates such texts or rarely experiences difficulty relating ideas or making inferences. Ability to comp-

prehend many sociolinguistic and cultural references. However, may miss some nuances and subtleties. Increased ability to translate unusually complex structures and low-frequency idioms; however, accuracy is not complete.

In rendering translations, able to write the language in a few prose styles pertinent to professional/ educational needs. Not always able to tailor language to suit original material. Weaknesses may lie in poor control of low-frequency, complex structures, vocabulary or the ability to express subtleties and nuances.

Level 4

Able to translate fluently and accurately all styles and forms of the language pertinent to professional needs. Can translate more difficult prose and follow unpredictable turns of thought readily in any area directed to the general reader and all materials in his/her own special field, including official and professional documents and correspondence. Able to translate precise and extensive vocabulary, including nuances and subtleties, and recognize all professionally relevant vocabulary known to the educated nonprofessional native, although may have some difficulty with slang. Can translate reasonably legible handwriting without difficulty. Understands almost all sociolinguistic and cultural references.

In rendering translations, able to write the language precisely and accurately in a variety of prose styles pertinent to professional/ educational needs. Errors of grammar are rare, including those in low-frequency complex structures. Consistently able to tailor language to suit material and able to express subtleties and nuances.

Level 4+

Increased ability to translate extremely difficult or abstract prose. Increased ability to translate a variety of vocabulary, idioms, colloquialisms and slang. Strong sensitivity to sociolinguistic and cultural references. Increased ability to translate less than fully legible handwriting. Accuracy is close to that of an educated translator, but still not equivalent.

In rendering translations, able to write the language precisely and accurately, in a wide variety of prose styles pertinent to professional/educational needs.

Level 5

Can translate extremely difficult and abstract prose (i.e., legal, technical), as well as highly colloquial writings and the literary forms of the language. Translates a wide variety of vocabulary and idioms, colloquialisms, slang and pertinent cultural references. With varying degrees of difficulty, can translate all kinds of handwritten documents. Able to understand how natives think as they produce a text. Accuracy is equivalent to that of a well-educated translator.

In rendering translations, has writing proficiency equal to that of a well-educated native. Without nonnative errors of structure, spelling, style or vocabulary, can translate both formal and informal correspondence, official reports and documents and professional/educational articles, including writing for special purposes which might include legal, technical, educational, literary and colloquial writing.

APPENDIX D: PORTUGUESE TECHNICAL DICTIONARIES

General Dictionaries

The Oxford-Duden Picture Dictionary: (English- Brazilian Portuguese) Oxford University Press 2000

Dicionário de Expressões Populares Portugueses, Simões, G. A., Lisbon: Dom Quixote 1993 *Portuguese-Portuguese*

The New Michaelis Dictionaries, São Paulo: Edições Melhoramentos 2000 *A series of dictionaries. The **Novo Michaelis** Portuguese-English, English-Portuguese is a good comprehensive dictionary.*

Dicionário Escolar de Português-Inglês /Dicionário Escolar de Inglês-Português, 2 vols., sold separately, Lisbon: Porto Editora 1989

Novo Dicionário Aurélio da Língua Portuguesa, 2nd ed., Buarque de Holanda, A., Ferreira: J.E.M.M. Editores, Ltda. 1986 *Portuguese-Portuguese. Essential.*

A Portuguese-English Dictionary, Taylor, J., Stanford University Press 1970

A Dictionary of Informal Brazilian Portuguese, Chamberlain, B., Washington, D.C.: Georgetown University Press 1984

Webster Dicionário Inglês-Português, Houaiss, A. and Cardim, I.,. Record 1982

Dicionário de Expressões Idiomáticas, Pugliesi, M., Editora Parma Ltda. 1981 *Portuguese-Portuguese.*

The New Appleton Dictionary of the English and Portuguese Lan-guages, Houaiss, A., New York: Appleton-Century-Crofts 1967

Dicionário Estrutural, Estilístico e Sintático da Língua Portuguesa, Ramalho, E., Porto: Lello & Irmão
Though published in Portugal, it is still useful for Brazilian texts.

Portuguese: Computers

Computer Dictionary: English-Portuguese/Portuguese-English, French & European Publications 1998

Dicionário de Informática, Inglês-Português, Português-Inglês. Microsoft Press, Editora Campus 1993

Dicionário Enciclopédico de Informática, Fragomeni, A.H., 1986 *English-Portuguese/Portuguese-English*

Dicionário de Informática, Society of Computer and Peripheral Equip-ment Users, Rio de Janeiro 1985

Dicionário de Informática, Lisbon: Publicacões Dom Quixote 1984

Portuguese: Economics

Dicionário de Termos de Negócios Inglês-Português/Português-Inglês, Pinho, Manuel Orlando M. Editora Atlas 1995

Michaelis Dicionário Executivo Inglês-Português. Melhoramentos 1989

Dicionário Bancário Português-Inglês, Correia da Cunha, A., Portugal: Publicações Europa-América 1988
Excellent but small.

Dicionário de Economia e Gestão, Lima, G. et al, Porto: Lello & Irmão, Editores 1984

Dictionary of Economic and Commercial Terms, Cavalcante, J.C. Marques, 1982 *English-Portuguese*

Dicionário Técnico Contábil, Altmann, M.R., 1980
English-Portuguese/Portuguese-English

Portuguese: Law

Enciclopédia do Advogado, 5th ed., Soibelman, L., Rio de Janeiro: Luso-Brazilian Books 1995 *Portuguese-Portuguese Essential for legal translation.*

Noronha Legal Dictionary / Dicionário Jurídico, de Noronha Goyos, D., Editora Observador Legal 1993
Portuguese-English/English-Portuguese. An absolute necessity.

Dicionário Jurídico Português-Inglês/Inglês-Português, Chavez, M., Rio de Janeiro: Barrister's Editora 1989

Vocabulário Jurídico, 2 vols., DePlacido e Silva, Rio de Janeiro 1961 *Portuguese-Portuguese*

Portuguese: Medicine

Medical Dictionary: English, Spanish, Portuguese, Notte-Schlegel,I., New York: Springer-Verlag 2001

Dicionário Médico, Rio de Janeiro: Editora Guanabara-Koogan 1979

Dorland (Pocket) Dicionário Médico, New York: ibd Ltd. 1996

Portuguese: Metallurgy

Dicionário Metalúrgico, Inglês-Português, Português-Inglês, Taylor,
J.L., São Paulo: Assoc. Brasileira de Matais 1981

Portuguese: Technical

Dicionário Verbo de Inglês Técnico e Científico, Farinha dos Santos Tavares, J., Lisbon:Editorial Verbo 1994
English-Portuguese/ Portuguese-English

Dicionário de Termos Técnicos, Mendes Antas, L., São Paulo: Traco Editora 1980

DePina Dicionário Técnico (Inglês-Português/Português-Inglês) Araujo, Avelino de Pina. MAKRON Books,
Editora McGraw-Hill 1978

APPENDIX E: SOURCES OF TRANSLATION WORK

> This book includes a CD (inside the front cover) with lists of translations companies and international corporations who do a large volume of translation in all languages.

If you choose freelance translation, you should consider yourself a one-person translation company. Your main concern will be where to find work. The need for freelance translation is greater than anyone can estimate, and is clearly growing at a rapid rate. Worldwide, translation is a multibillion dollar industry. But finding translation work on your own is easier said than done. The main problem is that translation is hardly ever a steady, ongoing function of any particular work source, such as an embassy, a company, a government agency, or even a publisher. None of those needs translation every day of the year. Each of them may need a great deal of translation all at once (more than any one person can handle within the given time-frame), and then none for a long time. And, if any one of them needs translation on an ongoing basis, chances are a decision will be made to hire an in-house translator rather than farm out the work.

The fact remains, however, that a well-rounded freelancer can earn well over $50,000 a year, and, in the case of highly specialized technical translators in major languages like Spanish, German, Japanese or Russian, even $100,000 or more. The secret to all of this is establishing for yourself a good clientele. There are two ways of doing this. The first, and by far the hardest, is finding your own clients and working with them directly. You may want to contact embassies, law firms, publishers, government agencies and so on, and solicit work directly from them. If you are fortunate enough to find some good steady clients on your own, you will be doing quite well. But the problem often lies in the word "steady." What seems to be a steady client today may not be so steady tomorrow.

This brings us to the second, and by far the safer option, which is translation agencies. There are hundreds of them in the United States, and they handle huge amounts of translation business every year. In this chapter we will discuss translation agencies, as well as direct sources of translation available to the freelancer.

Translation Agencies

Translation agencies, also known as translation companies, or translation bureaus, are for the most part privately owned commercial establishments ranging in size from one or two employees to ten or more, but hardly ever larger than ten. Some are divisions of larger companies, such as Berlitz, which is primarily a language school and publisher, offering translation as a secondary function. Some specialize in one language only, such as Spanish, German, or Japanese. Most offer several languages, and quite a few bill themselves as offering "all languages." This last type is somewhat pretentious, since there are more languages in the world than any one person can identify. But what they really mean is that they will make the effort to find a translator in almost any language they may be called upon to translate.

As a general rule, translation agencies employ relatively few in-house translators, since the flow of work in any given language is usually uneven. Instead, they rely on the services of a network of hundreds of freelancers who can handle a great variety of subjects. Those freelancers are located all over the United States and even abroad. The ones who are most reliable and professional get the major share of the work, and some of them earn the above-quoted figures.

As a freelancer, you need to cultivate at least one such agency, preferably two or three. The problem in working with only one is that, with few exceptions, there may not be a steady flow of work coming out of any given agency in any given language, in subjects you are equipped to handle. Two or three will give you better coverage, and assure a better flow. On the other hand, you may find yourself in a situation where all three ask you to do something at the same time, and you may not be able to do it. You need to establish an understanding with your agencies that would make an allowance for such a scenario, so that you don't spoil your relationship with any one of them.

The worst thing you can do as a freelancer working with translation agencies is to overcommit yourself. Your most important personal asset is your reliability. Once you fail to meet deadlines (keep in mind—the agency stands to lose a client if deadlines are not met), your reliability becomes questionable, and if you do it once too often, you may soon find out that those phone calls from the agency offering you work assignments stop coming.

Where do you look for translation agencies? Below you will find a listing of hundreds of such agencies. You can find more in the Yellow Pages, or through the ATA (American Translators Association), which has local chapters around the country. My suggestion is to start with those close to home. In this day and age of international electronic communications, distance has little meaning. But then again, close to home still works, because you can meet the people there, befriend them, and in some instances even avail yourself of their dictionaries and other resources.

Keep in mind that a translation company has overhead, and also needs to make some profit to stay in business. They do the hard work of finding translation assignments, and therefore share with you the profit from the job. You can usually make more money by going directly to the client, and if you have enough of your own clients you don't need a translation company to send work your way. But most freelance translators do need those companies, which invariably provide a more steady flow of work than what a freelancer can get on his or her own.

The two things all translation companies appreciate and reward in a freelancer are honesty and loyalty. If you agree to a deadline, stick to it. Don't renege on it at the last minute. That's a sure prescription to spoil your association with your company. Equally important is not to go behind the company's back and try to solicit its own clients directly. Some companies will make you sign an agreement to this effect. Others will rely on the honor system. Don't abuse their trust. It usually doesn't pay off.

Direct Sources of Work

Working with translation agencies usually does not stop you from finding your own clients, as long as there is no conflict of interest with the agency's clients. It would be impossible to list here all the potential sources of direct translation work, since they include practically the entire human race (everyone needs a document translated at some point). But there are some major sources which ought to be mentioned, and here are some of the more important ones.

Law Firms

Law firms are a major source of translation work. Some of the larger firms hire full-time translators or staff members who are bilingual, especially if they do business on a regular basis with a foreign entity. Most firms use translators on an as-needed basis. Legal translation is a specialized field in which you need to acquire experience working with legal documents. There are several legal specialties, such as patent law, international law, immigration, and so on. Each specialty has its own style and terminology, which a translator needs to become acquainted with. As a freelancer, adding legal translation to your list of specialties is an excellent idea. You will find out that your volume of translation will increase considerably by doing so.

Quite often, a law firm needs both document translation and interpretation. Keep in mind that interpretation is a discipline separate from translation, and that there is a big difference between one-on-one consecutive interpreting and simultaneous conference interpreting. If asked by a law firm to do both text translation and interpreting, be sure to find out first exactly what the assignments consist of.

Industry

Corporations doing business in other countries have to deal with documents originated in the languages of those countries or English documents that need to be translated into those languages. Here again we find the two approaches of either hiring translators or farming out work to freelancers and to translation services (or a combination of both). This field is perhaps the fastest growing source of translation in the closing years of the twentieth century. More and more major American companies are turning to international business as a way to offset the decline of business at home and to gain a share of the world market. Their need for translation is growing every day, and even those who have in-house translators are finding themselves using freelancers because of their volume of translation work.

If you are fortunate enough to form a relationship with a major company doing business overseas, you may find yourself in the enviable position of dealing with a major, steady source of translation. How does one get work with major corporations? If you have a special expertise in their field of work, say you are a telecommunications expert and you would like to translate for Sprint, find out who handles outside vendors or services, and give them a call or drop them a note. It also helps to know someone in the company, who can do some of the legwork for you and put you in touch with the right people. As a general rule, this is not easy to do. But persistence does pay off some of the time, and even if only a few respond, it is worth the effort.

The U.S. Government

For several decades following World War Two, translation in the federal government enjoyed a boom. The onset of the Cold War resulted in wide-scale translation activities on the part of the U.S. Department of Defense (DoD), all the branches of the service (particularly the Army, Navy, and Air Force), and the Central Intelligence Agency (CIA). In addition, such multilingual organizations as the Voice of America (which started broadcasting in 1942 in 40 languages), sprang into being. These and other organizations employed a host of translators, and farmed out millions of words every year to be translated. Looking back, those were the feast years of government translation. During the nineties, however, a major shift has been taking place. Since 1992, there has been a sharp decline in government translations, and those translation agencies and freelancers who were dependent on government work for their bread and butter, are hurting. This is not to say that the U.S. Government is no longer a source of employment for translators. There are still many opportunities for translation in the government, offered by such bodies as the Language Services division of the U.S. Department of State (for in-house as well as freelance translators and interpreters), the Library of Congress, the U.S. Patent and Trademark Office, and so on (see list of U.S. Government Agencies, Appendix 4).

My translation company, Schreiber Translations, Inc. (STI), started out in life as a full-service translation company for the federal government. This was in the early eighties, when the boom was still on. We provided translation from and into over 50 languages and dialects, as well as interpreting, transcription, voice-over, graphics, and editing. Luckily for us, we realized early on that, as the world was changing, we were better off not being locked into government work, and we were able to develop a lucrative practice in the nongovernmental sectors. Today, government work makes up less than 50% of our total translation work.

What does all of this mean to linguists seeking translation work in the closing years of the twentieth century? There is no one simple answer. The government has been known to swing like a fast-moving pendulum. This author believes that before long the federal government will be launching new major translation projects, in such sectors as world trade and international relations. American interaction with other cultures and languages is far from diminishing. If anything, it is increasing day by day. One good example is the American space program, conducted by the National Aeronautics and Space Administration (NASA). Back in the sixties, there were two major space programs in the world—the Soviet and the American. Today, many countries in Western Europe and Asia have an active space program, and many of them are involved in cooperative efforts. NASA is actively involved in this new international space scene, and the need for translation in this particular organization should not be underestimated. But all of this, of course, is speculative. The federal government is making a historical effort to reduce its enormous deficit, and since the lawmakers of our land are not necessarily attuned to the critical importance of translation, translation may well be a casualty of the budget wars. Translators would be well advised not to write off doing translation for the government, since it is, and will continue to be, the single biggest employer around. But they should put at least as much, if not more, effort into finding translation work outside the government, where indeed the field is all but limitless.

What are the pros and cons of translating for the government? For many linguists over the years, the government has offered job security. I know some fine translators who have worked for the government for many years and had interesting and fulfilling careers. On the other hand, career translators in the government are not paid exceptionally high salaries. Quite a few freelance on the side in an effort to supplement their income. As for freelancers who contract with the government, here we have mixed results. Some have found themselves a cozy niche and are kept busy on a fairly regular basis. Others go through the "feast and famine" syndrome. Some have been frustrated by spending a long time hunting for government assignments, with little result. To freelance effectively for the government, one should, in most instances, work in one of the top five

languages the U.S. Government is interested in (Spanish, Russian, German, French and Japanese). Any other language, even Chinese or Italian, may not offer enough of a flow. One should also make many contacts.

On the downside, government agencies, with few exceptions, are notorious for not paying on time. A few years ago, the government passed a "prompt payment" act, which mandates 30-day net payment, with interest accruing thereafter. The problem is, more than a few agencies take at least another 30 days to process an invoice, claiming that it takes that long to get your invoice "into the system." Others take even longer, and simply neglect to add interest. If you try to get it, you may soon find out you waste more time going after it than it's worth. In some extreme cases—which are by no means rare—it can take six to twelve months to get paid. Your invoice simply gets lost in the system. Your remedy is to contact your congressperson, who will call that particular government office to make sure you get paid. The problem is, those folks in the finance office often resent being put on the spot in this manner, and while they will expedite your payment, you may not get work next time. It all sounds shocking, but having been there, it is my civic duty to let you know.

Another drawback of government freelancing is the incredible amount of paperwork you are asked to fill out in doing some of those jobs. I have done five and ten dollar jobs that required three detailed forms filled out, plus an invoice in six copies, mailed to three different offices (finance, procurement, and contract). It took me longer to do the paperwork than to translate, and clearly the whole thing was not worth my while. If you do a fair amount of freelancing for the government, you learn to overlook these excesses. Otherwise, you may have to decide whether it's all worth it.

A third major drawback to doing government work is the fact that quite often the translation standards of a particular agency may be quite low. As a result, you run the risk of developing poor translation habits, lack of attention to details, lack of sufficient editing and proofing, and so on. What that means in a practical sense is that when a more demanding job comes along, especially in the private sector, you may find out your performance is not satisfactory, and you may lose your client.

Having said all this, it behooves me to add that during the last seventeen years I have interacted with hundreds of government employees and dozens of agencies, and many of those have been a delight to work with, and overall I have been very fortunate to have this unique opportunity to take part in many historical events, including the peace treaty between Israel and Egypt, the Gulf War, the disarmament agreement with the former Soviet Union, the Bosnian peace agreement, and many more. Thus, working with the government as a linguist is by no means a dull experience, and if you learn how to take some of the problems in your stride, you can do quite well.

State and Local Government

Government at all levels, from the municipal to the federal, needs translation. At the local level we find more and more city and county government translating their pamphlets, brochures and other documents into the languages of their immigrant populations, notably Asian languages and Spanish. In addition, local government has an ongoing need for interpreters, mostly for the court system, but also for social services, hospitals, and other local institutions. At this time of tight budgets, this may not be the most lucrative field, but it is definitely worth exploring, since it is local, and mostly uses local linguists.

Major Organizations

Among the largest organizations that use a great deal of translation one should mention the United Nations, The World Bank, the World Health Organization, the Organization of American States, to cite only some of the better-known ones here in the U.S. Surely there are more in Europe, such as the World Court, the European Community, NATO, and many more. Most of these organizations use in-house linguists, and do not farm out translation work if they can help it. But quite often they have more documents to translate than they can handle in-house, and they look for outside help.

Publishers

Book publishers use freelance translators in many different ways. This is not an easy field to break into, particularly for the beginner. Many publishers turn to academia for translators, and if you are in academia and can translate from or into another language in your field of expertise, there is a chance you can get the work. Others turn to established translators with name recognition. But it is certainly worth trying, to query publishers and find out if they need your services.

Software Localization Companies

A fast-growing area of translation is software localization, or translation of software-related text into other languages and adapting the text to the target culture. Software localization companies specialize in computer subjects and in English-into-foreign language translation. They employ in-house translators, but they also use freelancers from time to time. Their work encompasses everything from computer manuals to localization of web-sites.

Networking

An excellent source of work for freelance translators is personal contacts with other translators. The ATA's local chapters are one place where translators meet and get to know each other. The annual conference of the ATA holds a networking session, which is very valuable. One also meets translators through personal contacts in the translation field.

The latest way to meet translators is on the Internet. Entities such as the Foreign Language Forum on CompuServe bring together translators from all over the world. All you need to do is post a message on one of those programs, and before you know it you get a response from someone in your own town or half way around the world.

Keeping in touch with other translators is a prime means of finding out about work sources and assignments. There are clearly many advantages to networking in the translation field, and the more contacts one has the better.

The following is a list of translation companies who use freelance translators. The companies are not rated. It is up to you to find out which are best suited to your needs.

-A-

A L Madrid & Associates, 165 Ponce de Leon Boulevard , Coral Gables, FL 33134 Phone: (305)448-8985 Fax: (305)448-7519 e-mail: info@almadrid,com Web site: www.amlogos.com Contact: Alberto Lares Member: ATA

A & M Logos International, Inc., 40 Rector Street, Ste. 1504, New York, NY 10006 Phone: (212)233-7061 Fax: (212)233-7167 e-mail: trans@amlogos.com Web site: www.amlogos.com
Contact: Elena Gapeeva Member: ATA

A Perfect Translation, 3415 Waterview Trail, Rockwall, TX 75087 e-mail: aptrans@msn.com
Contact:Rianne Sanchez Member: ATA

AAA Worldwide Translation Services, 4820 Minnetonka Blvd., St. Louis Park, MN 55416 Phone: (612)922-7446 Fax: (612)922-2001 e-mail: aaawwide2@aol.com
Contact: Danny Freier Member: ATA

ABC Worldwide Translations & Interpretations, 8306 Wilshire Boulevard, Ste. 200, Beverly Hills, CA 90211
Phone: (310)260-7700 Fax: (310)260-7705 e-mail: info@wordexpress.com
Web site:www.wordexpress.net Contact: Muriel Redoute Member: ATA

ABS Translation & Interpreting Service, 1685 Hampton Road, Abington, PA 19001 Phone: (215)886-2219 Fax: (215)886-7671 e-mail: ABStrans@aol.com Contact: Aram Sarkisian Member: ATA

A.C.E. InfoTech Group, 1450 114th Ave SE, Ste. 1-230, Seattle, WA 98004 Phone: (425)453-4444 Fax: (425)453-0188 Web site: www.aceinfotech.comContact: Maya Vengadasalam Member: ATA

AE Inc. Translations, 15995 N. Barkers Landing, Ste. 111, Houston, TX 77079 Phone: (281)870-0677 Fax: (281)556-9737 e-mail: translations@aetrans.com Web site: www.aetrans.com
Contact: Stephen D. Ross, President Member: ATA

ABLE International, Inc., 8 Wright Acres Road, Bedford, NH 03110
Phone: (603)625-2253 Fax: (603)625-0950 Web site: www.ableint.com Member: ATA

Academy of Languages Translation & Interpretation Services, 216 First Ave. South, Ste. 330, Seattle, WA 98104 Phone: (206)521-8601 Fax: (206)521-8605e-mail: trasnalte@wal.org Web site: www.wal.org Contact: Mercedes Creelman Member: ATA

Academy of Legal and Technical Translation, Three Continental Towers, 1701 Golf Road, Ste. 604, Rolling Meadows, IL 60008
Phone: (847)364-7700 Fax: (847)364-7883e-mail: info@transexpert.com Web site: www.transexpert.com
Contact: Hema Desai Member: ATA

Academy Translations, P.O. Box 357, East Berlin, CT 06023
Phone: (860)828-9615 Fax: (860)828-3965
e-mail: acadtran@pobox.com
Contact: David J. Marsh, Director of Operations
Founded 1996. Member: ATA, NAJIT. Translates all languages, both from and into English. Emphasis on all areas of translation, with specialties in Business and Finance, Insurance and Banking, Manufacturing, Immigration and Naturalization and Broadcast and Print Journalism. Prospective translators should demonstrate proficiency in their languages, and be able to verify their education and experience. ATA or other accreditation is preferred. Resumes are evaluated, and if qualified, translators are sent a letter with a subcontractual agreement. Maintains a pool of over 1800 translators.

Accent on Language, 160 East 56th St., 5th Fl., New York, NY 10022 Phone: (212)486-6790 Fax: (212)486-2439
e-mail: info@accentonlanguage.com Web site: www.accentonlanguage. com
Contact: Brian E. McDermott Member: ATA

Accent Typography & Translation, 1086 Rainberry Court, Neenah, WI 54956 Phone: (920)751-8260 Fax: (920)729-5843
e-mail: accent@athenet.net
Contact: Kimberlee A. Heier, President Member: ATA

Accento, The Language Company, 5527 Dyer St., Dallas, TX 75206 Phone: (214)363-5353 Fax: (214)363-0067
e-mail: accento@accento.net Web site: www.accento.net Contact: James Mahler Member: ATA

Access Transport & Translation Services, Inc., 528 S North Lake Boulevard, Ste. 1000, Altamonte Springs, FL 32701
Phone: (888)748-7575 Fax: (407)330-7959 e-mail: gengelman@accessontime.com Web site: www. accessontime.com
Contact: Stacey L. Whidden Member: ATA

Accomplished Translation Services, 305 Broadway, Ste. 408, New York, NY 10007 Phone: (212)227-7440 Fax: (212)227-7524 e-mail: kungarsohn@hotmail.com Web site: www.accomplishedtranstion.com
Contact: Ken ungarsohn Member: ATA

Accu Trans, Inc., 4517 Minnetonka Boulevard, Ste. 200, Minneapolis, MN 55416 Phone: (612)823-1231 Fax: (952)925-4772 e-mail: attranslation@yahoo.com Contact: Ken ungarsohn Member: ATA

Accura International Translations 12862 Cherry Way, Thornton, CO 80241 Phone: (303)280-1292 Fax: (303)280-1489 e-mail: accutrans.com Contact: Tanja M. Tombaugh Member: ATA

Accurapid Translation Services, Inc., 806 Main St., Poughkeepsie, NY 12603 Phone:(845)473-4550 Fax: (845)473-4554 Web site: accurapid.com Contact: Gabe Bokor
Founded 1978. Member: ATA. Translates German, Spanish, French, Hungarian and Japanese both from and into English, and Portuguese and Russian from English. Emphasis on Engineering, Patents, Law, Business and Finance trans-lation. Prospective translators should demonstrate competence and a professional attitude. Resumes are filed for future reference. The company pioneered the use of technological tools in the industry. The company counts freelance translators from Europe, Asia and the Americas in its professional pool. Maintains a pool of 600 translators.

Accurate Spanish Translations by Spanish Business Services, Inc., P.O. Box 720519, Dallas, TX 75372
Phone:(214)821-2050 Fax: (214)821-7065 e-mail: sbscorp@swbell.net Web site: www.spanishbusiness.com
Contact: Robert H. Brandao Member: ATA

ACCUWORLD, LLC, 200 West Madison St., Ste. 230, Chicago, IL 60606
Phone:(312)641-0441 Fax:(312)641-7370 e-mail: ts@inlinguachi.com   Contact: Human Resources Department
Founded 1968. Member: ATA. Translates all languages, both from and into English. Covers all areas, with specialties in foreign language voice-overs and technical manual translation. Resumes are compiled in a database according to area of expertise. The company, headquartered in Bern, Switzerland, has over 300 worldwide locations. It provides language training, cultural training, translation/interpretation services, and foreign language typesetting and voiceovers. Maintains a pool of 800+ translators.

Acentos, Marketing & Advertising & Translations, 400 E. Lake St., Minneapolis, MN 55408 Phone: (612)824-6109 Fax: (612)825-1729 e-mail: acentos@compuserve.com   Contact: Franklin Curbelo   Member: ATA

AD-EX WORLDWIDE, 525 Middlefield Rd., Ste. 150, Menlo Park, CA 9402 Phone: (800)223-7753 Fax: (650)325-8428   e-mail: ADEXTRAN@compuserve.com Web site:www.ad-ex.net   Contact: Robert Addis
Founded 1957. Member: ATA. Translates in all major languages, in all industrial fields, especially in the power and aerospace industries. Prospective translators must have demonstrable years of experience and written evidence of competence, including resumes and work samples. Resumes are responded to with a request for samples which are then thoroughly examined. The company is always glad to hear from veteran professional translators. Their client base is worldwide. Maintains a pool of "hundreds" of translators.

Adams Translation Services, 10435 Burnet Rd., Ste. 125, Austin, TX 78758 Phone:(512)821-1818
Fax:(512)821-1888 e-mail: mdavila@adamstrans.com Web site: adamstrans.com   Contact: Martha Davila
Founded 1982. Member: ATA, AATIA, AITA. Translates all European as well as Asian languages, including Italian and Hebrew. Emphasis on Hardware, Software, Legal, and Engineering translations. Prospective translators should be native speakers with college/graduate degree in their language/s and training or experience in specialized technical area/s and be familiar with C.A.T. tools. Resumes are entered in a database and called as possible jobs come up. The company also has desktop publishing and hypertext services. Maintains a pool of 1000+ translators.

Adaptive Language Resources, Inc., 45 Mount Auburn St., Watertown, MA 02139 Phone: (617)924-0554
Fax:(617)924-0280 Web site: www.adaptivelanguage.com   Contact: Adrian Spidle   Member: ATA

Advance Language Studios, 500 N. Michigan Ave., Chicago, IL 60611 Phone:(312)782-8123 Fax:(312)782-8356
Contact: Patrick Schoorlemmer
Founded 1963. Member: ATA. Translates from English into Spanish, French, German, Italian, Portuguese, Dutch, Japanese, Korean, Mandarin, Russian, and Polish. Emphasis on Technical, Advertising, Financial, Legal, and Commercial translations. Prospective translators should be born and raised in country of target language. Resumes are entered in a database. Company services include Translation, Interpreting, Desktop Publishing, Video dubbing in in-house studio. Maintains a pool of 1000+ translators.

Advanced Communication and Translation, Inc., 6404 Stratford Rd., Chevy Chase, MD 20815   Phone: (301)654-2890 Fax: (301)654-2891 e-mail: act@act-translate Website: www.at-translate.com
Contact: Monique-Paule Tubb   Member: ATA

Advanced Global Services, Inc., P.O. Box 965, Chesterton, IN 46304 Phone: (219)921-1733   Fax: (219)921-0640 e-mail: fruslcs@gte.net   Web site: www.FR-USA.COM Contact: Sylvie Prudhomme   Member: ATA

Advanced Language Translation, 564 E Ridge Road, Ste. 105, Rochester, NY 14621
Phone: (716)342-1250 Fax: (716)342-1270 e-mail: info@advancedlanguage.com
Web site: www.advancedlangauge.com
Contact: Scott Bass Member: ATA

Affinity Language Services, 101 S. Fairview Ave., Wind Gap, PA 18091 Phone: (610)863-3955   Fax: (610)863-8571 e-mail: info@affinity-languages.com   Web site: www.affinitylanguages.com   Contact: Michelle Zuccarini
Founded 1998. Member: ATA. Works in Spanish, German, French, Italian, and Dutch. Also in Japanese. Main areas: Technical, sci-tech, legal, medical, and business. Also provides interpretation, editing, proofreading, transcription, and copywriting. Uses translators worldwide.

Agnew Tech-II, 741 Lakefield Rd., Ste. C, Westlake Village, CA 91361 Phone: (805)494-3999 Fax: (805)494-1749 e-mail: agnewi @agnew.com Web site: agnew.com Contact: Irene Agnew Founded 1986. Member: ATA, NAWBO, WITI. Translates Spanish, Chinese, French, German, Japanese, Russian, Vietnamese, etc. from English. Also scripts and voiceover. Covers all technical areas. Prospective translators should have a B.A. degree or higher and 2-3 years experience. Resumes received via e-mail, reviewed, graded and scheduled for a translation test. The company is a full-service translation bureau, as well as providing desktop publishing, web page design, multimedia, and audiovisual services. Maintains a pool of 300-400 translators.

AimTrans, Inc., 14752 Beach Blvd, Ste. 201, La Mirada, CA 90638 Phone: (714)522-8200 Fax: (714)522-7773 Web site: www.aimtrans.com Contact: Irene Agnew member: ATA

Airspeed Translations, 4200 Westheimer Road, Ste. 201, Houston, TX 77027 Phone: (713)586-2577 e-mail: rknauth@att.net Web site: www.airspeedtranslations.com Contact: Rick Knauth

Alanguage Bank, Inc., 150 Lafayette St., 5th Floor, New York, NY 10013 Phone: (212)213-3336 Fax:(212)685-7263 e-mail: peiwens@alanguagebank.com Web site: www.alanguagebank.com Contact: Pei Wen Shih Member: ATA

Albanian Translation Services, 11880 Barclay Dr., Moreno Valley, CA 92557 Phone: (909)275-9278 Fax:(909)684-3134 e-mail: tirana@email.msn.com Contact: Mirela S. Kuhn Member: ATA

Albors and Associates, Inc., P.O. Box 5516 Winter Park, FL 32793 Phone: (800)785-8634 Fax: (407)657-7004 e-mail: rene@albors.com Web site: www.albors.com Contact: René A. Albors, President Founded 1996. Member: ATA, NAJIT, Hispanic Chamber of Commerce, Orlando Chamber of Commerce. Translates Spanish, French, Portuguese, Japanese, German, Chinese, Russian, Polish, Italian and Italian, both from and into English. Emphasis on Legal, Medical and Business translations. Prospective translators should be experienced, expert with terminology, and prompt in their delivery of finished work. Accepts unsolicited resumes for translation and inter-pretation. Resumes are computer-filed, and a letter of thanks is sent to acknowledge receipt. Maintains a pool of 5300 translators.

Alexandria Translations, 8827 Fort Hunt Rd., Alexandria, VA 22308 Phone:(703)799-7606 Fax:(703)799-7607 e-mail: 102554.3407 @compu-serve.com Contact: Lidia Terziotti Member: ATA Translates and edits documents in a variety of languages.

All-Language Services, 545 Fifth Ave., New York, NY 10017 Phone: (212)986-1688 Fax: (212)986-3396 e-mail: alsny@idt.com Web site: all-language.com Contact: Miriam Edgelow, Personnel Founded 1959. Uses freelance translators and interpreters. Accepts unsolicited resumes. If interested, asks for work sample, and offers a small initial assignment. Applicant must be a professional translator. Main languages (both ways) are Spanish, French, Italian, German, Portuguese, Chinese, Korean, Japanese, Dutch, and Russian. In total, some 59 languages. Main subjects are finance, law, advertising, banking, including brochures, annual reports, and manuals. Uses 80 translators in house, and some 1000 on call.

All Language Translations, 656 Lansing St., Schenectady, NY 12303 Phone: (518)372-6804 Fax: (518)374-6174 e-mail: cezary@netcom.com Contact: Cezary Drzymalski Member: ATA

Allegro Translations, 4513 Vernon Blvd., Madison, WI 53705 Phone: (608)233-3208 Fax: (608)233-3511 e-mail: info@allegro.com Web site: www.allegro-translation.com Contact: Yaël Bratzlavsky Founded 1993. Member: ATA. Translates English into Spanish, German, French, Japanese, Chinese, Russian, Italian, Brazilian Portuguese, Hmong and Laotian. Technical manuals, user manuals, employee handbooks, and marketing. Has over 100 translators.

Allen Translation Service, Box 1529, Morristown, NJ 07962 Phone: (973)292-2737 Fax: (973)292-3954 Contact: Jeanette C. Fredericks Member: ATA

Allslavic Translation Services, 4930 NW 84th Ave., Ft. Lauderdale, FL 33351 Phone: (800)775-5504 Fax: (954)741-3898 e-mail: info@slavprom.com Web site: www.slavpromc.com Contact: Stanka Moskov Member: ATA

ALLSPEAK Interpreting Services, P. 0. Box 1606, Glendale, CA 91209
Phone: (818)246-1515 Fax: (818)246-4211 e-mail: allspeakint@aol.com Contact: Tatiana E. Vorobieff
Member: ATA

Allworld Language Consultants, Inc., P.O. Box 2128, Rockville, MD 20847
Phone: (301)881-8884 Fax: (301)881-6877 Web site: www.alcinc.com
Contact: Carlos Scandiffio Member: ATA

ALTA Language Services, 3355 Lennox Rd. NE, Ste. 510, Atlanta, GA 30326 Phone: (404)240-1810 Fax: (404)239-9516
e-mail: robert@altalang.com
Contact: Robert Jones
Company founded 1982. Member: ATA, AAIT. Uses freelance translators and interpreters. Accepts unsolicited resumes. Resumes are filed by language. Requires outstanding translation skills. Main languages (both ways) are Spanish, German, French, Japanese, Portuguese, Dutch, Italian, Chinese, Korean, and Russian. Main subjects are legal, medical, and general. Does multilingual typesetting in addition to translation and interpretation. Engages around 300 translators.

ALTCO Translations, 1426 Ridgeview Rd., Columbus, OH 43221 Phone: (614)486-2014 Fax: (614)486-6940
e-mail: trudypeters@compuserve.com Contact: Trudy E. Peters, Owner.
Founded 1982. Member: ATA. Uses freelancers for translation and interpretation. Accepts resumes, and enters the more promising ones into a database. Applicants must be experienced. Main languages (both ways) are Spanish, French, German, Russian, and Japanese. Also translates into other languages, notably Italian. Main subjects are patents, business documents, manuals, certificates, brochures. Uses dozens of translators.

Always Ready Translation Services, 11026 Ventura Blvd., Room 10, Studio City, CA 91604 Phone: (800)240-6601 Fax: (818)755-8959 e-mail: language@worldnet.att.net Contact: Dan Prescott, President
Founded 1985. Accepts resumes. Translates Spanish, Asian languages, Russian, Armenian, and other European languages.

Ambassador Translating, Inc., 442 Route 202-206 N., #PMB200, Bedminster, NJ 07921 Phone: (908)429-0200 Fax: (908)429-0333 e-mail: rosa@am-translating.com Web site: www.am-translating.com
Contact: Rosa A. Stevenson Member: ATA

America Translating Services, P.O. Box 800272, Santa Clarita, CA 91380 Phone: (800)535-0555 Fax: (800)316-2230 e-mail: rstevenson@aol.com Web site: am-translating.com Contact: Rosa A. Steventon, Coordinator Member: ATA
Founded 1984. Member: ATA, CCIA. Translates all languages, both from and into English. Emphasis on Legal, Technical and Medical translation. Prospective translators should provide sample translations, reference list. Resumes are listed in a database. Specializes in voiceover work. Maintains a pool of over 1,000 translators.

American Bureau of Professional Translators, 8401 Westheimer Rd., Ste. 115, Houston, TX 77063
Phone: (713)789-2500 Fax: (713)789-8920 e-mail: abpt@abpt.com Web site: www.abpt.com Contact: Ms. Lu Waterhouse Member: ATA

American Business Concepts, LLC, P.O. Box 212942, Columbia, SC 29221
Phone: (803)749-2060 Fax: (803)407-3010 e-mail: abctranslation@aol.com Contact: Taeko T. Kerr
Member: ATA

American Education Research Corp., Box 996, West Covina, CA 91793
Phone: (626)339-4404 Fax: (626)339-9081e-mail: aerc@cyberg8t.com
Web site: www.credencialsevaluation.comContact: John A. Sheety Member: ATA

American Translation Partners, 839 Albany St., Boston, MA 02119
 Phone: (617)989-9989 Fax: (617)989-9919 e-mail: info@americantranslationpartners.com
Web site: www.americantranslationpartners.com Contact: Scott Crystal
Founded 1998. Member: ATA, NAJIT, NETA, MMIA, LPDAM, FIT, TTI, LISA, AIIC. Accepts resumes. Requires language proficiency and experience as well as computer proficiency. Translates Spanish, Portuguese, French, German, Italian, Japanese, Chinese, Korean, Vietnamese, Haitian Creole, Afrikaans, and all Indian dialects. Works in government, legal, medical, insurance, technical, financial, software subjects in more than 200 language pairs. Has 1500 translators in New England and 3500 worldwide.

e-mail: tieu_o'brien@alticor.com Contact: Tieu O'Brien
Company founded 1959. Member: ATA. Translates Spanish, French, German, Italian, Dutch, Japanese, Chinese, Korean, Portuguese, Hindi, Polish, Hungarian, Czech, Slovak, Slovene, Turkish, Indonesian, Vietnamese, Malay, and Russian both from and into English. Bulk of work in Spanish and French. Emphasis on Marketing literature, Legal documentation, Product-related materials (Labels, brochures), Technical documentation (chemical and biological topics). Prospective translators should have at least 3-5 years full-time experience as a translator and/or interpreter. ATA accreditation preferred. Resumes are placed in a database. Maintains a pool of 200-300 translators.

ANDALEX International, Inc., 10101 SW Barbur Blvd, Ste. 101, Portland, OR 97219
Phone:(503)241-9756 Fax:(503)243-6815 e-mail: info@andalexintl.com   Web site: www.andalexint.com
Contact: Andrei Lupenko   Member: ATA
Antiquariat Literary Services, Inc., 12042 Trumbull Way, Reston, VA 20190
Phone:(703)707-8531 Fax:(703)707-8532
e-mail: alstranslation.com Web site: www.alstranslation.net Contact: Rebecca Marie Hindrichs   Member: ATA

Antler Translation Services, 48 Woodport Rd., Sparta, NJ 07871 Phone: (201)729-8465 Fax:(201)729-9389

e-mail: antler@sparta.csnet.net Web site: www.quikpage.com Contact: Patrick W. Clevenger
Founded 1988. Translates in all languages. Emphasis on Technical, Medical, and Chemical translation. Prospective translators should provide evidence of competence and experience. Resumes are added to a database. Maintains a pool of 100 translators.

APS International Ltd, 7800 Glenroy Rd., Minneapolis, MN 55439 Phone: (612)831-7776 Fax: (612)831-8150
e-mail: trans@aps-now.com   Contact: Ann Mickow Member: ATA

Arab American Translators, 5827 Columbia Pike, #415, Falls Church, VA 22041
Phone: (703)820-5612 Fax: (703)820-1318 e-mail: info@translateItalian.com   Web site: www.translateItalian.com
Contact: Radwan Hakim   Member: ATA

ArchiText Inc., 240 Pleasant St., Methuen, MA 01844
Phone: (978)688-7200 Fax: (978)688-7222 e-mail: hansf@architext-usa.com Web site: www.architext-usa.com
Contact: Hans Fenstermacher   Member: ATA

Argo Translation, Inc., 3747 S. Howell Ave., Milwaukee WI 53207 Phone: (414)615-6000 Fax: (414)615-6005
e-mail: sales@argotrans.com Web site: www.argotrans.com Contact: Jacqueline LaCarelli
Founded 1995. Member: ATA. Uses freelance translators and interpreters. Accepts unsolicited resumes. Works in all languages and subjects, viz., medical, technical, legal, commercial. Always on the lookout for professional translators. Has 575 translators.

Around The World, Inc., 12281 Butterfield Drive NW, Pickerington, OH 43147
Phone: (614)575-2424 Fax: (614)575-2423 e-mail:atw@nls.com   Web site: www.atwtranslation.com
Contact: Gary West   Member: ATA
Founded 1998. Member: ATA, BBB. Translates all languages, mainly technical, advertising, business and legal. Has satellite offices in Kansas City, Columbus, Brussels (Belgium), and Paris (France). Translates and typesets for private and business sectors. Utilizes over 5000 translators.

ASET International Services Corporation, 2009 North 14th St., Ste. 214, Arlington, VA 22201 Phone:(703) 516-9266 Fax:(703)516-9269 e-mail: Khendzel@asetquality.com Web site: asetquality.com
Contact: Kevin S. Hendzel, Director of Language Services
Founded 1987. Member: ATA. Translates in over 100 languages, both from and into English. Emphasis on Equipment Manuals, Pharmaceuticals and Medical Equipment, Software Localization, Nuclear, Chemical, Industrial and Structural Engineering, Law and Legislation, Regulations and Codes, Education and Consumer Goods translation. Prospective translators are required to have 10 years professional translating experience and formal technical training in a specialty area. Resumes are archived in database and assignments given when appropriate match arises. Resumes *must be faxed or submitted by e-mail*. The company also works with engineering drawings and specifications and possesses full AutoCad and full-color printing capabilities. They provide interpreting services and are an authorized Master Distributor for the Philips interpreting equipment series. Welcomes voice-over talent. Maintains a pool of 1000 translators.

Asian Link Corp., 1108 W Valley Blvd., Ste. 4, Alhambra, CA 91803
Phone: (626)300-9191 Fax: (626)300-8955 e-mail:sophia@asialink.com   Contact: Sophia N. Yang   Member: ATA

Asian Translation Service, 7393 S. Locust St., Midvale, UT 84047
Phone: (801)565-8281 Fax: (801)565-0320   e-mail:ats@asiantranslation.com   Web site: www.asiantranslation.com
Contact: Steve Stevens
Founded 1992. Member: ATA. Translates English into Hmong, Vietnamese, Cambodian, Thai, Korean, Japanese, Chinese, Tagalog, Malay, and Indonesian, mainly health-related, business, personal documents, and product catalogues. Provides full range of translation and interpretation. Uses about 30 translators.

Asian Translations, Inc., 3702 E. Lake St., Ste. 102, Minneapolis, MN 55406
Phone: (612)712-5432 Fax: (612)721-5778   e-mail: atrans@asiantranslations.com
Web site: www.asiantranslations.com   Contact: Sokunthea (Sue) Hendry   Member: ATA

ASIST Translation Services, 4663 Executive Drive, Ste. 11, Columbus, OH 43220   Phone: (614)451-6744 Fax: (614)451-1349
e-mail: asist@asisttranslations.com   Contact: Elena Tsinman, President
Founded 1983. Member: ATA. Uses freelance translators and interpreters. Accepts unsolicited resumes. All resumes are entered in a database. If qualified, translator is contacted immediately. Applicant must be experienced, native speaker, and have a university degree. Main languages are English into French, Spanish, Chinese, Japanese, Russian, Italian, German, Somali, Portuguese and Italian. Additional languages are Dutch, Swedish and Danish. Does 2-3 million words a year. Does also typesetting, Web site translation, software translation, localization, audio-visual productions, and desktop publishing. Maintains pool of 2000 translators.

ATL Ultrasound, P.O. Box 3003, Bothell, WA 98041
e-mail: tony.messent@philips.com   Contact: Tony Messent, MS 264   Member: ATA

Atlantic International, Translators, Inc., 4956 Vermack Rd., Atlanta, GA 30338
Phone: (770)350-9050 Fax: (770)350-9051   e-mail: atlanticit@aol.com   Web site: www.atlanticitinc.com
Contact: Rogelio Cipriano   Member: ATA

Atlas Translation Services, 336 North Central Ave., Ste. 6, Glendale, CA   91203   Phone: (818)242-2400   Fax: (818)242-2475   e-mail: atlas @atlaspvs.com   Contact: Sorina Kalili
Founded 1993. Uses freelancers for translation. Accepts unsolicited resumes. Main languages (both ways) are Farsi, German, Spanish, French, Italian, Chinese, and Japanese. Main subjects are legal, business, and scripts. Also does legal interpretation.

Audio To Go, Inc., 42 West 89th St., New York, NY 10024
Phone: (212)721-1183 Fax: (212)721-1273   e-mail: info@a2g.com   Web site: www.a2g.com   Contact: Gayle Goldfarb
Founded 1991. Member: NYCT. Accepts resumes. Requires certification, experience, native speakers in target language. Translates all languages. Translates audio and video programs with narrators in their native language.

Avant Page, 1138 Villaverde Lane, Davis, CA 95616
Phone: (530)750-2060 Fax: (530)750-2024   e-mail: luis@avantpage.com   Web site: www.avantpage.com
Contact: Luis Miguel, President
Founded 1996. Member: ATA. Accepts resumes. Requires 3 years exp., certification/accreditation where available. Translates English into Spanish, Japanese, Chinese (simplified and traditional), Korean, French, German, Vietnamese, Italian, Hebrew, Italian, and Portuguese. Also Farsi, Thai, and Tagalog. Main areas are business, hi tech, biotechnology, and government documents. Does multilingual desktop publishing. Does over one million words per year. Utilizes over 200 translators.

Avantext, 614 Grand Avenue, Ste. 203, Oakland, CA 94610
Phone: (510)832-1608 Fax: (510)832-1617   e-mail: info@avantext-usa.com   Web site: www.avantext-usa.com

BBC Multilingual Translations, 1231 Somerset Drive, McLean, VA 22101 Phone: (703)448-0893 Fax: (703)448-8077
e-mail: mansourf@aol.com

Babel Tower, Inc., P.O. Box 491023, Ft. Lauderdale, FL 33349
Phone: (954)731-9180 Fax: (954)731-1366 e-mail: babeltower@aol.com Web site: www.babeltowerinc.com
Contact: Sandra Fernandez Founded 1996. Member: ATA. Translates all languages.

Barinas Translation Consultants, Inc., 1100 NW Loop 410, Ste. 700, San Antonio, TX 78213 Phone: (210)545-0019 Fax: (210)545-4731 160424 E-mail: info@barinas.com Web site: www.barinas.comContact: Sonia Barinas, President
Company founded 1980. Member: MPI, AAHA, TSHE, SATC, San Antonio Chamber of Commerce, GSHMA, ISMP, THMA. Uses freelance translators and interpreters. Accepts unsolicited resumes. Resumes are checked for quality and experience, then filed by language and areas of expertise. Please submit sample with resume, and indicate degree in translation and/or interpretation. Degree in law, medicine etc. is a plus. Main language pairs are Spanish/English, French/ English, French/ Spanish, Portuguese/English, German/English, Chinese/English, Japanese/English. Main subjects are legal, medical, technical, telecom. Specializes in simultaneous interpretation for meetings and conventions. Does about 350 projects a year. Uses hundreds of freelancers.

Berkeley Scientific Translation Service, Inc., P.O.Box 150, Berkeley CA 94701 Phone:(510)548-4665 Fax: (510)548-4666 e-mail: marlo@berksci.com Web site: www.berksci.comContact: Dr. Marlo R. Martin
Founded 1974. Member: ATA, NCTA. Translates Japanese, Korean, Chinese, and other major European and Asian languages, both from and into English. Emphasis on Mechanical, Automotive, Chemical and Chemical Engineering, Computers and Software, Electronics, Biotechnology, Pharmaceuticals, Physics and Patent translations. Prospective translators should be able to produce authoritative translations into their native language within a specialized area. Resumes are screened for educational background and subject expertise as related to translation experience. The company was founded by a physicist and engineer and seeks translators with similar qualifications. Maintains a pool of 70-100 translators.

Berlitz GlobalNet, 132 W. 31st St., New York, NY 10001
Phone: (917)339-4890 e-mail: james.keller@nyc.berlitz.com Web site: www.berlitz.com Contact: Beatriz Almonte
Founded 1882. Member: ATA. **Berlitz** is an international organization of language schools which offer translation services as a sideline. Most of its branches use the services of freelance translators. Berlitz is very active in the localization of software. Prospective translators should definitely consider Contacting this company. Check out its Web site at: www.berlitz.com.

Betmar Languages, 6260 Highway 65 NE, Ste. 308, Minneapolis, MN 55432 Phone: (612)572-9711 Fax: (612)571-3467 e-mail: best@betmar.com Contact: Elizabeth A. Loo Member: ATA

Bilingual Services, 9707 Chapel Down, Austin, TX 78729 Phone: (512) 258-1932 Fax:(512)258-2131
email: 71754.2717@compuserve.com Contact: Vivian Carmona-Agosto, President
Member: ATA, AATIA. Translates Spanish, French, German, Vietnamese, Russian, Chinese (Taiwanese & Mandarin/Cantonese), Italian, and Portuguese, both from and into English. Emphasis on advertising, PR, merchandising, computer, health, social services and petroleum. Prospective translators should have ATA or other accreditation or license. Resumes are filed according to language, and, within languages, according to equipment. Translators must have computer/fax/modem/etc. Resumes are also welcome from Texas-based interpreters. Uses professionals whose work will reflect well on both the company and its clients.

BioMedical Translators, 3477 Kenneth Drive, Palo Alto, CA 94303 Phone:(650)494-1317 Fax:(650)494-1394
e-mail: biomed@biomedical.com Contact: Monique Vazire
Founded 1992. Member: ATA, NCTA. Main languages translated are French, German, Italian, Spanish, Dutch, Swedish, Portuguese, Danish, Japanese, and Chinese. Emphasis is on Medical and Biological translation, including equipment, studies and software. Prospective translators should possess at least one year experience, have knowledge of the medical field, and have access to medical dictionaries. Their equipment should include a PC and modem or e-mail; software should include Word and WordPerfect. Resumes are reviewed by the recruiting department and responded to with a test translation, which is then evaluated. The company specializes exclusively in the medical field and its peripherals. Their services also include desktop publishing. Maintains a pool of 500+ translators.

Bloomberg L.P., 100 Business Park Drive, P.O. Box 888, Princeton, NJ 08542   Phone:(609)279-4955
Contact: Elsa Shilling

Bowne Translation Services, 345 Hudson St., New York, NY 10014 Phone: (212)924-5500 Fax: (212)229-3410
e-mail: lisa.dimeglio@bowne.com   Web site: www.bowne.com   Contact: Lisa Di Meglio
Company founded 1989. Member: ATA. Uses freelance translators and interpreters. Accepts unsolicited resumes. Applicants
sign a confidentiality agreement and are sent a test. If successful, they are given small assignments at first, leading to larger
ones. Main language pairs are English into Spanish, Ger-man, French, Chinese, Japanese, and Portuguese, and Spanish, French,
German, and Japanese into English. Additional languages are Italian, Dutch, Swedish, Danish, Norwegian, Greek, Polish,
Hungarian, Czech, Bulgarian, and Tagalog. Main subjects are financial, legal, corporate, and industrial, as well as documents
related to IPO/mergers and acquisitions. Keeps about 400-500 translators in its pool.

BRADSON Corporation, 1735 Jefferson Davis Highway, Ste. 705, Arlington, VA 22202   Phone: (703)413-3050
Fax: (703)413-3056   Contact: John S. Horner

BRIDGE-LINGUATEC LANGUAGE SERVICES, 915 South Colorado Blvd., Denver, CO 80246   Phone:
(303)777-7783
Fax:(303)777-7246 e-mail: translators@bridgeschool.com   Web site: www.bridge-linguatec.com
Contact: Michelle Duvall
Founded 1981. Translates mainly Spanish, French, German, Italian, Dutch, Russian and Portuguese. Emphasis on
legal and medical. Prospective translators should, by preference, be native speakers. Resumes are filed by language
and translators contacted by need.. The company also provides ESL training for executives, foreign language
instruction, and interpretation services. Maintains a pool of 150-200 translators

The Bridge-World Language Center, Inc., 110 2nd Street S, Ste. 213, Waite Park, MN 56387   Phone: (320)259-
9239 Fax:(320)654-1698   e-mail: co@bridgelanguage.com   Web site: www.bridgelanguage.com
Contact: Francisco Almarza   Member: ATA

Brigham and Women's Hospital, 75 Francis St., Boston, MA 02115   Phone: (617)732-6640 Fax: (617)975-0813
e-mail: igarcia@partners.org   Contact: Ileana Jimenez Garcia   Member: ATA

Bromberg & Associates, 28475 Ranchwood Drive, Southfield, MI 48076
Phone: (248)827-7164 Fax: (248)827-3621 e-mail: jinny@linguacity.com   Web site: www.linguacity.com
Contact: Jinny Bromberg   Member: ATA

Bruce International, Inc., 10550 SW Allen Blvd., Ste. 123, Beaverton, OR 97005   Phone: (503)643-8448   Fax:
(503)643-7174   e-mail: info@bruceinternational.com   Web site: www.bruce international.com   Contact: Oscar
Andrino
Member: ATA

Bureau of Translation Services, 30 Washington Ave., Haddonfield, NJ 08033 Phone: (609)795-8669 Fax:
(609)795-8737   e-mail: wschrieks@btsinc.com Web site: btsinc.com   Contact: Wim Schrieks   Member: ATA

Burg Translation Bureau, Inc., 29 South LaSalle, Ste. 936, Chicago, IL 60603 Phone:(312)263-3379 Fax:(312)263-
4325   e-mail: burg@interaccess.com Web site: www.burgtranslations.com   Contact: Lodovico Passalacqua,
President
Founded 1936. Member: ATA. Emphasis on technical translation. Prospected translators are "evaluated." Provides
translation and typesetting services.

CC Scientific. Ltd., Rancho Las Palmas Office Park, 42-600 Bob Hope Drive, Ste. 404, Rancho Mirage, CA 92270 Phone: (760)341-7544 Fax: (760)341-7514 e-mail: CCSLtd@aol.com Contact: Jaime R. Carlo-Casellas Member: ATA

C.P. Language Institute, 225 West 57ᵗʰ St., Ste. 404, New York, NY 10019 Phone: (212)246-2054 Fax: (212)247-2258
e-mail: info@cpli.com Web site: www.cpli.com Contact: Yuki Saito
Founded 1980. Member: ATA. Translates Chinese, Japanese, Korean, Spanish, Italian, Russian, French, German, Hebrew, Hindi, Urdu, Vietnamese, Italian, Portuguese, Thai, Khmer, Tagalog and Indonesian, both from and into English. Emphasis on Advertising, Technical, Patent, Financial, Medical, Legal, Personal Document and Textbook translation. Prospective translators should show proficiency in English and the target language and should be experienced. Resumes are responded to with a call-in or an e-mailed test translation in order to assess the candidate's ability. The company has two departments - programs and services. Programs is a language school providing small group and private language instruction. Services comprise translation, typesetting, formatting, interpretation, voiceovers and subtitling. Maintains a pool of 300 translators.

CTS Language Link TM, 911 Main St., Ste. 300, Vancouver, WA 98660
Phone: (360)693-7100 Fax: (360)693-9292 e-mail: jennyt@ctsll.com Contact: Jenny Tallis-Grow Member: ATA

Calvin International Communications, Inc., 869 Plymouth Rock Drive, St. Louis, MO 63131 Phone: (314)821-5033 Fax: (314)821-5035 e-mail: calvinint@cs.com Contact: Beatriz E. Arauco-Calvin Member: ATA

Carolina Polyglot, Inc., PO Box 36334, Charlotte, NC 28236
Phone:(704)366-5781 Fax:(704)364-2998 e-mail: wdepaula@carolinapolyglot.com
Web site: www.carolinapolyglot.com Contact: Dr. William DePaula
Company founded 1971. Member: ATA, CATI. Accepts unsolicited resumes. Resumes are filed by language pair. E-mail and fax filed electronically. Requirements for applicants include academic degree, previous experience, professional affiliation/ accreditation, references. Main languages (both ways) are French, Spanish, Italian, Portuguese, Romanian, German, Dutch, Italian, Chinese, Viet-namese, and Japanese. Also translates Turkish, Farsi, Afrikaans, Hindi, Danish, Norwegian, Swedish, and Finnish. Main subjects are immigration, education, law, business, medicine, insurance, theology, ecology, literature, and computers. Uses over 30 translators.

Caterpillar, Inc., Dealer Capability Dept., Corp Translation, 501 SW Jefferson Ave., Peoria, IL 61630
Phone: (309)494-5216 e-mail: opherk_jorg@CAT.com Contact: Dr. Jorg Opherk Member: ATA

CDNOW, Inc., 1005 Virginia Drive, Fort Washington, PA 19034
Phone: (215)619-9696 Fax: (215)619-9559 e-mail: emcpartland@cdnow.com Web site: www.cdnow.com
Contact: Erica A. McPartland Member: ATA

Certified Interpreters & Translators (CIT), PO Box 390006, San Diego, CA 92149 Phone: (619)475-8586 Fax: (619)472-2157
Company founded 1983. Uses freelance translators and interpreters. Accepts unsolicited resumes. Resumes are filed by language and geographical area. Interpreters have to be certified. Main language pair is English-Spanish, followed by English into German and Tagalog, Russian, Italian, and Japanese into English. Also Portuguese, Polish, and Vietnamese into English. Main subjects are legal, medical, technical, literary, commercial, as well as manuals. Does conference interpreting. Also does translator and interpreter training.

Certified Languages International, 4700 SW Macadam Ave., #200, Portland, OR 97201
Phone: (503)525-9601 Fax: (503)525-9607 e-mail: bill@clilang.com Web site: www.clilang.com
Contact: William Graeper Member: ATA

Certified Translation Services, One Harbison Way, Ste. 105, Columbia, SC 29212
Phone: (800)730-9970 Fax: (803)781-5052 e-mail and web site: certifiedtranslationservices.com Contact: Ed Crosby
Member: ATA

Cherry Creek Language Centre, Inc., 1071 Jersey St., Denver, CO 80220
Phone: (303)756-2520 Fax: (303)782-5686 e-mail: ignacio@translationlinks.com Web site: www.translationlinks.com
Contact: Ignacio Jimenez

Chicago Multi-Lingua Graphics, Inc., 960 Grove St., Evanston, IL 60201 Phone: (847)864-3230 Fax: (847)864-3202
e-mail: infor@multimedia.com   Web site: www.multilingua.com   Contact: Yi Han   Member: ATA

Choice Translating & Interpreting, 8701 Mallard Creek Rd., Charlotte, NC 28262   Phone: (704)717-0043 Fax: (704)717-0046 -mail: hr@choicetranslating.com Web site: www.choicetranslating.com
Contact: Sophie David-Gunn   Member: ATA

CinciLingua, Inc., 322 East Fourth St., Cincinnati, OH 45202 Phone: (513)721-8782 Fax:(513)721-8819
email: translat@cincilingua.com Web site: www.cincilingua.com   Contact: Michael Sum
Founded 1972. Member: ATA, ASME. Translates in Spanish, French, German, Chinese, Japanese, etc., both from and into English. Prospective translators should have college degree, professional experience in a technical specialty, and references. Should have a computer. Resumes are reviewed by the Project Manager and entered in a database. Qualified candidates may be asked to translate a short sample for additional information.

CITI Translation Center, Inc., 1000 Quayside Terrace, PH8, Miami Beach FL 33138 Phone: (305)868-1746
Fax: (305)868-1748 e-mail: info@cititran.com   Web site: www.cititran.com   Contact: Fernando Velez-Pardo
Founded 1987. Member: ATA, FLATA. Translates German, Russian, Japanese, Chinese, French, Italian and Spanish, both from and into English. Emphasis on Technical, Communication Manuals, Medical, Business and Personal Documents translation. Prospective translators should be experienced, preferably with accreditation and/or certification. Resumes are reviewed and the applicant contacted if there is a specific need for that language or specialty area. The company supports markets in the Americas, Europe and the Pacific Rim. Maintains a pool of 60 translators.

CME Corporation, 2945 Three Leaves Drive, Mount Pleasant, MI 48858
Phone: (517)773-0377 Fax: (517)773-1105   Contact: Fumiko Lobert   Member: ATA

Columbia Language Services, 11818 SE Mill Plain Blvd., #307, Vancouver, WA 98684
Phone: (360)896-3881 Fax: (360)896-4074 e-mail: mail@columbia-language.com
Web site: www.columbia-language.com   Contact: Sveltana Linchuk   Member: ATA

CommGap International Comm Services. 5369 S Baker St., Murray, UT 84107
Phone: (801)262-8984 Fax: (801)262-8996 e-mail: info@commgap.com   Web site: www.commgap.com
Contact: Lelani P. Craig   Member: ATA

Community Interpreter Services, Catholic Charities/Greater Boston, 270 Washington St., Somerville, MA 02143
Phone: (617)629-5767 Fax: (617)629-5768 e-mail: inna_persitsgimelberg@ccab.com Web site: www.ccab.org
Contact: Inna P. Gimelberg, Program Manager
Founded in 1986. Member: ATA, MMIA, NETA. Accepts resumes. Translates Haitian Creole, Spanish, Cape Verdean Creole, Vietnamese, Russian, Khmer, Portuguese, Cantonese-Chinese, Vietnamese, Polish, Farsi, Bosnian and Albanian. Also Somali, Swahili, Italian, French, Italian, Khmer and Laotian. Emphasis on Personal Document translation. Prospective translators should live in Massachusetts or a bordering state, and possess at least a Bachelor's degree, past
translating experience, and fluency in at least two languages. Mostly certificates and correspondence. Qualified resumes are responded to with an interview appointment. They are a nonprofit service operated by Catholic Charities. Maintains a pool of 200 translators and interpreters.

ComNet International, 31255 Cedar Valley, Ste. 212, Westlake   Village, CA 91362 Phone:(818)991-1277
Fax:(818)991-1699 Web site: comnetint.com   Contact: Dr. Elias Agel
Founded 1989. Member: ATA. Translates all languages, in all subjects. Prospective translators should have extensive experience and should provide references. Resumes are reviewed and entered into a database. The company also provides desktop publishing, art production and printing services. It also does voice-overs and dubbing. Specialties include Middle East consulting services, electronic update filing and interagency network cooperation. Maintains a pool of 600 translators.

Comprehensive Language Center, 4200 Wilson Blvd., Ste. 950, Arlington VA 22203   Phone: (703)247-0700   Fax: (703)247-4295   e-mail: kjdresen@comlang.com Web site: www.comlang.com   Contact: Kelly Jones Dresen   Company founded 1980 as CACI. Member: ATA. uses freelance translators and interpreters. Accepted unsolicited resumes, but not unsolicited phone calls. Qualified applicants are sent a database form which is processed and are called upon when needed in their area of expertise. Requirements include college degree, 2 years professional experience as linguist, or appropriate certification/specialized degree. Over 100 languages. Main areas are technical, legal, promotional, business. Company also does training, transcription, software and web page localization, and video narration.

Contact International Inc., 717 Light St., Baltimore, MD 21230   Phone: (800)333-3812 Fax:(800)333-5637   e-mail: Contact@cicenter.com Web site: www.cicenter.com   Contact: Greg Bathon   Member: ATA

Continental Book Company, 625 E. 70th Ave. #5, Denver, CO 80229   Phone: (303)289-1761 Fax:(303)289-1764   e-mail: cbc@continentalbook.com Web site: www.continentalbook.com   Contact: Karen A. Manville   Member: ATA

Continental Communications Agency, 5775 East Los Angeles Ave., #226, Simi Valley, CA 93063   Phone:(805)527-4446 Fax:(805)527-4460   e-mail: cca_inc@ix.netcom.com   Contact: Peter Charbonneau   Member: ATA

Continental Interpreting Services, Inc., 3111 N. Tustin Ave., Ste. 235, Orange, CA 92865   Phone:(800)201-7121   Fax:(714)283-9045   e-mail: info@wespeakyourlanguage.com   Web site: www.wespeakyourlanguage.com   Contact: Kevin McQuire   Member: ATA

Copper Translation Service, 530 Franklin St., Ste. 207, Schenectady, NY 12305 Phone: (518)372-8940 Fax: (518)372-8952   -mail: angelos@coppertranslation.com   Web site: www.coppertranslation.com   Contact: Angelos G. Tzelepis
Company founded 1971. Member: ATA. Uses freelance translators and interpreters. Accepts unsolicited resumes. Applicant must be native speaker of target language. Main areas are legal, medical, and business. Over 700 translators in pool.

Corporate Translations, Inc., 1300 Aviation Blvd., Redondo Beach, CA 90278   Phone: (310)376-1400 Fax: (310)376-1394   e-mail: translators@corporatetranslations.com   Web site: www.corporatetranslations.com   Contact: Toni Andrews
Founded 1995. Member: ATA, SCATIA. Accepts resumes. Requires experience, ATA accreditation and references. Translates all languages.

Corporate Translations, 1300 Aviation Blvd., Redondo Beach, CA 90278
Phone: (860)450-0405 Fax: (860)450-0409   e-mail:ctoomey@corptrans.inc.com   Web site: www.orptrans.inc.com
Contact: Carolyn Toomey   Founded 1995. Member: ATA

Cosmopolitan Business Communication, 8025 Marshall Circle, Arvada, CO 80003   Phone: (303)422-6702   Contact: Maya León Meis

Cosmopolitan Translation Bureau, 53 West Jackson Blvd., Ste. 1260, Chicago, IL 60604 Phone: (312) 726-2610   Fax: (312)427-8591   Contact: Emanuel H. Steen   Member: ATA

Coto Interpreting, Translating & Graphics, 447 Burchett St., 2nd Floor, Glendale, CA 91203   Phone: (818)551-4545 Fax: (818)551-1123   Contact: Melanie Coto-Trevor   Member: ATA

Course Crafters, 44 Merrimac St., Newburyport, MA 01950   Phone: (978)465-2040 Fax: (978)465-5027   e-mail:lise@coursecrafters.com   Web site: www.coursecrafters.com   Contact: Lise B. Ragan   Member: ATA

Creo International, 520 Marquette Ave., Ste. 700, Minneapolis, MN 55402
Phone: (612)342-9800 Fax: (612)342-9745 e-mail:cthudson@creo-works.com   Web site: www.creo-works.com
Contact: Christa Tiefenbacher   Member: ATA

Counterpoint Language Consultants, Inc., PO Box 6184 Bridgewater, NJ 08807 Phone: (908)231-0991 Fax: (908)231-8266 e-mail: ctpt@ctpt.com Web site: www.counterpoint Language.com Contact: Dr. Lynne R. Judd Founded 1979. Member: ATA. Company uses freelance translators and interpreters. Accepts unsolicited resumes. Main languages (both ways) are French, German, Spanish, Chinese, Japanese, Portuguese, Russian, Greek, Hindi and Italian. Also Thai, Swahili, Gujarati, Czech and Slovak. Main areas are pharmaceuticals, telecom, and lega. Provides worldwide business language training. Uses over about 110 translators.

Crimson Language Services, Inc., 258 Harvard St., Ste. 305, Brookline, MA   02146 Phone: (617)731-6920 Fax: (617)731-5244   e-mail: crimson@tiac.net   Contact: John Connors Founded 1992. Member: ATA. Resumes are responded to with calls and/or tests on an as-needed basis.

Cross Cultural Comm Systems, Inc., 50 Cross St., P.O. Box 860, Winchester, MA 01890 Phone: (781)729-3736 Fax: (781)729-1217 e-mail:cccs@icnt.comContact: Zarita Araujo   Member: ATA

Crossword Translation Services, 16350 Park Ten Place, Ste. 201, Houston, TX 77084   Phone: (281)578-1300 Fax: (281)578-1334 e-mail:language@crosswordtranslation.com   Contact: Office Staff Founded 1997. Member: ATA. Accepts resumes. Translates and interpreters most languages in all fields. Uses many translators and interpreters.

Cybertec USA, Inc., 153 West Westfield Ave., Roselle Park, NJ 07204-1816 Phone:(908)245-3305 Fax:(908)245-5434 e-mail: cybertec_inc @compuserve.com Web site: www.cybertecusa.com Contact: Joseph Nunes Founded 1990. Member: ATA, NYCT. Uses freelance translators and interpreters. Accepts unsolicited resumes. Resumes are filed by language and specialty. Translators are required to be experienced professional translators. Accreditation and/or diploma preferred. Translates mainly Portuguese, Spanish, French, Italian, and German. Also Chinese, Japanese and Korean, technical, industrial, business and legal. Does over 5 million words per year. Over 100 translators in company's pool.

CyraCom International Inc., 7332 N Oracle Rd., Tucson, AZ 85704 Phone: (520)745-9447 Fax: (520)745-9022 Web site: www.cyracom.com Contact: Paul Burns Company founded 1997. Member: ATA. Provides telephonic interpretation services on demand 24 hours a day, 7 days a week in about 150 languages. Has a secure system that provides rapid access to interpreters.

-D-

DFP Translating Service, 42 Frederick Place, Bergenfield, NJ 07621 Phone: (201)343-2258 Fax: (201)343-4155 e-mail: info@ translationservices.netWeb site: www.translationservices.net   Contact: Doris Pacheco

DTS Language Services, Inc., 308 W. Rosemary St., Ste. 210, Chapel Hill, NC 27516   Phone: (800)524-0722 Fax: (919)942-0686 e-mail: sales@dtstrans.com   Web site: www.dtstrans.com Contact: Lucia Apollo Shaw Founded 1972. Member: ATA, DIA, STC. Accepts resumes only electronically. Requires 5 years min. professional technical translation experience with related degree. Translates mainly Portuguese, French, Spanish, German, Italian, Czech, Vietnamese, Japanese, and Korean. Also Dutch, Finnish, Norwegian, Swedish. Mainly technical, medical, marketing, patents.

Detroit Translation Bureau, 30800 Telegraph Rd., Ste.1930, Bingham Farms, MI 48025 Phone: (248)593-6710 Fax: (248)593-6720 e-mail: info@dtbonline.com   Web site: www.dtbonline.com Founded 1946. Member: ATA, LISA, SAW. Accepts resumes. Translates mainly Spanish (Mexico, Spain), Canadian French, German, Japanese, Italian, Norwegian, Dutch, Finnish and Korean. Mainly automotive – technical, training and marketing. Uses hundreds of translators.

Digital Publishing, Inc., 1805 Hicks Rd., Rolling Meadows, IL 60008 Phone: (847)776-0200 Fax: (847)776-0249e-mail: translation@digitalpub.com   Web site: www.digital pub.com Contact: Debbie Shulman

Digitek International, Inc./SAKHR, 7631 Leesburg Pike, Ste. B, Fall Church, VA 22043   Phone: (703)883-0134 Fax: (Contact: Youb Benyoucef

Diplomatic Language Services, 1901 N. 19th St., Ste. 600, Arlington, VA 22209 Phone:(703)243-4856 Fax:(703)358-9189 e-mail: resume@dls-inc.com Web site: www.dls-inc.com
Founded 1985. Member: ATA, NCATA, NAJIT. Accepts resumes. Requires 5 years professional experience. Translates all languages. Provides all translation and interpretation services as well as language training.

DocuTrans, Inc., 4712 S. 2675 W, Roy, UT 84067 Phone: (801)776-6510 Fax: (801)776-4027 e-mail: translate@docutrans.com Web site: www.docutrans.com Contact: Gabariele H. Johnson Member: ATA

Dragon Crest Associates, Inc., 11026 Ventura Blvd., Ste. 10, Studio City, CA 91604 Phone: (800)240-6601 Fax: (818)755-8959 e-mail: language@worldnet.att.com Contact: Dan Prescott Member: ATA

DrTango.com, Inc., 20 Mansell Court East, Ste. 100, Roswell, GA 30076d Phone: (770)649-0298 Fax: (770)649-0299 e-mail:cecilia@drtango.com Web site: www.drtango.com Contact: Cecilia Santamarina Member: ATA

Dynamic Language Center, Ltd., 15215 52nd Ave. S., Ste. 100, Seattle, WA 98188 Phone:(206)244-6709 Fax:(206)243-3795 e-mail: dynamic@d-l-c.com Web site: www.d-l-c.com Contact: Ricardo Antezana
Founded 1985. Member: ATA, SOMI (Society of Medical Interpreters), WITS, NOTIS. Translates Spanish, French, German, Italian, Chinese, Japanese, Russian, Korean, Italian, and Vietnamese both from and into English.Total of over 85 languages. Emphasis on Technical Manuals, Industrial Project Specifications, Contracts and Patents, Legal Documentation, Commercial Correspondence, Promotional Brochures, Technical Presentations, Software Support Materials, Business Cards and Credentials translation. Prospective translators should be ATA accredited, have college-level education in both source and target languages, native speaker in target language. New translators must do a test translation. Not all resumes will receive a response. The company also provides text and graphics conversion, composition and layout, design and illustration, phototypesetting, scanning and HTML publishing services. They also do foreign language tape transcription and foreign language voiceovers. The company additionally provides interpreting and instructional services. Maintains a pool of over 600 translators.

-E-

800-Translate, 865 United Nations Plaza, New York, NY 10017 Phone: (800)872-6752 Fax: (888)872-6752 Web site: Contact: Ken Clark

East West Institute, 110 North Berendo St., Los Angeles, CA 90004 Phone: (213)389-7944 Fax: (213)382-0757 e-mail: ewincc@mindspring.com Web site: www.ewincc.com Contact: Danny Ree, Personnel Manager
Company founded 1989. Uses freelance translators and interpreters. Accepts unsolicited resumes. Translates all languages, both from and into English. Mainly Korean, Spanish, Japanese, Cheinese, Vietnamese. Prospective translators should be U.S. residents. Resumes are kept and applicants called if necessary. Interpreters provided only in Southern California.

echo international, Three Gateway Center, Floor 14 W, Pittsburgh, PA 15222 Phone: (412) 261-1101 Fax: (412) 261-1159 e-mail: dutka@echotrans.com Contact: Leslie A. Dutka

Echo Translation, P.O. Box 15301, Minneapolis, MN 55415 Phone: (612) 822-3473 Fax: (612) 371-9398 e-mail: echobea@aol.com Contact: Bea Cabrera

Eiber Translations 65-11 174th St., Fresh Meadows, NY 11365
Phone: (718) 463-2900 Fax: (718) 359-4073 e-mail: ibertrans@aol.com Contact: Edna H. Eiber

El Andar Translations, P.O. Box 7745, Santa Cruz, CA 95061
Phone: (831) 457-8353 Fax: (831) 457-8354 e-mail: translations@elandar.com Web site: www.elandar.com
Contact: Marga Vaquer

Elance.com, 820A Kifer Rd., Sunnyvale, CA 94086   Phone: (408) 524-759   Fax: (408) 524-4814
e-mail: Daniel@elancc.com   Web site: www.elance.com   Contact: Daniel L. Shapiro
Elocale, Inc., 815 Park Blvd., Ste. 255, Boise, ID 83712
Phone: (208)336-5530   Fax: (208)343-1336   info@elocale.com   Web site: www.elocale.com
Contact: Cary Clark

Encompass Globalization, 4040 Lake Washington Blvd. NE, Ste. 205, Kirkland, WA 98019   Phone: (425)828-2079   Fax: (425)828-2088   e-mail: nataliez@encompglobal.com   Web site: www.encompglobal.com
Contact: Nathalie H. Zimmerman

Eriksen Translations Inc., 32 Court St., 20th Fl., Brooklyn, NY 11201 Phone: (718)802-9010 Fax: (718)802-0041
e-mail: info@ erikseninc.com Web site: erikseninc.com   Contact: Leah Riggiero
Founded 1986. Member: ATA, NYCT, STC. Translates mainly Spanish, French, Portuguese, Japanese, Chinese, German, Danish, Finnish, Norwegian and Swedish. Emphasis on Legal, Financial, Advertising, Medical and Computers. Translators are encouraged to register on web site . The company also provides editing and typesetting services and Web site development. Maintains a pool of 2000 translators.

eTranslations, 222 Milwaukee St., Ste. 302, Denver, CO 80206   Phone: (303)388-4488 Fax: (303)388-2255
e-mail: info@etranslations.com   Web site: www.etranslations.com   Contact: Stephen Blum

Eurasia International, 16530 Ventura Blvd., Ste. 206, Encino, CA 91436   Phone: (818)907-9718   Fax; (818)907-9763
e-mail: VMordukhay@worldnet.att.net   Web site: www.eurasia-usa.com   Contact: Violetta Mordukhay
Founded 1993. Member: ATA. Accepts resumes. Translates mainly Spanish, German, Hebrew, Russian, French, Italian, Farsi and Indonesian. Also Romanina, Slovak, Malay, Japanese, Polish, Czech and Chinese. Mostly immigration, legal, and book publishing. Pool of over 200 translators.

Eureka-Foreign College Evaluators & Translators, 5308 West Lawrence, Chicago, IL 60630 Phone:(773)545-1700
Fax:(773)545-1716 e-mail: eureka@interaccess.com   Web site: www.polishtranslations.com
Contact: Maria Drewicz, Executive Director
Founded 1992. Member: The Translators and Interpreters Guild. Translates Polish, both from and into English, and German and Spanish into English. Emphasis on University Admission Documents, Immigration & Naturalization, Business, Technical, Medical and Legal translation. Prospective translators should have IBM-compatible PC, Word Perfect 5.1 DOS or Windows, minimum Bachelor's Degree. Resumes are reviewed, and qualified persons contacted. The company specializes in credential evaluation and Polish-American consulting services for business cooperation, cultural and marketing advisement, and is currently looking for Polish translators and interpreters. Maintains a pool of 10 translators.

EuroNet Language Services, 295 Madison Ave., 45th Fl., New York, NY 10017 Phone:(212)271-0401
Fax:(212)271-0404
e-mail: euronet@mindspring.com   Contact: Anouk, HRM
Founded 1989. Member: NYCT, ATA. Uses freelance translators and interpreters. Accepts unsolicited resumes. Translates Spanish, French, Portuguese, Italian, Dutch, German, Swedish, and other European languages, both from and into English. Translates all subjects. Prospective translators must be native speakers with bilingual capacity in English and possess a university degree. Resumes are reviewed and added to a database. Maintains a pool of 300 translators.

Excel Translations, Inc., 564 Market St., Ste. 705, San Francisco, CA 94104 Phone: (415)434-4224 Fax: (415)434-4221
e-mail: info@xltrans. com Web site: www.xltrans.com   Contact: Hervé Rodriguez
Founded 1995. Member: ATA, NCTA, TAALS, STC, HTML Guild, SPA. Translates French, Spanish, German, Japanese, Portuguese, Italian, Chinese and Dutch, all from English. Emphasis on Software Localization and Legal and Medical translation.

Prospective translators should have three years' translation experience and a specialty field. They should be native speakers and have access to the Internet. Resumes are screened and entered into a data base if passed. Applicants are notified by postcard. The company works with both freelancers and in-house translators and provides full DTP services. Maintains a pool of 500 translators.

Executive Linguist Agency, Inc., 500 S. Sepulveda Blvd., Ste. 300, Manhattan Beach, CA 90266   Phone: (310)376-1409   Fax; (310)376-9285   e-mail: executivelinguist@earthlink.net   Contact: Ronald R. Randolph

Expert Language Services, Inc., 745 Kirkton Court, Rochester Hills, MI 48307   Phone: (810)656-4220   Fax: (810)656-2733   e-mail:els@rust.net   Contact: Lori Ann Elzerman

-F-

FLS, Inc., 3609 A-5 Memorial Parkway SW, Huntsville AL 35801 Phone: (205)881-1120 Fax: (205)880-1112 e-mail: mail@flstranslation.com Web site: www.flstranslation.com   Contact: Judith H. Smith
Company founded 1979. Member: ATA. Uses freelance translators and interpreters. Unsolicited resumes accepted. Translates over 60 languages, mainly Japanese, Spanish, French, Chinese, Korean, German and East European languages. Mostly technical and legal. Over 200 translators.

Federal News Service, 620 National Press Building NW, Washington, DC 20045 Phone: (202)347-1400 Fax: (202)626-2630   e-mail: info@fednews.com Web site: www.fednews.com   Contact: Marina Makanova
Founded 1987. Accepts resumes. Requires college degree. Translates mainly Spanish, French, Russian, Chinese, and Italian. Uses 63 translators. The company is a news wire that provides government transcripts, online newsclipping, news monitoring services, and translations in almost any language.

First Translation Services, 3072 Brighton, 1st St., Brooklyn, NY 11235
Phone: (718)372-7723   Fax: (718)265-6653   Contact: Jack Kleyman   Member: ATA

Foreign Exchange Translations, Inc., One Richmond Square, Providence, RI 02906   Phone: (401)454-0787 Fax: (401)454-0789   e-mail: adnresh@fxtrans.com   Web site: www.fxtrans.com   Contact: Andres Heuberger
Member: ATA

Foreign Ink, Ltd., 5735 Washburn Ave. S, Minneapolis MN 55410 Phone: (612)920-4884 Fax: (612)924-9075 e-mail: greg@fornink.com Web site: fornink.com   Contact: Gregory Stricherz Member: ATA

-G-

GES Translation Services, 836 Manhattan Ave., Brooklyn, NY 11222
Phone: (718)389-8453   Fax: (718)389-4442 e-mail:ges@flashcom.net   Contact: Richard Rzeznik

Garcia-Shilling International, 1402 Corinth, L.B. 139, Dallas, TX 75215   Phone: (214)428-4428 Fax: (214)428-4458   e-mail: acento@swbell.net Web site: www.garciashillinginternational.com   Contact: Luis A. Garcia, Sr.
Gateway Direct, 45 W. 34th St., Ste. 203, New York, NY 10001   Phone: (202)695-5394 Fax: (202)695-5106 e-mail: gatewaydirect@earthlink.com   Contact: Sergiy Orlov

Gene Mayer Associates, 9 Depot St., 2nd Fl., Milford, CT 06460   Phone: (203)882-5990 Fax: (203)882-5995 e-mail: info@design4language.com
Founded 1985. Member: ATA, AIGA, Design Management Institute, National Investor Relations Institute, CT Art Directors Club. Provides graphic design, translation and production of complex printed material used by global corporations. Emphasis on business (employee information, annual reports, marketing brochures, corporate policy manuals). The firms handles translation, design, book layout and production in 30 languages. Prefers to work with agencies or with translators with a qualified track record with large corporate clients.

The Geo Group, 6 Odana Court, Ste. 205, Madison, WI 53719 Phone: (608)230-1000 Fax: (608)230-1010 e-mail: translation@thegeogroup.com Web site: www.thegeogroup.com Contact: Translation Manager

Founded 1991. Accepts resumes. Requires min. 3 years translation/inter-preting experience. Main languages are French, German, Hmong, Italian, Portuguese, Spanish, Japanese, Chinese and Dutch. Also other European languages. Main subjects are medical, automotive, marketing, computers, dairy equipment, legal and audio/video. Uses a pool of over 500 translators.

Geotext Translations, 352 7th Ave., New York, NY 10001
Phone: (202)631-7432 Fax: (202)631-7407 -mail: translations@geotext.com Web site: www.geotext.com
Contact: Joseph Duncan

German Language Services, 2658 48th Ave., SW, Seattle, WA 98116   Phone: (206)938-3600   Fax: (206)938-8308
e-mail: GermanLanguage@GermanLanguageServices.comWeb site: www.GermanLanguageServices.com
Contact: Maia Costa
Founded 1979. Member: ATA, NOTIS, GALL. Accepts resumes only in electronic form. Requires formal training in translation or interpretation and 5 years experience. Only translates German.

Global Advanced Translation Services, Inc., 501 S. Fairfax Ave., #212, Los Angeles, CA 90036
Phone: (323)937-1525 Fax: (323)937-6568 e-mail: mteper@aol.com   Contact: Marina Teper   Member: ATA

Global Impact Inc., 13570 Grove Drive, #212, Maple Grove, MN 55311   Phone: (763)424-7449 Fax: (763)424-7407
e-mail: info@global-impactinc.com Web site: www.global-impactinc.com   Contact: Kathi Winger   Member: ATA

The Global Institute of Languages and Culture, Inc., 7301 NW 4th st., Ste. 110, Plantation, FL 33317 Phone: (954)327-1662 Fax: (955)327-8116 e-mail: globalin@gate.net Web site: www.globalinstitute.com
Contact: Antonieta Mercado
Member: ATA. Translates Spanish, Portuguese, Italian, French, Ger-man, etc., both from and into English. Emphasis on General, Computer, Medical and Legal translation. Prospective translators should have a college degree, experience, and should be native speakers of the target language. Resumes are responded to based on the applicant's qualifications and the company's needs. Maintains a pool of 20 translators.

Global Languages & Cultures, Inc., 680 N. Lake Shore Drive, Ste. 919, Chicago, IL 60611   Phone: (312)981-4444 Fax: (312)981-4445   -mail: yozturk@e-translation.com Web site: www.e-translation.com   Contact: Sedef Olcer

Global Language Solutions/The Russian Word, Inc., 19800 MacArthur Blvd., Ste. 520, Irvine, CA 92612
e-mail: info@globallanguages.com Web site: www.globallanguages.com   Contact: Inna Kassatkina

Global Software Solutions, 210 SW Morrison St., Ste. 300, Portland, OR 97204   Phone: (503)827-0787 Fax: (503)827-0790 e-mail: kirsteens@g11n.com   Web site: www.G11N.com Contact: Kirsteen Scott

Global Translation Systems Inc., 910 Airport Rd., Chapel Hill, NC 27514 Phone:(919)967-2010 Fax:(919)929-1333
e-mail: mike@globaltranslation.com Web site: www.globaltranslation.com Contact: Michael Collins Member: ATA

Global Visions LLC, 4820 Eastwind Rd., Virginia Beach, VA 23464
Phone: (757)495-3719 Fax: (757)495-6398 e-mail: globalvisions60@hotmail.com   Contact: Kristi B. Emerson
Member: ATA

The Global Word, Inc., 63 Grand Ave., River Edge, NJ 07661   hone: (201)343-0015 Fax: (201)343-4155
e-mail: info@globalword.com   Web site: www.globalword.com Contact: Michael Fundaro   Member: ATA

Global Works.Com, 129 W. 27ᵗʰ St., New York, NY 10001 Phone; (212)414-1300 Fax: (212)414-8700 e-mail: emantello@globalworks.com Web site: www.globalworks.com Contact: Elisabeth Mantello Member: ATA

GlobalDoc Inc., 1800 Peachtree St., Ste. 370, Atlanta, GA 30309 Phone:(404)350-6740 Fax:(404)350-6747 e-mail: mail@globaldoc.com Web site: www.globaldoc.com Contact: Michael W. Cooper
Founded 1990. Member: ATA, STC. Translates all Major European languages plus Japanese, both from and into English. Emphasis on Technical, Telecommunication, Hardware/Software, and Office Products translation. Prospective translators should be ATA member, possess translation experience, and have modern word-processing capabilities, fax and modem. Candidates should have high levels of technical knowledge and be reliable, accessible, and able to work quickly. Resumes are entered into a database with notes regarding qualifications.

Go Global Translations, Inc., 19515 Rosedale Ave., Excelsior, MN 55331 Phone: (952)474-6413 Fax: (952)474-3756 e-mail:TeresaGoGlobal@cs.com Web site: www.goglobalranslations.com Contact: Teresa A. Crespo Member: ATA

The Golf Channel, Inc., 7580 Commerce Center Drive, Orlando, FL 32819 Phone: (407)248-3344 Fax: (407)248-1344 e-mail: jkrisand@tgcinc.com Contact: James R. Krisanda Member: ATA

Grammaton, LLC, 137 Cambridge St., Ste. 100, Burlington, MA 01803 Phone: (781)365-4000 Fax: (781)365-1000
e-mail:wally.rodriguez@grammaton.com \Web site: www.grammaton.com Contact: Walter A. Rodriguez

Groupe Mistral, 522 Brewers Mill Rd., Harrodsburg, KY 40330 Phone: (859)366-4211 Fax:(630)477-0438 e-mail: mistral@groupmistral.com Web site: www.groupmistral.com Contact: Sylvie Gadness
Founded 1996. Accepts resumes. Translates French, Spanish, German, Haitian Creole, Italian, Oromo, Chinese, Japanese, Korean and Farsi, as well as all Indian languages and dialects and more. Emphasis on Engineering, Financial, Medical and Advertising translation. The company does not work with freelance translators; it is rather a consortium of in-house personnel. Prospective translators should be local, within driving distance, and should have translation experience. Specializes in French Computer translation. Maintains a pool of 120 translators.

-H-

HG Translations, P.O. Box 31372, Seattle, WA 98103 Phone: (206)374-2403 Fax: (206)374-2403 e-mail: admin@hgtranslation.com Web site: www.hgtranslations,com Contact: Gary M. Gilligan Member: ATA

H&K Translations, LLC, 701 Brickell Ave., Suite 3000, Miami, FL 33131 Phone: (305)789-7521 Fax: (305)789-7799 Contact: Maury M. Scharrer Member: ATA

Health Outcomes Group, 435 Middlefield Rd., Palo Alto, CA 94301 Phone: (650)321-4336 Fax: (650)321-4510 e-mail: hog_usa@compuserve.com Contact: David Himmelberger Member: ATA

Hernandez & Garcia, LLC, 7360 N. Lincoln Ave., Ste. 100, Lincolnwood, IL 60712 Phone: (847)676-4445 Fax: (847)676-1420 e-mail: mhernandez@hernandezgarcia.com Contact: Maritza Hernandez Member: ATA

Hightech Passport Limited, 1590 Oakland Rd., Ste. B202, San Jose, CA 95131 Phone: (408)453-6303 Fax: (408)453-9434 e-mail: magdalena@htpassport.com Web site: www.htpassport.com
Contact: Magdalena Enea, VP of Market Development
Founded 1992. Member: ATA, NCTA. Translates French, German, Spanish, Italian, Portuguese, Swedish, Dutch, Russian, Japanese, Chinese, and all Scandinavian from English. Emphasis on Computer Software, Documentation (both printed and online), Marketing Materials, Tapes, and Computer Training Literature translations. Complete range of internationalization and localization services, mainly to IT and medical industry. The company also provides software localization and testing, videotape localization, and desktop printing services. Maintains a pool of 150 translators.

Honda R&D North America, Inc., 21001 State Route 739, Raymond, OH 43067   Phone: (513)645-6164   Fax: (513)645-6341   e-mail: knason@oh.hra.com   Contact: Kay T. Nason

-I-

IDEM Translation, 614 Greer Rd., Palo Alto, CA 94303   Phone: (415)329-0170 Fax: (41)329-0266
e-mail: idem@compuserve.com   Contact: Mariam Nayiny   Member: ATA

IRU Language & Translation Services, 2909 Hillcroft Ave., Ste. 538, Houston, TX 77057 Phone: (713)266-0020 Fax: (713)266-1716 e-mail: iru@aol.com   Web site: www.iru-services.com   Contact: Dagmar Beck
Founded 1989. Member: ATA, HITA. Translates mainly German, Spanish, Portuguese, French, Italian, Russian, Japanese, Dutch, Bosnian and Italian, as well as all other languages. Emphasis on commercial, financial, technical and business. Prospective translators should have prior experience and excellent computer literacy, as well as the ability to deliver in a timely manner. Resumes are reviewed and entered into a data base by language. The company also provides language classes, chaperon services and cross-cultural seminars, with emphasis on Spanish and German. Maintains a pool of over 60 translators.

ISI, 3501 Market St., Philadelphia, PA 19104   Phone: (215)386-0100 Fax: (215)243-2208
e-mail: ellen.boyar@isinet.com   Web site: www.isinet.com   Contact: Ellen A. Boyar

ISI (Interpreting Services International Inc.), 6180 Laurel Canyon Blvd., #245, N. Hollywood, CA 91606
Phone: (818)753-9181 Fax: (818)753-9617   e-mail: info@isitrans.com   Contact: Cathi Rimalower

INAWORD, 811 W. 7ᵗʰ St., Ste. 204, Los Angeles, CA 90017   hone: (213)688-6200 Fax: (800)805-7994
e-mail: info@inaword.net Web site: www.inaword.net   Contact: Stella Fridman   Member: ATA

Information Builders, Inc., Two Penn Plaza, New York, NY 10121
Phone: (212)736-4433 Fax: (212)967-6404 Web site: www.ibi.com   Contact: Georgina Channer   Member: ATA

The Information Foundry at Robert Bently, Inc., 1734 Massachusetts Ave., Cambridge, MA 02138
Phone: (617)528-4043 Fax: (617)876-9235 e-mail: john.harthborne@infofoundry.com
Web site: www.infofoundry.com   Contact: John Harthborne   Member : ATA

Inline Translation Services. Inc., 100 W. Broadway, Ste. 250, Glendale, CA 91210   Phone: (818)547-4995
Fax: (818)547-4013   e-mail: inlinela@inlinela.com Web site: www.inlinela.com   Contact: Richard S. Paegelow
Member: ATA

Inlingua, Inc., 171 East Ridgewood Ave., Ridgewood, NJ   07450 Phone: (201)444-9500 Fax: (201)444-0116
e-mail: ridgewood@inlingua.com   Web site: www.inlingua.com   Contact: Sandra Stern, Translation Services Coordinator
Founded 1977. Member: ATA. Accepts resumes from translators and interpreters.. Requires ATA accreditation. Main languages are Spanish, French, Portuguese, German, Italian, Chinese, Japanese, Russian, and Italian. Also Hindi, Hungarian, Polish, Romanian and Dutch. Mainly legal, pharmaceutical, financial. Uses some 150 translators.

Inlingua Language & Intercultural Services, 4500 Park Glen Rd., Ste. 120, Saint Louis Park, MN 55416
Phone: (952)929-9155 Fax: (952)929-0020   e-mail: info@inlingua-mn.com
Web site: www.inlingua.com/minneapolis.htm
Cosntact: Carolyn W. Leavenworth   Member: ATA

Inlingua Language Service Center, 1901 N. Moore St., Arlington, VA 22209   Phone: (703)527-8666 Fax: (703)527-8693
e-mail: intpschool@inlinguadc.com Web site: www.inlinguadc.com Contact: Harry Obst   Member: ATA

Inlingua Translation Service, 95 Summit Ave., Summit, NJ 07901 Phone: (908)522-0622 Fax: (908)522-1433 e-mail: summit@inlingua.com   Contact: Becky Miller

Founded 1968. Uses freelance translators and interpreters. Accepts unsolicited resumes. Resumes are kept on file for future jobs. Applicants must have computer, fax, and modem. Ten top languages are Spanish, French, Italian, Port-uguese, Russian, German, Chinese, Japanese, Danish, and Polish. Also translates Korean and Romanian. Main areas are licenses, birth certificates, and transcripts. Has pool of some 30 translators. Operates as language school with translation services.

Inlingua Translation Service, 230 S. Broad St., 7th Fl.,   Philadelphia, PA 19102   Phone:(215)735-7646 Fax:(215)735-4188 e-mail: acassidy@inlingua.com Web site: www.inlingualv.com   Contact: Angela Cassidy Member: ATA

Translates French, German, Japanese, Chinese, both from and into English. Emphasis on Legal and Pharmaceutical translation. Prospective translators should be ATA certified, with at least 3-5 years experience. Resumes are responded to with a letter of receipt. Maintains a pool of 200 translators.

Intela Services, 19146 Stare St., Northridge, CA 91324   Phone: (800)209-1663 Fax: (818)998-3993 e-mail: david@intela.com   Web site: www.intela.com   Contact: David Deaussin   Member: ATA

Interclub, 4200 N. Central Ave., Chicago, IL 60634   Phone: (773)777-ABCD Fax: (773)202-0012 e-mail: Contact@interclubabdc.com Web site: www.translationsusa.com Member: ATA

Intermark Language Services Coporation, 2555 Cumberland Pkwy, Ste. 295, Atlanta, GA 30339 Phone: (770)444-3055 Fax: (770)444-3002 e-mail: info@intermark-languages.com Web site: www.intermark-languages. com

Contact: Tom West

Founded 1995. Member: ATA. Accepts resumes. Interested in translators with a law or business degree. Translates mainly French, Spanish, German, Portuguese and Swedish. Emphasis is on Law and Business translation. Prospective translators *must* provide a sample translation in every combination they wish to translate; ATA accreditation is preferred.

InterNation, Inc., 299 Broadway, Ste. 1400, New York, NY 10007 Phone:(212)619-5545 e-mail: info@ internationinc. com Web site: www.internationinc.com

Founded 1990. Member: ATA, NYCT, BBB. Uses freelance translators and interpreters. Accepts unsolicited resumes. Prospective translators should have experience, adequate hardware and software. Resumes are reviewed, and a questionnaire mailed with a request for samples. The samples are then reviewed. Translates Spanish, French, German, Japanese, Chinese, Russian, Italian, and other major languages, both from and into English. Emphasis on Commercial Document, Legal Document, Video voice-over and subtitling, Advertising Copy, Scientific Material, Medical and Pharmaceutical translation. Specialties in Foreign Language Voiceovers and Subtitling. The company specializes in voiceovers for corporate sales, training and safety videos. It does post-production in over 25 languages. Also employs narrators and character actors in the New York City area. Maintains a pool of some 5000 translators.

International Bureau of Translations, Inc, 10291 North Meridian   St., Ste. 350, Indianapolis, IN 46290 Phone: ((317)581-0060 Fax: (317) 581-1160 e-mail: ibtinc@ibtworld.com Web site: www.ibtworld.com   Contact: Christian Gecewicz

Founded 1976. Member: OTIAQ, Indianapolis Chamber of Commerce, IUPUI, Indian University. Translates French, Spanish, German, Portuguese, Dutch, Italian, Japanese, Chinese, Korean and Russian, both from and into English, as well as various Slavic, Scandinavian, Eastern European and Asian languages. Emphasis on Business Correspondence, Medical, Technical, Legal and Personal Document translation. Prospective translators should be native speakers with access to a computer, modem, or fax. They should send a rate chart with their resume. Resumes are filed and the translator contacted as the need arises. The company does foreign videos, court interpretation, cultural presentations, and conducts language classes. They research the cultural acceptability of company names, product names and slogans, and are the official translators for the International Violin Competition. Maintains a pool of 150 translators.

International Communication by Design, Inc., 1726 North First St., Milwaukee, WI 53212 Phone:(414)265-2171 Fax:(212)265-2101   -mail: info@icdtranslation.com   Web site: www.icdtranslation.com   Contact: Jennifer Marquardt, Office Manager
Founded 1991. Member: ATA, Wisconsin World Trade Center, STC. Translates mainly Italian, Spanish, French, German, Portuguese, Dutch, Italian, Greek, Japanese and Chinese. Also Korean, Russian and Swedish. Emphasis on Technical Manuals, medical and Legal translation. Also web site localization. Prospective translators should be native speakers and ATA accredited, with a specific area of expertise and must be able to send projects in via CompuServe. Resumes are filed and used as a resource for new translators, interpreters and typesetters. It is a translation service company with a wide range of clients, from large corporations to smaller cottage industries. The company is actively community involved. Maintains a pool of over 60 translators.

International Contact, Inc., 351 15th St., Oakland, CA 94612   Phone:(510)836-1180 Fax:(510)835-1314 e-mail: info@intl Contact.com Web site: www.intl Contact.com Contact: Accounting   Member: ATA

International Effectiveness Centers, 690 Market St., Ste. 700, San Francisco, CA 94104 Phone:(415)788-4149 Fax:(415)788-4829 e-mail: iec@ie-center.com   Web site: www.ie-center.com Contact: Taryk Rouchdy
Founded 1972. Member: ATA, NCTA. Translates Spanish, Chinese, Russian, and Portuguese, both from and into English, French and Vietnamese from English, and Japanese into English. Emphasis on Legal, Technical and Children's Book translation. Uses freelance translators and interpreters. Accept unsolicited resumes. Prospective translators must have at least 3 years experience and be tested unless they hold current ATA accreditation. Resumes are screened for qualifications and appropriate equipment and, if qualified, entered into a data base The company also does desktop publishing in all languages, as well as voiceovers, dubbing, promotional work, crosscultural and language training, and international business consulting. Maintains a pool of 7000 translators in its data base, 170 of whom are used regularly.

International Institute of Wisconsin, 1110 N. Old World 3rd St., Milwaukee, WI 83203   Phone: (414)225-6220 Fax: (414)225-6235 e-mail: iiw@excpc.com Web site: www.iiwisconsin.org Contact: Alexander P. Durtka, Jr.

International Language Center, 1416 S. Big Bend Blvd., St. Louis, MO 63117   Phone: (314)647-8888   Fax: (314)647-8889   e-mail: ilc@ilcworldwide.com Web site: www.ilcworldwide.com   Contact: Dede S. Brunetti

International Language Service. Inc., 1221 S. Shepherd, Ste. 200, Houston, TX 77019   Phone: (713)783-3800 Fax: (713)529-7717   e-mail: i4@houston.rr.com Web site: www.eworld-link.com   Contact: Kimberly K. Silverman

International Language Services, Inc., 5810 Baker Rd., Ste. 250, Minnetonka, MN 55345 Phone: (612)672-9600 Fax: (612)672-9400 e-mail: info@ilstranslations.com   Web site: www.ilstraslations.com   Contact: Phyllis Beatty
Founded 1982. Translates Spanish, French, German, Italian, Portuguese, Japanese, Swedish, Dutch, Danish, Chinese and most other languages from English. Emphasis on Medical, Technical, Business and Legal translation. Prospective translators should have ATA accreditation, references, a minimum 3-5 years experience, and be native speakers of the target language. Resumes are read and filed by language. Their primary focus is on biomedical instrumentation. Maintains a pool of over 300 translators.

International Language Source, Inc., P.O. Box 338, Holland, OH 43528 Phone:(419)865-4374 Fax:(419)865-7725
e-mail: ilsource @att.net Web site: www.ilsource.com   Contact: Ryan Stevens, Account Manager
Founded 1981. Member: TAITA, ATA. Uses freelance translators and interpreters. Accepts unsolicited resumes. Prospective translators should have a specialty area and the appropriate resources for projects in that area. Resumes are kept for 6 months in an active database. Contact may involve the paid translation of a short sample. Translates mainly French, Spanish, German, Italian and Chinese. Also Japanese, Portuguese and Hebrew. Emphasis on Glass Manufacturing and Retail, Automotive OEM and Aftermarket, Furniture, Legal, Industrial and Healthcare translation. In addition to translation services, the company provides video and interactive CD-ROM translation and voiceovers. The company is willing to consider internships and cooperative projects with other translation companies.

International Translating & Typesetting Company, 2730 Stemmons Freeway, Ste. 302, Dallas, TX 75207-2248 Phone:(214)630-0840   Fax: (214)630-6482 e-mail: 102462.161@compuserve.com   Contact: Javier Galdeano, Translation Manager

Founded 1969. Member: Greater Dallas Chamber of Commerce. Translates Spanish, Chinese, French, German, Italian, Russian, Japanese, Portuguese, Kore-an, Vietnamese, Bulgarian, Cambodian, SerboCroatian, Czech, Danish, Dutch, Farsi, Finnish, Greek, Gujarati, Hebrew, Hindi, Indonesian, Kurdish, Latin, Norwegian, Polish, Punjabi, Romanian, Hungarian, Swedish, Tagalog, Thai, Turkish, Ukrainian, and Urdu, both from and into English. Emphasis on Petroleum, Electronics, Legal, Business, Advertising, Food Export, Chemical, and Civil Engineering translations. Prospective translators must accept work *only* from translation companies, and *never directly from end users*. They must have either IBM or Macintosh computers, a modem and a fax. Resumes are filed until a need arises. In addition to translation, the company also provides high-resolution typesetting in most languages. Maintains a pool of 200 translators.

International Translating Bureau, 16125 West 12 Mile Rd., South-field, MI 48076-2912 Phone:(248)559-1677 Fax:(248)559-1679 e-mail: itbinc @itbtranslations.com   Contact: Mariano Pallarés, President

Founded 1977. Translates all language pairs. Emphasis on Automotive, Engineering, Machine Tool, Legal, Medical, and Public Relations translation. Prospective translators should be native speakers of the target language, have at least 5 years residence in the source-language country, and have academic training or on-job experience in a specialized field. Candidates must have computer, fax and current software, particularly WordPerfect and Word for Windows for PC or Mac. Resumes are scanned for qualifications in which the company is interested and filed for future use. The company offers accurate, native-like translations. Maintains a pool of 250 translators.

International Translation Service, P.O. Box 188331, Sacramento, CA 95818   Phone: (530)753-7482 Fax: (530)753-7482 e-mail: its@yolo.com Web site: www.geocities.com/its worldwide   Contact: Garry Pratt

Founded 1970. Uses freelance translators and interpreters. Accepts unsolicited resumes. Prospective translators must be experienced in both their languages and specialty fields, and should possess a variety of means of communications, including phone, fax and e-mail; they should have computers with the appropriate language fonts. Resumes are filed by language and the summiteers contacted. Translates mainly Scandinavian, German, Spanish, and French, and also Estonian, Irish, Italian, Russian, Finnish, Portuguese, Polish, Dutch and more. Translates mainly legal, scientific, commercial, and medical. Maintains a pool of some 80 translators.

International Translation Services, P.O. Box 1707, Taos, NM 87571 Phone: (505)758-3444 Fax: (505)737-5484 e-mail: its2leslie@compuserve.com   Contact: Leslie G. Haynes

International Translation Solutions, 10 S. 5th St., Ste. 320, Minneapolis, MN 55402   Phone: (612)339-4660 e-mail: translate@intransol.com Web site: www.intransol.com   Contact: Cary Rothschild

Founded 1987. Member: ATA, STC, NADTP, GBCC. Translates Spanish, French and German, both from and into English, and Portuguese, Korean, Japanese, Chinese, Italian, Indonesian and Eastern European languages, from English. Emphasis on Commercial, Legal, Technical and Medical translations. Prospective translators should have professional experience, subject specialties, and possess computer, fax, modem, e-mail and other technologies. Resumes are reviewed and replied to with an application form requesting additional information. The company also provides multilingual typesetting and desktop publishing, graphic design, and audio and video production services. Maintains a pool of over 3,000 translators.

Interpretations, Inc., 8665 W. 96th St., Ste. 201, Overland Park, KS 66212   Phone: (913)338-2434   Fax: (913)338-2636 e-mail: interp@accessus.net Web site: www.exactwords.com   Contact: Gloria J. Donohue

Founded 1991. Member: ATA, MICATA, International Trade Club, International Relations Council, Women's Resources Network. Translates mainly Spanish, French, German, Portuguese, Russian, Dutch, Swedish and Italian. Also Danish, Finnish and Korean. Emphasis on Instructional and Technical, Legal, Advertising, Video Script and Educational Materials translation. Prospective translators must be native speakers and have five years' experience; ATA accreditation is a must. They should be up-to-date on hardware and software. Resumes are reviewed and filed; a select number are asked to provide samples of their work and/or translate short paragraphs. The company also provides interpreters for meetings, conferences and telephone conferencing. Maintains a pool of about 100 translators.

Interpreters' Index.com, P.O. Box 880872, San Diego, CA 92168   hone: (619)850-8279 Fax: (619)334-9473 e-mail: info@interpretersindex.com   Web site: www.interpretersindex.com   Contact: Juana Esther Blanco Member: ATA

Interpreters International & Translations, 123-40 83rd Ave., Ste. 9D, Kew Gardens, NY 11415-3431 Phone: (718)544-0224 Fax:(718)261-3864 e-mail: mzinola@nyct.net   Contact: Maria Zinola
Founded 1986. Member: ATA. Accepts resumes with college degree and 5 years experience. Translates mainly Italian, Chinese, French, German, Hebrew, Japanese, Korean, Portuguese, Russian and Spanish. Also Czech, Dutch, Farsi, Greek, Haitian Creole, Hindi, Hugarian, Italian, Polish, Romanian, Serbian, Croatian, Turkish, Vietnamese and Yiddish. Mostly business, insurance, legal, marketing, medical and technical. Uses some 55 translators.

InterSol, Inc., Three Point Drive, Ste. 301, Brea, CA 92821   Phone: (714)671-9180 Fax: (714)671-9188 email: solutions@intersolinc.com Web site: intersolinc.com   Contact: Susana Turbitt
Founded 1996. Member: ATA. Accepts resumes. Translates mainly French, Italian, German, Spanish, Portuguese, Japanese, Chinese, Danish, Swedish and Finnish. Mostly medical, electronics, computers, automotive, general business, travel and sports. Also software localization. Uses some 30 translators.

Interspeak Translations, Inc., 114 East 32nd St., New York, NY 10016 Phone: (212)679-4772 Fax: (212)679-5084
Contact: Silvia Zehn   Member: ATA

Intertech Translations, Ltd., 671 S. Gulph Rd., King of Prussia, PA 19406 Phone: (610)265-7776 Fax: (610)337-4994 e-mail: intertechltd@compuserve.com   Contact: Carole K. Kenney   Member: ATA

IRCO/International Language Bank, 10301 NE Glisan St., Portland, OR 97220 Phone: (503)234-0068 Fax: (503)233-4724   e-mail: translation@mail.irco.com   Web site: www.irco.org   Contact: Translation Services Supervisor
Founded 1976. Member: ATA, NOTIS. Uses freelance translators. Accepts unsolicited resumes. Applicants should own PC or Mac, fax machine and e-mail, and have experience with the Internet and desktop publishing. Resumes are sorted by language and applicant's last name and filed for future use. Translates Spanish, Russian, Romanian, Serbo-Croatian Vietnamese, Cambodian, Laotian, Mien, Hmong, Chinese, Japanese, Amharic, Tigrigna, Creole and Thai, all from English. Emphasis on community translation projects, such as government forms, employee manuals, social service literature, and translation for refugee and immigrant communities in the U.S. They specialize in refugee-related documents and languages. IRCO is the Immigrant and Refugee Community Organization and is a nonprofit agency. ILB has grown from providing language services to refugee communities to a full-service translation and interpreting agency. Maintains a pool of over 100 translators.

Italian Language Connection, Inc., 5225 Pooks Hill Rd. Ste. 504-S, Bethesda, MD 20814 Phone: (301)897-3728 Fax: (301)897-0872 e-mail: ItaTranslations@cs.com   Contact: Mark L. Pisoni
Founded 1991. Member: ATA. Accepts resumes. Only translates Italian. Main subjects are economics and finance, legal, business, marketing and medical. Uses 15 translators.

Iverson Language Associates, Inc., P.O. Box 511759, Milwaukee, WI 53203 Phone:(414)271-1144 Fax:(414)271-0144 e-mail: steve@iversonlang.com Web site: www.iversonlang.com   Contact: Steven P. Iverson, President
Founded 1986. Member: ATA, STC, ASTD. Translates French, Spanish, Japanese, Italian, Italian, Dutch, and Korean from English, and Portuguese, German, Polish, Chinese and all other languages, both from and into English. Emphasis on Technical Manuals (large machines), Medical Operators' Manuals, Spec Sheets, Financial, Software, Advertising Packaging, and Legal translations. Prospective translators should have computer, fax, current software, e-mail. Must be native speakers in the target language, with a technical background and formal training in a specific field of concentration. Three years experience in the industry and good writing skills are preferred. Resumes are reviewed internally for the required criteria. If so, they are sent a Translator Profile to fill out, and the completed form made available to project managers for use on new projects. The company provides translation, interpretation, typesetting and video narration services in most major languages, as well as technical writing and illustration. Typesetting capabilities include Chinese and Japanese. Maintains a pool of 600 translators.

-J-

JBT Translations & Localization, 115 U. St., Salt Lake City, UT 84103 Phone: (801)355-0518 Fax: (801)355-1873
e-mail: juttabrandt@compuserve.com   Contact: Jutta Brandt   Member: ATA

J. D. Edwards, One Technology Way, Denver, CO 80237   Phone: (303)334-1638 Fax: (303)334-1679
e-mail: loy_searle@jdedwards.com   Contact: LoyAnne Searle   Member: ATA

JLS Language Corporation, 135 Willow Rd., Menlo Park, CA 94025 Phone: (415)321-9832 Fax: (415)329-9864
e-mail: info@jls.com   Web site: jls.com   Contact: Ms. Rikko Field, President
Founded 1977. Member: ATA. Translates Japanese, Chinese, German, French and Spanish, both from and into English, with other languages on request. Emphasis on High Tech translation. Prospective translators should have ATA accreditation, education and industry experience. Resumes are screened and filed, and the promising applicants tested. In addition to High Tech, the company also does Agribusiness, Biomedical and Patent translations, and provides Chinese and Japanese desktop publishing. Maintains a pool of "hundreds" of translators.

JTG, Inc., 105 N. Washington St., Ste. 300, Alexandria, VA 22314   hone: (703)548-7570 Fax: (703)548-8223
e-mail: hr@jtg-inc.com   Web site: www.jtg-inc.com   Contact: Muriel Jérôme-O'Keeffe   Member: ATA

Japan-America Management, Ltd., 2020 Hogback Rd., Ste. 17, Ann Arbor, MI 48105   Phone: (734)973-6101 Fax: (734)973-1847   e-mail: jamltdmi@ameritech.net   Contact: Landon Bartley   Member: ATA

Japan Communication Consultants, 236 E. 47th St., 28th Fl., New York, NY 10017 Phone: (212)759-2033 Fax: (212)759-2149 e-mail: jcc@japancc.com Web site: www.japancc.com Contact: Mariko N. O'Hare   Member: ATA

Japan Pacific Publications, Inc., 419 Occidental Ave. S. #509, Seattle, WA 98104 Phone: (206)622-7443 Fax: (206)621-1786 -mail: andrewt@japanpacific.com   Web site: www.japanpacific.com Contact: Andrew Taylor, President
Founded 1983. Member: ATA. Uses freelance translators and interpreters. Accepts unsolicited resumes. Resumes are entered into database and evaluated for skills and experience. Main language is Japanese. Also translates Chinese and Korean. Main areas are agriculture, business, bio-med, tourism, marketing, software and wood products. Maintains pool of 35 translators. Translation, DTP, pre-press, image setting.

John Benjamins Publishing Company, P.O. Box 27519, Philadelphia PA 19118-0519 Phone: (215)836-1200 Fax: (215)836-1204 email: paul@ benjamins.com   Contact: Paul Peranteau Member: ATA

Josef Silny & Associates, Inc., 1320 South Dixie Highway, Ste. 775, Coral Gables, FL 33146 Phone: (305)273-1616 Fax: (305)83601204   e-mail: translation@jsilny.com Web site: www.jsilny.com   Contact: Josef

Silny Member: ATA

-K-

K19.Com, P.O. Box 91927, Austin, TX 78709   Phone: (512)301-6623   Fax: (512)301-6624
e-mail: info@k19.com   Web site: www.k19.com   Contact: Albert Kadosh   Member: ATA

The Kaiser Permanente Medical Group, 2241 Geary Blvd., Rm. 146, San Francisco, CA 94115
Phone: (415)202-2888   Fax: (415)202-3829   -mail: gayle.tang@kp.org   Contact: Gayle Tang   Member: ATA

Kern Corporation, 230 Park Ave., Ste. 925, New York, NY 10169 Phone: (212)953-2070   Contact: Eric Schloss

Kotru Direct, 1001 Avenue of the Americas, #1214, New York, NY 10018   Phone: (212)840-2300   Fax: (212)840-0004
e-mail: kdiny@aol.com   Contact: Ravi Kotru   Member: ATA

Kramer Translation, 893 Massasso St., Merced, CA 95340 Phone: (209)385-0425 Fax: (209)385-3747
e-mail: keith@thailinguist.com Web site: www.thailinguist.com Contact: Keith & Marisa Ensminger   Member: ATA

LRA Interpreters, Inc., 5150 Wilshire Blvd., #506, Los Angeles, CA 90036   Phone: (323)933-1006 Fax: (323)933-1153
e-mail: lra2@flash.net   Web site: www. Flash.net/~lratrsln Contact: Abel Plockier   Member: ATA

LangTech International, 5625 SW 170th Ave., Aloha, OR 97007 Phone: (503)646-2478 (to fax, call first)
e-mail: LangTech@oregonvos.net   Web site: www.oregonvos.com   Contact: Douglas Foran, Owner
Founded 1994. Member: Latin American Trade Council of Oregon. Does not accept resumes. Translates French (European and Canadian), Spanish, Italian and Portuguese (Brazilian and Lusitanian), both from and into English. Emphasis on Scientific/Technical, Mechanical, Electronics, Automotive, Agricultural, Legal, Health Care/Medical and Employee Relations translation. Also interpretation and audio/visual narration.

Langua Translations, Inc., 30150 Telegraph Rd., Ste. 339, Bingham Farms, MI 48025 Phone: (810)645-6663
Fax: (810)645-5376 e-mail: rneely@languatutor.com   Web site: www.languatutor.com   Contact: R.P. Neely

Language Associates, 4924 N. Miller, Oklahoma City, OK 73112 Phone: (405)946-1624 Fax: (405)946-1302
e-mail: cessyevans@aol.com   Contact: Cecilia Evans, General Manager
Founded 1980. Member: ATA, NAJIT. Uses freelance translators and interpreters. Accepts unsolicited resumes. Resumes are entered in the system for future reference. Main languages (both ways) are Spanish, French, German, Russian, Japanese, and Korean. Also translates Chinese, Italian, Portuguese, Italian, and more.

The Language Bank, 875 O'Farrell St., Ste. 105, San Francisco, CA 94109 Phone: (415)885-0827 Fax: (415)885-1304 Contact: Yen Nguyen-le, Manager
Founded 1987. Uses freelance translators and interpreters. Accepts unsolicited resumes. Resumes are screened for qualifications. Main languages are Spanish, Chinese, Vietnamese, Russian, Tagalog, Thai, Laotian, Cambodian, and French. Emphasis on social services. Pool of more than 100 translators.

The Language Bank, Inc., 1323 Lancaster Drive, Orlando, FL 32806
Phone: (407)894-3300 Fax: (407)894-7825
e-mail: info@languagae-bank.com   Web site: www.language-bank.com
    Contact:Dennis Ray Merritt

The Language Center, 144 Tices Ln., E. Brunswick, NJ 08816
Phone: (732)613-4554 Fax: (732)238-7659
e-mail: tlc@thelanguagectr.com   Web site: www.thelanguagectr.com
    Contact: Mary Majkowski
Founded 1967. Member:ATA, TCD. Accepts resumes. Translates all languages. Main areas are health care, pharmaceutical, medical equipment and technical manuals.

The Language Center Inc., 7 Gilliam Ln., Riverside, CT 06878-0520 Phone: (203)698-1907 Fax:(203)698-2043
e-mail: thelanguagecenterinc@worldnet.att.net
    Contact: Siri Ostensen, President
Founded 1978. Translates (both ways) Spanish, French, German, Portuguese, all Scandinavian languages, Italian, Japanese, Chinese, and Russian. Emphasis on Technical, Commercial and Legal translation. Prospective translators should provide sample translations. Resumes are entered into a data base. Maintains a pool of 30 translators.

The Language Company, PO Box 42376, Houston, TX 77242   Phone: (713)952-6704 Fax:(713)952-5513
e-mail: language@pdq.net   Contact: Danielle Y. Pung, President
Founded 1981. Member: ATA, AATIA, HITA. Uses freelance translators and interpreters. Accepts unsolicited resumes. Translates French, Spanish, Russian, German, Portuguese, etc., both from and into English. Emphasis on Technical, Patent and Legal translation. Potential translators should have word processing and transmission capabilities. Resumes are reviewed and filed.

Language Company Translations, L.C., P.O. Box 721507, Norman, OK 73070   Phone: (405)321-5380 Fax: (405)366-7242   e-mail: 71564.2044 @compuserve.com   Contact: Nancy T. Hancock, Director
Founded 1982. Member: ATA. Translates all languages in all technical dis-ciplines. Potential translators should have experience and total fluency. They should be able to produce translations on disk if needed. Resumes are acknowledged and filed. Freelancers are contacted when appropriate work comes in. The company can take materials through final printing, working with commercial printers and supervising production. They also accept resumes from freelance interpreters. Maintains a pool of 40 translators.

The Language Connection, PO Box 1962, Laguna Beach, CA 92652 Phone: (949)497-9393 Fax: (949)497-7515 e-mail: languageconnection @compuserve.com Web site: www.languageconnection.com   Contact: J. Arturo Valdivia, President   Member: ATA

Language Direct, 9801 Westheimber, Ste. 302, Houston, TX 77042 Phone: (713)917-6870 Fax: (713)917-6806 e-mail: jylan@langdirect.com   Web site: www.langdirect.com Contact: Jylan Saleh-Maloy   Member: ATA

Language Doctors, 410 11th St. NE, #21, Washington, DC 20002   Phone: (202)544-2942 Fax: (202)547-2311 e-mail: languagedr@aol.com   Contact: Stuart Bennett   Member: ATA

Language Dynamics, 931 Howe Ave. #107, Sacramento, CA 95825 Phone: (916)920-4062 Fax: (916)920-3594 e-mail: juanvallej@aol.com   Contact: Rhody Vallejo
Founded 1979. Translates Spanish, French, Italian, Russian and Chinese and Hmong. All subject areas are translated. Prospective translators should be of high quality. Resumes are read and kept on file for contact on an as-needed basis.

The Language Exchange, Inc., P.O. Box 750, Burlington, WA 98233 Phone: (360)755-9910   Fax: (360)755-9919
e-mail: Langex@langex.com   Web site: www.langex.com Contact: Jaye Stover   Member: ATA

Language for Industry Worldwide, Inc., 186 South St., Boston, MA 02111   Phone: (617)451-1233   Fax: (617)451-2247   e-mail: smeek@lfiww.com   Web site: www.lfiww.com Contact: Sherri Meek   Member: ATA

The Language Group, 2421 Bowland Pkwy, Ste. 104-B, Virginia Beach, VA 23454   Phone: (757)431-9004 Fax: (75)431-0447 e-mail: info@thelanguagegroup.com Web site: www.thelanguagegroup.com Contact: Evelin Schuyler Founded 1999. Member: ATA, TCD, NAJIT, ASTM, NCMA, ABWA, NCATA. Accepts resumes via e-mail. Translates mainly Chinese, Croatian, Czech, French, German, Italian, Japanese, Norwegian, Polish and Spanish. Mostly technical, engineering, finance and marketing. Uses some 150 translators.

Language Innovations, LLC, 1225 I St. NW, Ste. 500, Washington, DC 20005   Phone: (202)682-4737   Fax: (202)682-3114   e-mail: Translate@languageinnovations,com Web site: www.Language.qpg.com   Contact: Brian S. Friedman   Member: ATA

Language Intelligence, Ltd., 16 North Goodman St., Rochester, NY 14607 Phone: (716)244-5578 Fax: (716)244-7880
e-mail: mail@languageintelligence.com   Contact: Irene White
Founded 1988. Member: ATA, STC. Accepts resumes. Main languages are French, Italian, German, Spanish, Dutch, Swedish, Danish, Japanese, Chinese and Portuguese. Emphasis on life sciences, web and CBT, marketing, pharmaceutical-medical, patents and software.

The Language Lab, 211 East 43rd St., #1904, New York, NY 10017 Phone: (212)697-2020 Fax: (212)697-2891 e-mail: info@thelanguagelab.com Web site: www.thelanguagelab.com Contact: Nicole Cee Member: ATA

Language Learning Enterprises (LLE), 1100 17th St. NW, Ste. 900, Washington, DC 20036 Phone: (202)775-0444 Fax: (202)785-5584 e-mail: hlacy@lle-inc.com Web site: www.lle-inc.com Contact: Heidi G. Lacy Founded 1979. Resumes are carefully screened; prospective translators and interpreters are then interviewed over phone, references checked, and then tried out on a small project first. Requires minimum 2 years experience. Translates all languages "from Italian to Zulu," both from and into English. Emphasis in all technical areas, with a specialty in medical interpretation. The company is the creator of LLE-Link, a 24-hour-a-day, 365 days-a-year telephone interpretation service using conference calling. Maintains a pool of 12 full-time people with 1000 linguists on call.

Language Line Services, 1 Lower Ragdale Drive, Bldg. 2, Monterey, CA 93940 Phone: (831)648-5819 Fax: (800)752-0073 e-mail: danyune@languageline.com Web site: www.languageline.com Contact: Daynune Geertsen

Language Link Corporation, 3100 Broadway, Ste. 110, Kansas City, MO 64111 Phone: (816)753-3122 Fax: (816)753-3262 e-mail: translation@languagelinkcorp.com Web site: www.languagelinkcorp.com Contact: Carrie Hewitt
Founded 1989. Member: ATA, ACTFL, MICATA, ASTM. Uses freelance translators and interpreters. Accpts unsolicited resumes. Main languages are Spanish, Russian, Chinese, Vietnamese, Italian, Croatian, Japanese, Somali, Korean and Farsi.

Language Matters, 1445 Pearl St., Ste. 215, Boulder, CO 80302 hone: (303)442-3471 Fax: (303)442-5805 e-mail: info@languagematters.com Web site: www.languagematters.com Contact: Rosangela Fiori
Founded 1992. Member: ATA. TCA. Accepts resumes. Translates mainly French, German, Italian, Spanish, Russian, Japanese, Chinese, Swedish, Greek and Dutch. Mostly technical, legal and advertisement. Has a pool of 800 translators.

The Language Network, Inc., 5151 Belt Line Rd., Ste. 452, Dallas, TX, 75240 Phone: (972)960-9980 Fax: (972)960-9904 -mail: Language@flash.net Contact: Christine J. Finck Member: ATA

Language One, 2305 Calverty St. NW, Washington DC 20008 Phone: (202)328-0099 Fax: (202)328-1610 e-mail: translations@languageone.com Web site: www.languageone.com Contact: Lorraine B. Smith Member: ATA

Language Plus,4110 Rio Bravo, Ste. 202, El Paso TX 79902 hone: (915)544-8600 Fax: (915) 544-8640 e-mail: langplus@aol.com Web site: www.languageplus.com Contact: Connie Gyenis Member: ATA

The Language Service, Inc., 806 Main St., Poughkeepsie, NY 12603 Phone: (845)473-4303 Fax:(845)473-4467 e-mail: info@tlsmedtrans.com Web site: www.tlsmedtrans.com Contact: Jeanne De Tar
Founded 1950. Member: ATA, FIT. Uses freelance translators and interpreters. Accepts unsolicited resumes. Qualified linguists are filed for future reference. Main languages (both ways) are German, French, Spanish, Italian, and Portuguese, and Japanese into English. Also Dutch and Swedish into English. Main areas are medical, pharmaceutical, chemical and environmental. Does about one million words a year. Works with various translators, but mainly with a steady group of about ten. Owner is co-founder and former president of the ATA.

Language Services Associates, Inc., 607 North Easton, C, PO Box 205, Willow Grove, PA 19090 Phone: (215)657-6571 Fax: (215)659-7210 e-mail: lschriver@lsaweb.com Web site: www.lsaweb.com Contact: Laura T. Schriver
Founded 1991. Member: ATA, DVTA, NAJIT, CHICATA, NOTA. Uses freelance translators and interpreters. Accepts unsolicited resumes. Resumes are acknowledged, kept, and used when needed. Applicants should have ATA accreditation. Main languages (both ways) are Spanish, German, French, Chinese, Japanese, Korean, Vietnamese, Russian, Hindi, Italian, and Tamil. Also Cambodian, Italian, Farsi, Hebrew, Dutch and more. Emphasis on Legal and corporate translation. Maintains a pool of 745 translators.

Language Services Consultants, Inc., P.O. Box 412, Ardmore, PA 19003   Phone: (610)617-8962 Fax: (610)617-9108

e-mail: ruth.karpeles@verizon.net   Contact: Ruth S. Karpeles

Founded 1992. Member: ATA, DVTA. Accepts resumes. Translates mainly Spanish, Vietnamese, Cambodian, Russian, Chinese, Korean, French, Portuguese, Greek, Dutch and Albanian. Mostly medical, education and social services. Uses some 150 translators.

Language Solution, Inc. The, 1700 North Dixie Highway, #114, Boca Raton, FL 33432 Phone: (561)395-5098 Fax:(561)393-6893 e-mail: jgo @languagesolution.com Web site: languagesolution.com Jean Giles Ordóñez, President Contact: Derya Guven, Manager

Founded 1991. Member: Women in International Trade, Greater Miami Chamber of Commerce, World Trade Center-Ft. Lauderdale, SEFAC. Uses freelance translators and interpreters. Accepts unsolicited resumes. Resumes are entered in database, and applicants are sent forms to fill out. They should have experience, computer, and e-mail capabilities. Resumes are reviewed, and if appropriate, entered into a database. No responses are sent. Translates (both ways) Spanish, Portuguese, and Korean, and English into German, French, Japanese, and Greek. Emphasis on marketing and training material, web site translations, manuals for products, and legal contracts. It uses both PCs and Mac, PageMaker, and Quark Express. It has a voice-over studio, does sound edits, produces CD-ROM masters for web courses and training programs. Maintains an active pool of 30-40 translators.

Language Source, 2208 N. 72nd St., Wauwatosa, WI 53213   Phone: (414)607-8766 Fax: (414)607-8767 e-mail: langsource@aol.com   Contact: Elizabeth Brudele-Baran

Languages International, Inc., 2849 Michigan St., NE #100, Grand Rapids, MI 49506   Phone: (616)285-0005 Fax: (616)285-0004 e-mail: dbertoni@iserv.net   Web site: www.lang-int.com   Contact: Delia L. Bertoni Member: ATA

The Languageworks, Inc.,1123 Broadway, Ste. 201, New York, NY 10010   Phone: (212)447-6060   Fax: (212)447-6257

e-mail: talwood@languageworks.com Web site: www.anguageworks.com Contact: Thomas Alwood   Member: ATA

Latin American Business Services, 16127 Bridge Hampton Club Dr., Charlotte, NC 28277   Phone: (704)543-0657 Fax: (704)543-4076 e-mail: letellez@cs.com Web site: www.cs.com Contact: Luis E. Tellez   Member: ATA

Latin American Translators Network, Inc.,1970 Cliff Valley Way NE, Ste. 208, Atlanta, GA 30329 Phone: (404)634-2635 Fax: (404)634-9683 e-mail: latn@latninc.com Web site: www.latninc.com Contact: Ann-Marie Bumbalo Member: ATA

Lazar & Associates, 2444 Wilshire Blvd., Ste. 411, Santa Monica, CA 90403   Phone: (310)453-3302   Fax: (310)453-6002 e-mail: languages@lazar.com   Web site: www.lazar.com Contact: Elaine Lazar

Founded 1995. Member: ATA. Accepts resumes occasionally.Main languages are Spanish, French, Chinese, Japanese and German. Mostly medical, pharmaceutical, IT, business, legal and technical equipment manuals. Has a pool of over 3000 translators.

Le Chateau Enterprises Group, Inc.   Phone: (941)574-5600   Fax: (941)574-3273 e-mail: info@letspeak.com   Web site: www.letspeak.com   Contact: Allendy Doxy   Member: ATA

Legal Interpreting Services, Inc., 21-50 44th Drive, Long Island City, NY 11101   Phone: (718)786-7890 Fax: (718)786-8034 e-mail: accutran@aol.com   Web site: www.accuratetranslation.com Contact: Alexandra Gerenburg Member: ATA

Leggett & Platt, Inc., Leggett Rd., #1, Carthage, MO 64836 Phone: (417)358-8131 Fax: (417)358-5840 Web site: www.leggett.com   Contact: Tomasita Hernandez   Member: ATA

Lemoine International, Inc., 339 E. 600 N., American Fork, UT 84003
Phone: (801)763-5644   Fax: (801)763-5660   e-mail: brigittem@lemoine-international.com
Web site: www.lemoine-international.com   Contact: Brigitte L. Morales   Member: ATA

LEXFUSION, 16855 W. Bernardo Drive, San Diego, CA 92127   Phone: (858)860-1000   Fax: (858)860-1001
e-mail: bobc@lexfusion.com   Web site: www.lexfusion.com   Contact: Bob Cocchia   Member: ATA

Liaison Language Center, 3500 Oak Lawn Ave., Ste. 110 LB 32, Dallas, TX   75219   Phone: (214)528-2731
Fax: (214)522-7167 e-mail: liaison@liaisonlanguage.com Web site: www.liaisonlanguage.com   Contact: Gerda Stendell
Founded 1978. Member: ATA. Uses freelance translators and interpreters.. Translated mainly Spanish, Portuguese, German, French, Italian, Korean, Japanese, Chinese (Madarin and Cantonese) and Vietnamese. Mostly legal, oil, insurance. Has a pool of around 100 active translators and interpreters.

Liaison Multilingual Services, 3261 Cherryridge Rd., Englewood, CO 80110   Phone: (303)762-0997   Fax: (303)762-0999   e-mail: liaison@ecentral.com Web site:eMultilingual.com Contact: Suzanne Robinson   Member: ATA

Lingo Systems, 15115 SW Sequoia Pkwy, #200, Portland, OR 97224   Phone: (503)419-4856   Fax: (503)419-4876
e-mail: info@lingosys.com Web site: www.lingosys.com   Contact: Maja Bailey
Founded 1992. Member: ATA. LISA, SAO. Accepts resumes. Requires 5 years experience and knowledge of CAT tools. Translates mainly French, German, Italian, Spanish, Japanese, Chinese, Korean, Dutch, Scandinavian languages and Eastern European. Also Asian. Mostly IT, computer hardware and software, web sites, marketing and training materials. Maintains some 500 translators.

Lingua Communications Translation Services, 9321 Lavergne, Ste. 101, Skokie, IL 60077 Phone:(847)673-1607
Fax:(847)673-1669 Con-tact: Alex Babich, General Partner
Founded 1989. Member: ATA. Translates Russian and German, both from and into English, and Polish, Ukrainian, Latvian, French and Japanese into English. Emphasis on all subject translations. Prospective translators should possess experience, speed and quality at market-level pricing. Resumes are filed against need; translators are then contacted. **Lingua** maintains a pool of 250 translators.

Lingua Language Center, 1730 Main St., Ste. 226, Weston, FL 33326   Phone: (954)349-8088   Fax: (954)349-1799
e-mail: info@linguaschool.com   Web site:linguaschool.com   Contact: Andreina Ojeda   Member: ATA

Lingualink Incorporated, 5777 W. Century Blvd., Ste. 1000, Los Angeles, CA 90045   Phone: (310)642-2920
Fax: (310)642-2945   -mail: lingualinkinfo@ccscom.com Web site: www.ccscom.com/ lingualink   Contact: Keir Milan Member: ATA

Linguistic Consulting Enterprises, Inc., 251 W. Marlboro Rd., Oro Valley, AZ 85737 Phone: (520)297-6420
Fax: (520)297-2629 e-mail: LCEAZ1@aol.com   Contact: Maria Elisa Rivera

Linguistic Systems, Inc., P.O. Box 390031, 130 Bishop Allen Drive, Cambridge, MA 02139 Phone:(617)864-3900
Fax:(617)864-5186 e-mail: info@linguist.com   Web site: www.linguist.com Contact: Martin Roberts, President
Founded 1967. Member: ATA. Uses freelance translators and interpreters. Applicants should have relevant education and experience. Translates mainly Spanish, French, German, Italian, Portuguese, Chinese, Japanese, Korean, Greek and Swedish. Mostly legal, medical and commercial. The company provides translation, interpretation, voiceover, and machine translation editing services. Maintains a pool of about 4000 translators.

Lionbridge, 301 Mission St., Ste. 350, San Francisco, CA 94105 hone: (415)546-6885 Fax: (415)495-4926
Web site: www.lionbridge.com   Contact: Allison Smith   Member: ATA

Littleton & Associates, Inc., 6006 W. 159th St., Bldg. C, Ste. 2 East, Oak Forest, IL 60452   Phone: (708)429-3336 Fax: (708)429-3414   e-mail: lcs62258@aol.com   Contact: James M. Littleton   Member: ATA

Lucent Technologies Global Translation, 2400 Reynolda Rd., Winston-Salem, NC 27106   Phone: (336)727-6218 Fax: (336)727-3221 -mail: mrhodes@lucent.com Web site: www.lucent.com/translations Contact: Marta C. Rhodes   Member: ATA

LUZ, 202 Potero Ave., San Francisco, CA 941103 hone: (415)241-0520 Fax: (415)241-0504 Web site: www.luz.com   Contact: Sanford Wright   Member: ATA

-M-

M² Limited, 9210 Wightman Rd., Montgomery Village, MD 20886   Phone: (301)977-4281   Fax: (301)926-5046 e-mail: info@m2ltd.com Web site: www.m2ltd.com Contact: Audrey Moyer
Founded 1979. Member: ATA, STC, World Trade Center. Accepts unsolicted resumes. Applicants should be native speakers of the target language, with 2-5 years minimum experience. Translates mainly Spanish, French, Italian, German, Portuguese, Chinese, Japanese, Korean, Dutch and Russian. Emphasis on Computer Software, technical documentation, web pages and localization. The company does not provide interpreting services. The company has become a specialist in the localization of computer-based equipment and software, and is heavily involved in software development, training, and adaptation of English-language materials for use in other cultures and languages. In addition to translators, the company is interested in proofreaders and editors in all languages. Maintains a pool of 2,000 translators.

M/C International, 7207 Chagrin Rd., Unit #4, Chagrin Falls, OH 44023 Phone:(440)247-2277 Fax:(440)247-0453   e-mail: mcinternational @stratos.net   Contact: Mrs. E. Marchbank
Founded 1969. Translates Spanish, French, German, Italian, Portuguese, Russian, Accepts resumes. Translates mainly French, German, Dutch, Italian, Portuguese, Spanish, Italian, Chinese and Japanese. Emphasis on technical, legal and commercial translation. The company is a full-service translation bureau. It also provides 4-color printing services, desktop publishing and typesetting, both to clients and to other translators. In addition, they operate their own travel agency. Maintains a pool of 50 translators.

MGE Lingual Services, 136 36th St. Drive SE, Ste. A-4, Cedar Rapids, IA 52403   Phone: (319)366-1038 Fax: (319)366-1047   e-mail: mike@mge-lingual.com   Web site: www.mge-lingual.com   Contact: Michael G. Elliff Member: ATA

MTS Multinational Translating Service, 928 Connetquot Ave., Central Islip, NY 11722   Phone: (631)581-8956 Fax: (631)224-9435   e-mail: mtsvc@optonline.net   Web site: www.mtssvc.qpg.com   Contact: Lisa Alesci Member: ATA

Madison Linguistic Services, 301 Keezell Hall, MSC 1802, Harrisonburg, VA 22807 Phone: (540)568-3512 Fax: (540)568-6904 e-mail: rethorcx@jmu.edu Web site: www.jmu.edu/forlang/trans Contact: Christophe Rethore Member: ATA

MAGNUS International Trade Services Corp., 1313 North Grand Ave., #280, Walnut, CA 91789
Phone: (909) 595-8488 Fax: (909)598-5852 Web site: www.manuscorp.com   Contact: Nora K. Schwartz
Member: ATA, PCLA, HPRMA, LA-FTA, NOTA. Translates Spanish, Chinese, Vietnamese, Tagalog, Korean, Portuguese, French, German and Russian from English, as well as Hindi, Farsi, Armenian, Hmong, Lao and Italian. Emphasis on Healthcare, Medical, Pharmaceutical, Engineering, Legal, Technical, and General Business translation. Prospective translators should have certification (if possible), appropriate education and field experience. Resumes are responded to with a standard contract, and contractors called as needed.

Mandarin Academy, The Crane Bldg., 40-24th St., Pittsburgh, PA 15222 Phone: (412)434-4771 Fax: (412)434-4772   e-mail: mandarin@stowgate.net   Contact: Helen Liu

Marion J. Rosley Secretarial, Transcription & Translation Services, 41 Topland Rd., Hartsdale, NY 10530
Phone: (914)682-9718 Fax: (914) 761-1384 e-mail: mrosley@rosley.com Web site: rosley.com
Contact: Marion J. Rosley, President
Founded 1977. Member: NYCT, World Trade Council of Westchester, Westchester County Assn., Westconn. Translates all languages. Emphasis on Legal, Medical, Technical, and Business Correspondence translation. The company provides interpreting services in all languages. Prospective translators should have excellent skills and reasonable prices. Resumes are filed for future use. Maintains a pool of "hundreds" of translators. The company provides secretarial, transcription and translation services, including cassette transcription of conferences.

MassLingua, LLC, 5 Stoddard Drive, Worcester, MA 01604 Phone: (508)752-7015 Fax: (508)752-7980
e-mail: ma_lingua@msn.com Web site: www.masslingua.com Contact: Rafael Martinez Member: ATA

MasterWord Services, Inc., 303 Stafford, Ste. 204, Houston, TX 77079 Phone:(713)589-0810 Fax:(713)589-1104
e-mail: masterword@ masterword.com Web site: www.masterword.com   Contact: Mila Green
Founded 1993. Member: ATA, Azeri Translators Association. Translates Russian, Spanish, Azeri, Brazilian Portuguese and Chinese, both from and into English. Emphasis on Oil and Gas, Drilling, Legal and Medical translations. Prospective translators should have significant translation experience, especially in the oil/gas or legal areas, and show quality performance on the company's certification exam. All resumes are acknowledged, and after prescreening, approximately 10% are sent an in-house certification exam, primarily in Russian or Spanish. They are then phoned for an in-person interview. The company also has offices in Baku, Azerbaijan, and is involved in ongoing projects in Europe, South America and Asia. They also have affiliates in Washington, DC, New York, London and Moscow. Maintains a pool of 35-50 translators.

Masua Funai Eifert & Mitchell, Ltd., 1701 Golf Rd., Ste. 800, Rolling Meadows, IL 60008
Contact: Yasuyo Wakuta Member: ATA

McDonald's Corporation, 2715 Jorie Blvd., Oak Brook, IL 60521 Phone: (630)623-6085 Fax: (630)623-6143
e-mail: nadia.gould@mcd.com Contact: Nadia F. Gould   Member: ATA

McNeil Multilingual, 6564 Loisdale Court, Ste. 800, Springfield, VA 22150   Phone: (703)921-1600 Fax: (703)921-1610
e-mail: rnelson@mcneilmultic.com Web site: www.mcneilmultic.com Contact: George E. Washington, Jr.
Member: ATA

ME Sharp, Inc., Publisher, 80 Business Park Drive, Armonk, NY 10504
Phone: (914)273-1800 Fax: (914)273-2106

e-mail: journals@mesharpe.com Web site: www.mesharpe.com Contact: C. P. Chetti   Member: ATA

Mena's International Corp., 2548 Nicollet Ave., S., Minneapolis, MN 55404   Phone: (612)872-8392 Fax: (612)872-7861
e-mail: menastrave@aol.com Contact: Maximo Mena Member: ATA

Mendoza-Harmelin, Inc., 525 Righters Ferry Rd., Bala Cynwyd, PA 19004   Phone: (610)668-2700 Fax: (610)668-8412
e-mail: MMendoza@Harmelin.com Contact: Mia Mendoza Member: ATA

Mercury Marine, W6250 West Pioneer Rd., Fond du Lac, WI 54936 Phone: (414)929-5299 Fax: (414)231-8916
email: Gary_Fenrich@mercmarine.com Contact: Gary Fenrich Member: ATA

Metropolitan Interpreters and Translators Worldwide, Inc., 110 E. 42ⁿᵈ St., Ste. 802, New York, NY 10017 Phone: (212)986-5050 Fax: (212)983-5998 e-mail: metlang@aol.com Web site: metlang.com
Contact: Joe Citrano
Founded 1990. Member: ATA, NYCT, NAJIT, IAFL. Uses freelance translators and interpreters. Accept unsolicited resumes. Resumes are entered in a database. Translates all languages. Emphasis on legal and law enforcement. About 500 in translator pool.

Monti Interpreting & Translation Services, Inc., 101 S. Wymore Rd., Ste. 315, Altamonte Springs, FL 32714 Phone: (888)686-6007 Fax: (407)830-1860 e-mail: montitrans@yahoo.com Web site: www.montitrans.com
Contact: Caroline Montalvo
Founded 1997. Member: ATA. Accepts resumes. Translates mainly Spanish, Creole, Vietnamese, French, Chinese, Italian, Bosnian, Croatian, Cambodian, Portuguese and Turkish. Mostly medical, legal and corporate literature. Maintains a pool of 50 translators and 500 interpreters.

MooreInterp, Inc., 1251 Century SW, Ste. 102, Grand Rapids, MI 49509 Phone: (616)247-4810 Fax: (616)247-5032
e-mail: mooreinterp@aol.com   Web site: www.mooreinterp.com   Member: ATA

Morales Dimmick Translation Service, Inc., 1409 W S Slope, Emmett, ID 83617   Phone: (208)365-2622
e-mail: projects@mdtranslation.com   Web site: www.mdtranslation.com   Contact: Chris
Founded 1989. Member: ATA, IMA. Accepts resumes. Main languages are Spanish, Bosnian, Laotian, Vietnamese and Italian. Mostly business, medical, legal and insurance. Maintains a pool of 65 translators.

Morgan Guaranty Trust Company, 60 Wall St., 34ᵗʰ Fl., New York, NY 10260   Phone: (212)552-5474 Fax: (212)552-8128 e-mail: lisa.gallo@chase.com   Contact: Lisa Gallo   Member: ATA

The Multi-Lingual Group, 8 Faneuil Hall Marketplace, 3ʳᵈ Fl., Boston, MA 02109 Phone: (617)973-5077 Fax: 617)787-3124   e-mail: multilg @aol.com   Contact: Felice Bezri
Founded 1994. Member: NAJIT. Translates Spanish, French, Italian and Portuguese, both from and into English, German, Swedish, Italian and Cantonese into English, and Japanese and Mandarin from English. Emphasis on Medical Studies, Computer, Legal and Military translation. Prospective translators should be ATA members with extensive experience in written translation and specialization in one or more fields. Resumes are reviewed on a regular basis with a particular eye to the experience of the candidate. The company also provides simultaneous interpreting in over 50 languages and offers cross-cultural consulting. Maintains a pool of approximately 320 translators.

MultiLing International, Inc., 32 W. Center St., Ste. 203, Provo, UT 84601 Phone:(801)377-2000 Fax:(801)377-7085 e-mail: translation@ultiling.com Web site: www.multiling.com
Contact: Michael V. Sneddon
Founded 1988. Member: ATA, STC, Utah Information Technology Assn., Software Publishers Assn. Translates Spanish, French, Dutch, German, Italian, Japanese, Chinese, Swedish, Danish, Russian and all other languages, both from and into English. Emphasis on High-Tech Product Localization and the translation of related documents. Prospective translators must be native speakers of the target language with an undergraduate and, preferably, a master's degree, with an area of special expertise. They should have a good software and desktop publishing background and several years of experience and accreditation. Resumes, when they meet company requirements, are sent a questionnaire with a request for a sample translation. The company works in all areas of translation, including working with translation software and aiding in its further development. Maintains a pool of1400 translators.

Multilingual Communications Corporation, P.O. Box 7164 Pittsburgh,   PA 15213 Phone:(412)621-7450 Fax:(412)621-0522 e-mail: mktg @mccworld.com Web site: www.mccworld.com Contact: Cathy Rosenthal
Founded 1977. Member: ATA. Translates Spanish, French, German, Chinese, Japanese, Russian, Italian, Korean, Portuguese, Italian and Korean, both from and into English. Emphasis on Technical, Legal and Medical Software translation. Prospective translators should possess native proficiency and background in a specialized field. Resumes are evaluated on receipt, then contacted and tested. Their services include software localization. Maintains a pool of 500 translators.

Multilingual Translations, Inc., 1510 Front St., Ste. 200, San Diego, CA 92101   Phone: (619)295-2682 Fax: (619)295-2984   e-mail: mcardenas@multitrans.com Web site: www.multitrans.com   Contact: Michael Ramírez Cardénas, J.D. Member: ATA

Multilingual Word, 2631 Salem Ave. S, Minneapolis, MN 55416 Phone: (952)929-4203 Fax: (952)922-4344 e-mail: mlivon@aol.com   Contact: Michelle Livon   Member: ATA

-N-

NCS Enterprises, Inc., 1222 Hope Hollow Rd., Carnegie, PA 15106 Phone: (412)278-4590 Fax: (412)278-4595 e-mail: cnagy@ncs-pubs.com   Web site: www.ncs-pubs.com   Contact: Stephanie Nagy
Founded 1992. Member: ATA. Uses freelance translators and interpreters. Accepts unsolicited resumes. All resume are reviewed and entered into database.

NiS International Services, 1913 Dundin Drive, Old Hickory, TN 37138 Phone:(615)758-6459 Fax:(615)758-6459   e-mail: Nisintl@aol.com   Web site: www.nisintl.com   Contact: Bill Hollaway
Founded 1987. Member: ATA. Translates Japanese, Korean, Chinese, Spanish, German, French, Italian, and Russian, both from and into English. Emphasis on Automotive, Electrical Engineering, Mechanical Engineering, Patent, Contract and Agreement, and other technical document translation. Prospective translators should send a sample of previous work. A specialized technical background is a plus. Resumes are saved in a database, and the translator contacted when a job is available. The company provides translation, interpretation, and teaching services. Maintains a pool of 600-700 translators.

N.O.W. Translations, 23054 Covello St., West Hills, CA 91307 Phone: (818)716-9112 Fax: (818)888-6962 e-mail: thomasc@nowtranslations.com Web site: www.nowtranslations.com Contact: Thomas Clement Member: ATA

Narragansett Translations & Interpreting, Inc., 32 East Ave., Pawtucket, RI 02860   Phone: (401)722-1222 e-mail: morra_red@ids.net   Contact: Mike D. Chea Member: ATA

Nelles Translations, 104 South Michigan Ave., Room 1004, Chicago, IL 60603   Phone: (312)236-2788 Fax: (312)236-0717   Contact: Lawrence R. Kramer, Product Manager
Founded 1956. Member: ATA, Chicagoland Chamber of Commerce, Chicago Convention & Tourism Bureau. Translates Spanish, French, German, Italian, Portuguese, Polish, Russian, Japanese, Chinese, Korean and numerous other languages, both from and into English. Emphasis on Patent, Print Advertising, Legal, Brochures and Manuals, and Personal Document translation. Prospective translators should be experienced with references. They may be tested at the discretion of the company. Resumes are acknowledged and promising applicants are contacted. The company provides interpreting and voiceover services in addition to translation.

NetworkOmni Multilingual Communications, 1329 E. Thousand Oaks Blvd., 2nd Fl., Thousand Oaks, CA 91362 Phone: (805)379-1090 Fax: (805)379-2467 e-mail: omni@networkomni.com
Web site: www.networkomni.com   Contact: Irena Stone

Founded 1978. Member: ATA. Translates French, Italian, German, Spanish, Chinese, Korean and Japanese, both from and into English. Handles a variety of subjects. Excellence is the primary requirement for prospective translators. Re-sumes are followed up with a call and a registration skills packet. The company has five separate divisions: Interpretations, Translations, Teleinterpretations, Transcriptions and Videointerpretations and all are supported by Omni's Quality Control staff. Maintains a pool of 800 translators.

New England Translations, 59 Temple Place, Ste. 204, Boston, MA 02111
Phone: (617)426-4868 Fax: (617)695-9349 e-mail: netranslations@langcenters.com
Web site: newenglandtranslations.com Contact: Ken Krall, Director
Founded 1986. Member: ATA. Uses freelance translators and interpreters. Accepts unsolicited resumes. Resumes are entered into database by language and specialty. Requires experience. Translates Spanish, Portuguese, French, German, Italian, Chinese,

Vietnamese, Korean and Japanese from English, and Spanish into English. Emphasis on Finance, Legal, Marketing, Industrial and Medical translation, with specialties in Financial and Medical. Prospective translators should have PC or Mac, fax, modem. A small sample translation should be sent with the resume. Resumes are entered into a database by language pair and technical specialty after qualifications are reviewed. The company is dedicated to the translation of all major languages. It also provides instruction in Spanish only.
Maintains a pool of 800 translators.

Newtype, Inc., 1259 Route 46 E, Bldg. 1, 2ⁿᵈ Fl., Parsippany, NJ 07054
Phone: (973)263-5000   Fax: (973)263-5522
e-mail: tbias@newtypeinc.com   Web site: www.newtypeinc.com   Contact: Thomas Bias   Member: ATA

Nikkei News Bulletin, 1325 Ave. of the Americas, Ste. 2401, New York, NY 10019   Phone: (212)261-6410   Fax: (212)261-6429   e-mail: nnbny@nikkel.com

Northwest Translations, 2636 E. Greentree Ct., Eagle, ID 83616   Phone: (208)938-5005   Fax: (509)351-7529
e-mail: sales@nwtranslations.com   Web site: www.nwtranslations.com   Contact: Jeff Scott Allen   Member: ATA

NovaTrans Enterprises, Inc., P.O. Box 3903, Boca Raton, FL 33427   hone: (561)368-0865   Fax: (954)255-5161
e-mail: mail@novatrans.net   Contact: Janet T. Aliaga   Member: ATA

-O-

Okada & Sellin Translations, LLC 1950 Addison St., Ste. 101, Berkeley CA 94704   Phone: (510)843-5600   Fax: (510)843-5603   e-mail: okada@ostrans.com   Web site: www.ostrans.com   Contact: Robert G. Sellin
Founded 1996. Member: ATA, STC. Uses freelance translators and interpreters.
Accepts unsolicited resumes. Resumes are reviewed and graded. Work sample are welcome. Requires e-mail. Translates all major Asian and European languages. Focuses on patents and other technical, scientific, pharma/biotech, and legal subjects.

Omega Translation Service, 331-A North Brand Blvd., Glendale, CA 91203 Phone: (818)545-3626 Fax: (818)545-0364
e-mail: omega2@earthlink.net   Contact: Jill Massehian
Founded 1985. Translates Spanish, French, German, Japanese, Italian and Chinese, both from and into English. Emphasis on Scientific, Business and Computer translation. Prospective translators should have good references. Resumes are filed by specialty and language. The company needs qualified translators and interpreters with various specialty fields. Maintains a pool of 1000 translators.

OmniLingua, Inc., 1010 First St. NW, Cedar Rapids, IA 52405   Phone: (319)365-8565   Fax:(319)365-7893
e-mail: omnilingua @omnilingua .com Web site: www.omnilingua.com   Contact: Elizabeth Miller
Founded 1980. Member: ATA, MACHETE, NCATA. Accepts resumes. Translates mainly French, Italian, German, Spanish, Portuguese, Chinese, Japanese, Korean, Greek and Russian. Mostly automotive, heavy equipment, medical products, IT, consumer durables and marketing. Prospective translators should complete a written application form and a short translation test. Experience and educational requirements vary; great emphasis is placed on test results. The company also provides desktop publishing services. Maintains a pool of 300 translators, editors, proofreaders, narrators, and word-counters, all freelance.
The One Technology Group, 18101 Von Karman Ave., #650, Irvine, CA 92612
Phone: (949)955-5318 Fax: (949)975-8450   e-mail: candida@theone.com   Web site: www.theone.com
Contact: Candida McCollam Member: ATA

OneWorld Language Solutions, 2909 Cole Ave., Ste. 300, Dallas, TX 75204   Phone: (214)871-2909 Fax: (214)871-2907 e-mail: flctans@connect.net   Web site: www.oneworldlanguage.com
Contact: Gabriele Hayes, Director
Founded 1990. Member: ATA, META. Uses freelance translators and interpreters. Accepts unsolicited resumes. Requires experience, prefers ATA members. Resumes are entered in database and applicants are contacted when the need arises. Translates (both ways) mainly Spanish, French, German, Italian, and Russian. Also Japanese, Dutch, and Chinese. Provides interpretation and language training. Maintains a pool of over 400 translators.

Openworld, 2673 NE University Village, Ste. 1, Seattle, WA 98105   Phone: (206)523-1100 Fax: (206)522-3345 e-mail: orders@openworldtranslations.com   Web site: www.penworldtranslations.com   Contact: Helen Tereshina Member: ATA

Origin - The Language Agency, P.O. Box 1648, Makawao, HI 96768   Phone: (808)573-1453 Fax: (808)573-6446 e-mail: info@origin.to   Web site: www.origin.to   Contact: Chelsea Hill Founded 1998. Member: ATA, Aquarius, Proz.com. Accepts resumes via web site. Translates mainly Chinese, Korean, Indian Languages, Spanish, French, Russian, German, Japanese, Ukrainian and Romanian. Mostly medical, computer-related, business, marketing, telecommunications, tourism, pharmaceuticals and automotive. Has a pool of 600 translators.

O'Sullivan Menu Corporation, 110 Triangle Blvd., Carlstadt, NJ 07072 Phone: (201)507-1449 Fax: (201)507-4920   Contact: Adriana Marton   Member: ATA

-P-

P.H. Brink International, 6100 Golden Valley Rd., Minneapolis, MN 55422 Phone:(763)591-1977 Fax:(612)542-9138 e-mail: bliaj@phbrink.com   Web site: www.phbrink.com   Contact: Belia Jimenez-Lorente Member: ATA. Uses freelance translators and interpreters. Accepts unsolicited resumes. Resumes are screened and best ones are called for test. Requires college degree and native speaking ability. Translates mainly English into major European languages and Japanese. Subjects are mostly technical. Employs 150 full-time translators.

PSC, Inc., 12330 Pinecrest Rd., Reston, VA 20191 Phone:(703)716-5000 Fax:(703)716-5005 e-mail: translat@pscusa.com   Contact: Fred Lothrop Founded 1988. Member: ATA. Translates Spanish (all dialects) to and from English, and Italian, Chinese (all dialects), Farsi, Haitian Creole, Russian, Serbo-Croatian, Japanese, and Central and West African languages into English. Emphasis on technical (computer, communications, radar), legal, and business translation. Specialty in transcription and translation for law enforcement agencies. Translators must have a specialized area and security clearance before being matched with an appropriate job. Unsolicited resumes for freelance work are processed through internal channels of selection. PSC, Inc. is a privately-owned firm with a major business area, also providing foreign language services for the private and public sectors. Maintains a pool of 1500 linguists.

Pacific Dreams, Inc., 2263 Judson St. SE, Salem, OR 97302   Phone: (503)588-7368 Fax: (503)588-7549 e-mail: pacific.dreams@viser.net   Web site: www.pacificdreams.org Contact: Ken Sakai   Member: ATA

Pacific Interpreters, Inc., 520 SW Yamhill, #320, Portland, OR 97204   Phone: (800)311-1232 Fax: (800)881-2565

e-mail: recruitment@pacificinterpreters.com   Web site: www.pacificinterpreters.com Contact: Joana Laitinen Founded 1992. Member: ATA, SOMI, NOTIS, NAJIT, ASTM. Accepts resumes. Translates mainly Spanish, Vietnamese, Chinese, Cambodian, Hmong, Laotian, Italian and Farsi. Mostly health care. Maintains pool of about 100 translators.

Pacific Ring Services, Inc., 1143 Christina Mill Drive, Newark, DE 19711   Phone: (302)269-1518 Fax: (302)269-1618 e-mail: pacific@dca.net   Web site: www.pacificring.com   Contact: Motoko Yuasa   Member: ATA **Pacolet International Translation Co.**, 11405 Main St., Roscoe IL 61073 Phone: (815)623-1608 Fax: (815)623-1907 e-mail: pacolet@inwave.com   Web site: www.pacolet.com   Contact: Julie Johnson McKee, President Founded 1993. Member: ATA, Greater Rockford Chamber of Commerce. Uses freelance translators and interpreters. Accepts unsolicited resumes. Resumes are reviewed for language skills and specialties, and entered in databse. ATA affiliation or translation degree required. Strong professional experience preferred. Translates mainly Spanish, French, Dutch, Italian, Portuguese, Swedish, Finnish, Chinese, Japanese, and Korean. Also other European and Asian languages, Italian and Farsi. Emphasis on technical subjects, heavy equipment, engines, aerospace, food service equipment, business contracts and proposals. Did one millions dollars worth of translation in 1988. Strong background in marketing communications and broadcasting. Company is family-friendly and develops long-term "partnerships" (company-translator-customer are a team). Maintains a pool of 300 translators.

Pangea Lingua, 3620 N. Washington Blvd., Indianapolis, IN 46250   Phone: (317)920-1600 Fax: (317)920-1601 e-mail: staff@pangealingua.com   Web site: www.pangealingua.com   Contact: Alessandra Matas
Founded 1994. Member: ATA. Accepts resumes. Translates mainly Spanish, Japanese, German, Chinese, French, Dutch, Portuguese and Russian. Mostly medical, pharmaceutical, promotional, legal and automotive. Maintains pool of over 1000 translators.

Para-Plus Translations, Inc., PO Box 92, Barrington, NJ 08007 Phone: (609)547-3695 Fax:(609)547-3345 e-mail: paraplus@erols.com Web site: www.para-plus.com   Contact: Sonia Santiago, President
Founded 1981. Member: DVTA, NAJIT, ATA. Translates Spanish, German, French, Creole, Chinese, Japanese, Korean, Italian, Russian, Vietnamese, Italian and Korean, both from and into English. Emphasis on Legal, Medical, Pharmaceutical and Technical translation. Prospective translators must be native speakers, college graduates, and have areas of special expertise. Candidates should submit a list of equipment available to them, as well as a sample of their work. Resumes are reviewed and a follow-up letter sent in response. The company also provides interpretation services in over 75 language and foreign-language tape translations and transcriptions. Maintains a pool of approximately 95 translators.

Paragon Language Services, 5657 Wilshire Blvd., Ste. 310, Los Angeles, CA 90036   Phone: (323)966-4655 Fax: (323)651-1867   e-mail: info@paragonls.com   Web site: www.paragonls.com Contact: Hanne R. Mintz Member: ATA

Peritus Precision Translations, Inc., 727 Industrial Rd., #710, San Carlos, CA 94070   Phone: (650)631-6667 Fax: (650)631-6664   e-mail: info@peritustranslations.com   Web site: www.peritustranslations.com   Contact: Dagmar Dolatshko   Member: ATA

Phoenix Translations, 6306 Highland Hills Drive, Austin, TX 78731   hone: (877)452-1348 Fax: (512)343-6721 e-mail: phoenixtranslations@ev1.net   Contact: Deborah K. Cooper   Member: ATA

Planet Leap, 220 Fifth Ave., 11th Fl., New York, NY 10001   Phone: (212)726-4061 Fax: (212)726-4020 e-mail: rceruzzi@planetleap,com   Web site: www.planetleap.com Contact: Rossana Ceruzzi   Member: ATA

Precision Translating Services, 150 W. Flagler St., Penthouse II, Miami, FL 33130   Phone: (305)373-7874 Fax: (305)381-7874   e-mail: vince@pretran.com   Web site: www.pretran.com Contact: Vicente J. de la Vega Member: ATA

Premier Translation Services, Ltd., 62 Stonicker Drive, Lawrenceville NJ 08648   Phone:(609)530-0230 Fax:(609)530-0079 e-mail: rzarelli@premiertranslationsusa.com   Web site: www.premiertranslationsusa.com Contact: Renée Zarelli, Esq., President
Founded 1994. Member: ATA. Accepts resumes. Translates mainly French, Italian, Spanish and Portuguese. Emphasis on legal translation and business. Prospective translators should be ATA members, accredited if applicable. Three + years full-time experience, college education or higher. Equipment should include WP or Word and modem. Resumes are reviewed on a monthly basis. The company specializes in using lawyers and individuals with a strong legal background, in both U.S. and other legal systems, for translation and editing. Ph.D.s in chemistry/physics and engineers are also used for patent translation. Maintains a pool of 150 translators.

Princeton Technical Translation Center, 333 Bolton Rd., East Windsor, NJ 08520 Phone: (609)443-6770 Fax: (609)443-6778   Contact: Charles Teubner, Director
Founded 1982. Member: ATA, STC. Translates French, German, Spanish, Italian, Portuguese, Chinese, Japanese, Russian and Scandinavian languages, both from and into English. Prospective translators should have advanced technical degrees and be proficient in Word/WordPerfect and related software.

Professional Translating Services Inc., 44 West Flagler St., Ste. 540, Miami, FL 33130 Phone: (305)371-7887 Fax: (305)381-9824 e-mail: translate@protranslating.com   Web site: www.protranslating.com Contact: Luis A. de la Vega
Founded 1973. Member: ATA. Accepts resumes. Translates mainly Spanish, Portuguese, French, Italian, German, Japanese, Russian, Chinese, Italian and Hebrew. Translations are in legal, technical, financial and advertising. Has a pool of over 350 translators.

Professional Translation Services, LLC, 2323 Vista Ave., Ste. 201, Boise, ID 83705   Phone: (208)343-1444 Fax: (208)422-9840 e-mail: daniella@languagesus.com   Web site: www.languagesus.com Contact: Daniella de la Torre Emerson   Member: ATA

ProTrans, Inc., P.O.Box 507, 74 Gov. Bradford Dr. Barrington, RI 02806   Phone: (401)245-9535
Fax: (401)245-9534 e-mail: protrans@ids.net   Web site: www.protrans1. com   Contact: H. Karin Weldy
Member: ATA
Founded 1989. Member: ATA, NETA, Greater Providence Chamber of Commerce, WACRI. Uses freelance translators. Accepts unsolicited resumes. Applicants should provide sample translations, references, work history; they need to be *full-time* translators. Resumes usually result in contact to ask questions, determine fees and check references. Main languages are English into Spanish, Portuguese, French, German, Italian, Japanese, Chinese, and Swedish. Also German, Dutch into English, and English into Cambodian and Laotian. Emphasis on technical manuals, automotive, legal, ad copy, educational, brochures, and catalogs. Maintains a pool of about 350 translators.

ProZ.com, 1448 Madison St., Apt. 410, Oakland, CA 94612   Phone: (510)682-3231
e-mail: henry@proz.com   Web site: www.proz.com   Contact: Henry J. Dotterer   Member: ATA

PTIGLOBAL, 9900 SW Wilshire, Ste. 280, Portland, OR 97225 Phone:(503)297-2165 Fax:(503)297-0655
e-mail: info@ptiglobal.com Web site: www.ptiglobal.com   Contact: Mollie Peters
Founded 1977. Member: ATA. Uses freelance translators and interpreters. Accepts unsolicited resumes. Resumes are reviewed, graded, and kept in database. Requires FrameMaker; Trados helpful. Main subjects are technical, software, and web applications.

-Q-

Quality Interpreting, 367 University Ave., Ste. 4, Saint Paul, MN 55103   Phone: (651)244-0066 Fax: (651)312-0270
Contact: Paul Yang   Member: ATA

Quantum, Inc., 240 S. 9th St., Philadelphia, PA 19107   hone: (215)627-2251 Fax: (215)627-5570
e-mail: www.quantumtrans@msn.com   Contact: Quan Pham Member: ATA

Quintana Multi-Lingual Services, Inc., 3050 W. Cermak Rd., Chicago, IL 60623   Phone: (773)277-0000
Fax: (773)277-1804 e-mail: quintana@compuserve.com   Contact: Gloria K. Quintana

-R-

RIC International, Inc., 955 Massachusetts Ave., PMB 342, Cambridge, MA 02139   Phone: (617)666-4555
Fax: (617)666-8896   e-mail: r-i-c.com   Web site: www.r-i-c.com Member: ATA

R.R. Donnelley Financial Translation Services, 75 Park Place, New York, NY 10007   Phone: (212)341-7416
Fax: (212)341-7532 e-mail: FBUTRansServ@rrd.com   Contact: Aouck F. Le Fur   Member: ATA

Ralph McElroy Translation Company, PO Box 4828, Austin, TX 78765   Phone: (512)472-6753 Fax: (512)472-4591 e-mail: tc@mcelroytranslation.com Web site: www.mcelroytranslation.com   Contact: Patricia Bown
Founded 1968. Member: ATA, STC. Accepts resumes. Translates mainly German, Japanese, French, Spanish, Italian, Portuguese, Russian, Chinese, Dutch and Korean. Mostly engineering, technical, medical, legal, pharmaceutical, chemical, patents, localization and high tech. Several hundred active translators.

Rancho Park Publishing, 2203 Balsam Ave., Los Angeles, CA 90064   Phone:(310)470-7488 Fax:(310)470-7930
e-mail: sales@ranchopark.com Web site: www.ranchopark.com   Contact: Stan Cheren
Founded 1988. Translates Spanish, French, German, Portuguese and German. Mostly sales and marketing, books and brochures. Prospective translators should have 10+ years experience and full computer /online capabilities. Resumes are filed for future projects. The company also has desktop publishing capabilities. Maintains a pool of over 700 translators.

Rapport International, 3 Stonegate Lane, #3 Middleboro, MA 02346 Phone: (508)946-3443 Fax: (508)946-3533
e-mail: rapport@rapportintl.com   Web site: www.rapportintl.com   Contact: Lisa Gavigan Member: ATA

Rennert Bilingual Translations, 216 East 45ᵗʰ St., 17ᵗʰ Fl. New York, NY 10025   Phone:(212)867-8700 Fax:(212)867-7666   e-mail: translations@rennert.com   Web site: www.rennert.com   Contact: Mikael Poulsen, Director

Founded 1973. Member: ATA, New York Circle of Translators. Translates all languages. Emphasis on all aspects of Patent Law, Marketing, Public Relations, Business and Finance, Videos and Educational Material translation, and web site localization. Prospective translators should possess training and experience in the specific fields. Resumes are reviewed for education and experiénce, and a Rennert application is sent to the translator for completion. Maintains a pool of 3000 translators.

Rescribe, P.O. Box 503981, San Diego, CA 92150   Phone: (858)487-5292 Fax: (858)487-5292 e-mail: erin@rescribe.com   Web site: www.rescribe.com   Contact: Erin Berzins

Founded 2001. Member: ATA. Accepts resumes. Translates mainly Spanish, French, Chinese, Vietnamese, Japanese, Italian, German, Korean and Russian. Mostly legal, insurance, medical, finance and insurance. Has a pool of several thousand translators.

Richard Schneider Enterprises, Inc., 27875 Berwick Drive, #A, Carmel, CA 93923   Phone: (831)622-0554 Fax: (831)622-0524   e-mail: service@idioms.com   Web site: www.idioms.com   Contact: Richard A. Schneider Member: ATA

Rosetta, 2261 Market St. #318, San Francisco, CA 94114   Phone: (415) 550-9151   Fax: (415)550-9162 e-mail: oshea@sirius.com   Contact: Christina O'Shea, Director

Founded 1995. Member: ATA. Translates Japanese, Chinese, French, German and Korean, both from and into English, and Italian, Spanish, Thai, Swedish, Norwegian, Polish, Danish, Dutch, Portuguese and Russian into English. Emphasis on Computer (hardware and software), Semiconductors, Chemical, Medical, Pharmaceutical, Automotive, Patent, Business, and Marketing translation. Prospective translators should have at least five years experience as translators, plus five years experience in a technical field or in business, and a degree in their area of specialization. Resumes are entered into a data base and sent a test if they fulfill company requirements. The company hires translators with technical specialties as opposed to "generalists" and has every document reviewed for accuracy by a technical editor. Maintains an "active" pool of 50 translators.

Rosetta Stone Associates, Inc., 34 Franklin St., Ste. 200A, Nashua, NH 03063   Phone: (603)883-9388 Fax: (603)595-8673 e-mail: translate@rosettastoneinc.net   Web site: www.rosettastoneinc.net   Contact: Jana Coughlin

Founded 1972. Member: ATA, STC. Accepts resumes. Translates mainly French, Italian, German, Spanish, Russian, Chinese, Japanese, Italian, Portuguese and Greek. Mostly industrial, medical, legal, scientific, marketing, computers, software and localization. Uses pool of over 2000 translators.

Russian and Slavic Language Services, 271 Madison Ave., 3ʳᵈ Fl., New York, NY 10016   Phone: (212)481-4980 Fax: (212)683-4801 e-mail: karina@russiantranslation.com Web site: www.russiantranslation.com   Contact: Karina Gukasyan   Member: ATA

RussTech, 1338 Vickers Rd., Tallahassee, FL 32303 Phone: (850)562-9811 Fax: (850)562-9815 e-mail: Contact: Cynthia Seaborn   Member: ATA

-S-

SBF Translation Services, Inc., P.O. Box 940818, Miami, FL 33194   hone: (305)553-1927 Fax: (305)551-6872 e-mail: SBFTrans@aol.com   Contact: Silvia B. Fernandez

Founded 1994. Member: ATA. Accepts resumes. Translates Spanish, Portuguese and Creole. Mostly legal, medical, immigration and Christian books. Has three translators.

SH3, Inc., 5338 East 115th St., Kansas City, MO 64137 Phone: (816)767-1117 Fax:(816)767-1727 e-mail: chubbard@sh3.com   Web site: www.sh3.com   Contact: Cathy Hubbard, General Manager
Founded 1980. Member: ATA, STC. Translates mainly French, German, Spanish, Italian, Dutch, Portuguese, Swedish, Chinese and Japanese. Emphasis on Agricultural and Industrial Equipment, and Consumer Equipment translation. Prospective translators should have Windows-based computer, modem and fax; they should have experience in the agriculture, industrial and mechanical areas. Translator's Workbench is a definite plus. Resumes are reviewed by subject specialty, experience, and language, and flagged for a future contact. Does around 20 million words a year. The company deals in high volume, highly technical manuals. Maintains an active pool of 70 translators.

Sally Low and Associates, 600 West Santa Ana Blvd., Ste. #208, Santa Ana, CA 92701 Phone: (714)834-9032 Fax: (714)834-9035 e-mail: slasehabla@aol.com   Contact: Lisa Hall
Founded 1979. Member: ATA. Accepts resumes. Translates mainly Spanish, Vietnamese, Korean, Italian, German, French, Italian, Japanese, Taglog and Chinese. Provides interpreter services. Has a pool of over 300 translators.

SARJAM Communications, Ltd., 4370 NE Hulsey St., Ste. 122, Portland, OR 97213 Phone:(503)287-9277 Fax:(503)287-9277 e-mail: 70314. 1226@compuserve.com   Contact: Seth A. Reames
Founded 1987.Member: ATA. Translates Japanese, Korean, Chinese, Spanish, German, French, Italian and Russian, both from and into English. Translates all subjects. Prospective translators should have 5+ years experience, a computer (MAC or PC), fax and modem. Resumes are examined and filed by language. The company also offers desktop publishing and graphic design. Their in-house computers are Macintosh. Maintains a pool of 40-50 translators.

Schreiber Translations, Inc., 51 Monroe St., Ste. 101, Rockville, MD 20850   Phone:(301)424-7737 Fax:(301)424-2336 e-mail: translation@schreibernet.com Web site: www.schreibernet.com
Contact: Walter Stankewick, Director, Translation Services
Founded 1984. Member: ATA. Uses freelance translators and interpreters. Accepts unsolicited resumes only on web site. Translates (both ways) mainly Japanese, Russian, German, French, Spanish, Chinese, Italian, Italian, Korean, Vietnamese, Hebrew, Polish, and Dutch, and close to 90 additional languages and dialects. Emphasis on patents, aerospace, law, medicine, communications, computers, engineering, public relations, military and maritime subjects, chemical subjects, and business and finance. Maintains a pool of over 1300 translators - 350 active, and 200 of those very active. In addition to translation and interpretation, the company produces multilingual brochures and advertisements, prints manuals and business literature in a variety of multinational fonts, and does voiceovers for video and films. Maintains a pool of over 1300 translators - 350 active, and 200 of those very active.

Scitran, 1482 East Valley Rd., Ste. 15, Santa Barbara, CA 93150 Phone: (805)969-2413 Fax:(805)969-3439 e-mail: 71046.1337@compu-serve.com   Contact: Revay Seifert
Founded 1972. Accepts resumes. Translates over 45 languages in all scientific disciplines.

Sebastian Lantos, LLC, 5111 East 89th Court, Tulsa, OK 74137 Phone:(918)481-1465 Fax: (918)481-0841 e-mail: language@gorilla.net eb site: lantosconsulting.com Contact: Tanya Shevchuk, Office Manager
Founded 1996. Member: NAJIT. Accepts resumes. Translates mainly Spanish, French, Italian, Chinese, Japanese, Russian, Ukrainian, Korean and German. Mains areas are medical, legal, and federal. The company also specializes in language tutoring, Hispanic personnel bilingual training. Maintains a pool of 20 translators.

Semantics Translations & Publishing, Inc., 3544 NW 99th Ave., Coral Springs, FL 33065   Phone: (954)341-4721 Fax: (954)341-8606 e-mail: getmeaning@sematicstp.com   Web site: www.sematicstp.com Contact: Pedro M. Liveira   Member: ATA

Semantix, 1660 International Drive, Ste. 400, McLean, Va 22102 Phone: (703)287-0091 Fax: (703)288-4003 e-mail: araswork@sematix.com   Web site: www.semantix.com Contact: Andy Ras-Work   Member: ATA

Siemens Medical-Ultrsound Group, 22010 SE 51ˢᵗ St., P.O. Box 7002, Issaquah, WA 98029
Phone: (425)392-9180 Fax: (425)557-1780 e-mail: marybeth.sloan@usg.sms.siemens.com
Web site: www.siemensultrasound.com Contact: Mary Beth Sloan Member: ATA

SimulTrans, LLC, 1370 Willow Rd., Menlo Park, CA 94025 Phone: (650)969-3500 Fax: (650)969-9959
e-mail: mark@simultrans.co Web site: www.simultrans.com Contact: Mark Homnack, President
Founded 1984. Member: ATA. Translates in all major languages. Covers all major technical areas. Prospective translators should have either a translation degree or professional experience, as well as native fluency. Resumes should be faxed or e-mailed. The company also offers formatting and typesetting services and possesses a digital typesetter for both European and Asian languages. They also provide software localization and desktop publishing. Maintains a pool of in-house translators (in French, German, Italian, Japanese, and Spanish), as well as using freelancers.

SinoMetrics International, Inc., 3503 188ᵗʰ St. SW, Lynnwood, WA 98115 Phone: (425)776-5648 Fax: (425)776-6648 email: info@sinomet.com Web site: www.sinomet.com Member: ATA

Speak Easy Languages, 757 South Main St., Plymouth, MI 48170 Phone:(734)459-5556 Fax:(734)459-1460
e-mail: selanguages@earthlink. net Contact: Cristina Clark
Founded 1980. Member: ATA. Translates all major language pairs. Emphasis on Automotive business, Brochure, Advertising and Legal translation. Prospective translators should be ATA accredited and possess fax and modem capabilities. Resumes are filed and the applicant called upon as the circumstance arises. The company also provides talent for voiceover work. Maintains a pool of 100 translators.

Spectrum Multilanguage Communications, 225 West 39ᵗʰ St., New York, NY 10018 Phone: (212)391-3940
Fax: (212)921-5246 e-mail: 76046.2123@compuserve.com Web site: www.come.to/spectrum Contact: Richard N. Weltz
Founded 1955. Member: ATA, DGA, IDIA. Translates Spanish, French, German, Italian, Japanese, Chinese, Russian, Italian, Dutch and all major business languages from English. Emphasis on Marketing, Advertising, Packaging and Public Relations translation. Prospective translators should exhibit a high degree of competence, reliability, and excellent writing style. They should possess a modem, fax, and word processing capabilities. Resumes are reviewed by the language resources manager. Provides complete ad-quality in-house typesetting and color pre-press capabilities in virtually all languages and alphabets.

Square D/Schneider Electric North American Division, 1415 S. Roselle Rd., Palatine IL 60067
Phone: (630)279-2395 Fax: (630)279-3687 email: schreibm@squared.com Web site: www.squared.com
Contact: Marie-France O. Schreiber Member: ATA

Star USA, 477 S. Main St., Plymouth, MI 48170 Phone: (734)416-1865 Fax: (734)416-1867
e-mail: jre@starusa-mi.com Web site: www.starusa-mi.com Contact: Jan R. Eisen Member: ATA

State Farm Insurance, One State Farm Plaza, SC-2, Bloomington, IL 61710 Phone: (309)766-3760
Contact: Joan Epperson Member: ATA

Superior Translations, 1924 Minnesota Ave., Duluth, MN 55802 Phone: (218) 727-2572 Fax: (218)727-2653
e-mail: towardinc@aol.com Web site: www.interpretazioni.com Contact: Elisa A. Troiani
Founded 1993. Member: ATA. Uses freelance translators and interpreters. Accept unsolicited resumes. Resumes for translation and interpretation should be mailed. Applicants are carefully screened and required to submit samples, references, and times tests. Requirements are honesty, accuracy, editing/proofing skills, reason-able rates, punctuality, and an eye for detail. Translates mainly Spanish, French, German, Japanese, Chinese, Russian, Portuguese, Italian, Polish and Hmong. Emphasis on all subject areas. Has 250-300 translators in its pool.

Suzuki, Myers & Associates, Ltd., P.O. Box 852, Novi, MI 48376 Phone:(248)344-0909 Fax:(248)344-0092 e-mail: language@suzukimyers.com Web site: www.suzukimyers.com Contact: Kumiko Oh
Founded 1984. Member: ATA, MITN, Japan-America Society. Translates Japanese and Korean only, both from and into English. Emphasis on Manufacturing-related translation (Autos, Engineering, Quality Design, Robotics, Plastics, Assembly, Electronics, Paint, Contracts, Product Liability).Prospective translators should be competent and diligent. Resumes are responded to with a phone call. The company provides translation, interpretation, and consultation services in North American-Japanese relations. They also provide DTP services. Maintains a pool of about 40 translators.

Sykes Enterprises, Incorporated, 5757 Central Ave., Ste. G, Boulder, CO 80301 Phone:(303)440-0909 Fax:(303)440-6369 e-mail: wpid@corp. sykes.com Web site: sykes.com
Contact: Recruiting Coordinator, Worldwide Product Information Development
Founded in 1977. Member: ATA, CTA, LISA, STC. Accepts resumes. Looks for linguists specialized in localization. Requires native language ability. Prefers translation degree. Applicants are tested. Must have full PC processing and communication ability. Main languages are English into all major Asian, Middle Eastern, Latin American, and European languages. Main areas are software, hardware, on-line help, and documentation. Provides information support services. Language services are coordinated from Boulder, Colorado, Edinburgh, Scotland, and Leuven, Belgium.

Synapse Intercultural Communications, 35560 Grand River Ave., Ste. 417, Farmington Hills, MI 48335
Phone: (248)473-4499 Fax: (248)473-1499 e-mail: synintcm@ix.netcom.com Contact: Curt Nielsen, Manager
Founded 1991. Translates German, French, Spanish, Italian, Japanese and Chinese from and into English. Emphasis on technical translations for the automotive industry. Resumes for freelance translation and interpretation are kept on file. Has a few dozen translators in its pool.

Syntes Language Group, Inc., 7465 E.Peakview Ave., Englewood, CO 80111 Phone:(303)779-1288 Fax:(303)779-1232
e-mail: linda.eaton@syntes.com Web site: www.syntes.com   Contact: Linda Eaton
Founded 1988. Member: ATA Translates Spanish, French, German, Japanese, Portuguese and Italian both from and into English, and Russian, Chinese and Vietnamese from English. Specialties in Legal, Oil & Gas Patents, Com-puters, Marketing Materials, Video Scripts, Engineering, Medical and Technical translation. The company's work is 60-70% translation and 30-40% interpreting. In addition to translators and interpreters, the company is interested in hearing from detail-oriented editors. Maintains a pool of 1600 translators.

-T-

Techno-Graphics and Translations, Inc., 1451 East 168th St., South Holland, IL 60473 Phone: (708)331-3333 Fax: (708)331-0003 e-mail: techno@wetrans4u.com Web site: www.wetrans4u.com Contact: Pinay Gaffney
Founded 1972. Member: ATA. Uses freelance translators and interpreters. Accepts unsolicited resumes. Resumes are entered in database. Requires native ability and technical background. Translates (both ways) mainly European, Asian, and Middle Eastern languages. Main areas are telecommunications, agriculture, industry, automotive, and medical. Worldwide pool of 200 translators.

TechTrans International, Inc., 2200 Space Park Drive, Ste. 410, Houston, TX 77058   Phone: (281)335-8000 Fax: (281)333-3503   e-mail: techtrans@tti-corp.com   Web site: www.tti-corp.com   Contact: Beth Williams
Member: ATA

Techworld language Services, Inc., 1250 W. 14 Mile Rd., Ste. 102, Clawson, MI 48017   Phone: (248)288-5900 Fax: (248)288-7900 e-mail: info@techworldinc.com Web site: www.techworldinc.com Contact: Fred Meinberg
Member: ATA

Tele-Interpreters On-Call, Inc., 447 W. Burchett St., 2nd Fl., Glendale, CA 91203   Phone: (818)638-2511 Fax: (818)543-6781   e-mail: dt@teleinterpreters.com   Web site: www.tele-interpreters.com   Contact: Daniel Trevor   Member: ATA

TerraSpan, Inc., 12647 Alcosta Blvd., Ste. 150, San Ramon, CA 94583
Phone: (925)866-3030 Fax: (925)866-3036 e-mail: galiloupour@terraspan.com   Web site: www.erraspan.com
Contact: Gloria Aliloupour   Member: ATA

TEXTnology CORPoration, 20 Trafalgar Square, Ste. 456, Nashua, NH 03063   Phone:(603)883-8398 Fax:(603)883-8998   e-mail: nadeau@textcorp.com   Web site: www.textcorp.com   Contact: Ronald Nadeau   Member: ATA

Thomas Computer Solutions, 21213-B Hawthorne Blvd., #5367, Torrance, CA 90503   Phone: (310)921-2611 Fax: (310)921-9676 e-mail: info@thomascomputersolutions.com Web site: www.homascomputersolutions.com Contact: Tracy Zehnder
Founded 1995. Member: ATA. Accepts resumes. Translates mainly Spanish, Russian, Armenian, Chinese, Thai, Italian, Hebrew, Farsi, Jamaican Patois and Korean. Mostly medical, banking and legal. Has a pool of 300 translators.

3 Way Talk, 2255 Skyfarm Drive, Hillsborough, CA 94010   Web site: www.3waytalk.com
Contact: Dr. B. Goldstein   Member: ATA

3DWord, Inc., 4325 Athens High Way, Ste. 4-13, Loganville, GA 30052 Phone: (770)613-0879 Fax: (770)849-9627
e-mail: julieMacgregr@3word.com   Web site: www.3word.com   Contact: Julie MacGregor   Member: ATA

TLS - Translation Service, 69 Broad St., Red Bank, NJ 07701 Phone: (732)530-4542 Fax: (732)530-6755 e-mail: trans90@aol.com Contact: Ingeborg Perndorfer
Founded 1982. Member: ATA. Uses freelancers and accepts unsolicted resumes. Resumes are check and filed until needed. Applicants must show experience. Translates all languages and all subjects. Maintains a pool of 30-50 translators.

Total Benefit Communications, Inc., 5775-B Glenridge Drive, Ste. 120, Atlanta, GA 30328   Phone: (404)256-5042   Fax: (404)256-5101   Contact: Anne McKillips Member: ATA

Total System Services, Inc., 1600 First Ave., TSYS Corporate Campus, 1st Fl., #1318, Columbus, GA 31901
Phone: (706)649-5450   Fax: (706)649-8148 e-mail: Evan Latham Contact: Member: ATA

Toward, 1924 Minnesota Ave., Duluth, MN 55802 Phone: (218)727-2572   Fax: (218)727-2653
e-mail: towardinc@aol.com   Web site: www.interpretazioni.com   Contact: Dr. Elisa A. Troiani   Member: ATA

TRADOS Corporation, 113 S. Columbus St., Ste. 400, Alexandria, VA 22314   Phone: (703)683-6900   Fax: (703)683-9457 e-mail: edith@trados.com   Web site: www.trados.com Contact: Edith Westfall   Member: ATA

Traducciones LinguaCorp, Poba International, #1-20072, P.O. Box 02-5255, Miami, FL 33102   Phone: 58(2)7625745 Fax: 58(2)7625745 e-mail: linguacorp@compuserve.com Contact: Francisco J. Pance   Member: ATA

Trans Global Translation & Immigration Services, 175 Fontainbleau Blvd., Ste. 2G 8, Miami, FL 33172
Phone: (305)552-9793 Fax: (305)223-4080   e-mail: trnsglobal@aol.com   Member: ATA

TransACT Inc., 8423 Mukilteo Speedway, Ste. 100, Mukilteo, WA 98275 Phone:(206)348-5000 Fax:(206)348-3095
e-mail: support @transact.com Web site: www.transact.com   Contact: Ms. Tomi Renshaw
Founded 1994. Member: ATA, NOTIS, Washington Software Assn., ASCD. Translates Spanish, Russian, Cambodian, Korean, Chinese, Lao, Thai, Italian, Japanese and Vietnamese from English. Emphasis on Education, Medical and Utilities translation. Prospective translators must have computer skills and PageMaker experience. Resumes are reviewed and applicants contacted if needed. The company specializes in translation and typesetting for school districts in the US. Their software division creates custom CD-ROMs for Mac/Win in all languages. Maintains a pool of 20 translators.

Trans-Caribe Communications, Inc., 9109 Queen Elizabeth Court, Orlando, FL 32818   Phone: (407)260- Fax: (407)260-6349   e-mail: transcc@aol.com   Web site: www.iotrak.com/trans-caribe.html   Contact: Sherry E. Allen-Diaz   Member: ATA

Transcend, 2043 Anderson Rd., Ste. C, Davis, CA 95616   Phone: (530)756-5834 Fax:(756)756-4810 e-mail: end@transcend.com   Web site: www.transcend.com   Contact: M. Mindlin
Founded 1991. Recruiting translators in Chinese, Korean, Cambodian, Farsi and Lao, from English, and Japanese into English. Prospective translators should have 3+ years experience, accreditation or certification, professional standards, and Internet/FTP capabilities. Resumes are accepted only by fax and only for the languages listed above.

Transemantics, Inc., 4301 Connecticut Ave. NW, Ste. 146, Washington, DC 20008 Phone: (202)686-5600 Fax: (202)686-5603   Contact: M-L Wax Cooperman   Member: ATA

Transfirex Translation Services, Inc., 12509 Village Sq. Terr., #201, Rockville, MD 20852   Phone: (301)984-9753 Fax: (630)604-8323 e-mail: info@transfirex.com   Web site: www.transfirex.com   Contact: Margaret Johnson
Founded 2001. Member: ATA. Accepts resumes. Main languages are Turkish, German, Spanish, Italian, French and Portuguese. Mostly scientific, engineering, social sciences, and safety, emergency and rescue. Has a pool of 12 translators.

TRANSGLOBAL Language Services, 534 Princeton Cove, Memphis, TN 38117   Phone: (901)680-0927
Contact: Robyn Hassell

TransImage Inc., 145 Hudson St., 9th Fl., New York, NY 10013 hone: (212)274-0501 Fax: (212)274-0503 e-mail: Joseph@transimage.com Web site: www.transimage.com Contact: Joseph Ruiz   Member: ATA

Transimpex Translations, 8301 East 166th St., Belton, MO 64012 Phone: (816)561-3777 Fax:(816)561-5515 e-mail: transmpx@sound.net Web site: www.transimpex.com Contact: Ingrid Pelger or Doris Ganser
Founded 1974. Member: ATA. Trade Club of Greater Kansas City. Uses freelance translators and interpreters. Accepts unsolicited resumes. Resumes are put in database until needed. Requires degree in linguistics or translation. Main languages translated are German, French, Spanish, Portuguese, Italian, Japanese, Russian, and Italian. Translates all subjects, with long experience in localization. Has overall pool of some 5000 translators, with about 150 active ones.

Translation Aces, Inc., 29 Broadway, Ste. 2301, New York, NY 10006 Phone: (212)269-4660 Fax: (212)269-4662   Contact: Serge Nedeltscheff
Founded 1952. Member: NY Circle, NY Chamber of Commerce. Translates Spanish, French, German, Japanese Italian, Portuguese, Russian and Greek, both from and into English, as well as *all* other language pairs. Emphasis on Legal, Patent, Medical Financial, Scientific, Advertising, Engineering, and almost all other areas of translation. Prospective translators should have "experience, experience, experience." Resumes are responded to with the company's ap-plication form. The company has 45 years experience in providing the legal, financial, advertising, medical and governmental communities with translation, interpreting, voiceover and consulting services. Maintains a pool of about 400 translators.

Translation Company of America, Inc., 10 West 37th St., New York, NY 10018   Phone:(212)563-7054 Fax:(212)695-2385 e-mail: trude@tcany.com   Web site: www.languagematters.com   Contact: Trudi Mathys Member: ATA

Translation Company of New York, Inc., 8 South Maple Ave., Marlton, NY   08053 Phone: (856)983-4733 Fax: (856)983-4595 e-mail: tcny2000@cs.com   Web site: www.tcny.net   Contact: Betsy Lussi
Founded 1983. Member: ATA. Uses freelance translators and accepts unsolicited resumes. Translates mainly French, German,Spanish, Italian, Japanese, Portuguese, Dutch, Russian, Chinese and Swedish. Main areas are pharmaceutical, chemical, medical, engineering, and electronics. Does about 7-8 million words a year. Has active pool of 200 translators.

Translation Services, Inc., 5860 Forward Ave., Office #1, Pittsburgh, PA 15217   Phone: (412)242-8240 Fax: (412)242-1241 e-mail: ATA-info@translations.us.com Web site: www.translations.us.com
   Contact: Lisa M. Heinrich   Member: ATA

Translation Services International, Inc., 417 E Blvd., Ste. 204, Charlotte, NC 28203   Phone: (704)375-8530 Fax: (704)375-8540   e-mail: info@tsitranslation.com   Web site: www.tsitranslation.com
Contact: Robert E. Krasow   Member: ATA

Translations & Language Consulting, 8105 Hearthstone Place, Antelope, CA 95843   Phone: (916)729-4222 Fax: (916)729-4232 e-mail: emorrow@trans-language.com Web site: www.trans-language.com Contact: Elena Morrow   Member: ATA

Translations Unlimited, 1455 Forest Hill SE, Grand Rapids, MI 49546 Phone: (616)942-5742 Fax: (616)957-8551 e-mail: lmathews@calvin.edu   Contact: Leslie Mathews, Director
Founded 1980. Member: ATA. Accepts resumes. Main languages are French, Spanish, German, Japanese, Portuguese, Italian, and Vietnamese. Main areas are patents, sales literature, video scripts, and voice-overs, employee handbooks, sales literature, legal documents, and technical specifications. Translator pool of 25-30.

translations.com, 3 Park Ave., 37th Fl., New York, NY 10016 Phone: (212)689-1616 Fax: (212)685-9797 e-mail: LRC@translations.com Web site: www.translations.com Contact: Pamela Kraljevich
Founded 1999. Member: ATA. Accepts resumes. Translates mainly Spanish, French, German, Chinese, Japanese, Portuguese, Italian, Korean, Norwegian and Swedish. Mostly software, IT-Telecom, finance, travel and medical. Provides full suite of globalization services. Pool of 500 translators.

Translation3, 49 Union Park, #2, Boston, MA 02118 Phone: (617)482-2223 Fax: (617)482-2121 e-mail: jjtranslation3@translation3.com   Web site: www.translation3.com   Contact: Jacqueline M. Jacquiot Member: ATA

The Translators, PO Box 303, Topsfield, MA 01983 Phone: (508)887-9234 Fax: (508)887-6657 e-mail: trnslate@shore.net   Web site: www.thetranslatorsinc.com Contact: Maria Salmon
Founded 1980. Accepts resumes. Translates all languages, mostly medical, patents, human resources, computer, sci-tech, legal, electronic and engineering. Unlimited translator pool.

Translingua, Inc., 5457 Twin Knolls Rd., Columbia, MD 21045 Phone: (410)730-9700 Fax: (410)730-9736 e-mail: moneill@translingua.com Web site: www.translingua.com Contact: Mary J. O'Neill
Founded 1984. Member: ATA, NCATA, STC, CATI. Translates French, Italian, German, Spanish, Japanese, Chinese, Korean, Swedish, Danish, Portuguese, Russian, Hebrew, and Italian from English. Emphasis on technical, scientific, medical, financial, software, packaging and labeling, marketing and advertising. Specialty in full-service graphics and high resolution double byte output. Prospective translators should have an area of expertise as well as a computer, email, modem, and fax. Resumes are screened, evaluated and databased. The company's translations, often large and multi-lingual, are aimed at publication and the end user. It provides services for the entire process from project management to printing. Maintains a pool of more than 1000 translators.

Transperfect, 2536 Barstow Ave., Clovis, CA 93611 Phone: (554)323-8915 Fax: (554)298-8996 e-mail: mortrans@lightspeed.net Web site: www.thetranslators.com Contact: Morton S. Rothberg
Founded 1992. Member: ATA, Fresno Chamber of Commerce, SJVITA, Hispanic Chamber. Uses freelance translators and interpreters. Accepts unsolicited resumes. Resumes are classified, graded, and filed. Requires college degree with specific language native ability, computer, e-mail. Main languages are Spanish, French, Portuguese, German, Chinese, Japanese, and Italian. Main areas are food industry and legal. Has affiliate offices in Europe, South America, and the Far East. Pool of 250 translators.

Transperfect Translations International, Inc., 3 Park Ave., 28th Fl., New York, NY 10016 Phone: (212) 689-5555 Fax: (212)251-0981 e-mail: info@transperfect.com Web site: www.transperfect.com Contact: Information Member: ATA

Transtek Associates, Inc., 599 North Avenue, Door 9, Wakefield, MA 01888 Phone: (781) 245-7980 Fax: (781)245-7993 e-mail: michele@transtekusa.com Web site: www.transtekusa.com   Contact: Michele Phillips
Founded 1964. Member: ATA. Uses freelance translators and interpreters. Accepts unsolicited resumes.

Tristan Translations, 1130 Taylor St., San Francisco, CA 94108 Phone:(415)474-2611 Fax:(415)928-4755 e-mail: tristant@ix.netcom .com   Contact: Marc de Tristan, Jr., Owner.
Founded 1978. Accepts resumes. Translates Spanish, German, Chinese, Japanese, Portuguese, French, Italian, and numerous other languages, both from and into English. Emphasis on Patents, Technical Document, Proposals and RFQ, Discovery Document and Insurance Claim translation. Prospective translators should exhibit fluency in the English resume or phone contact, education and word processing and file transfer skills. Resumes are read with an eye to flaws, and if approved, entered into a database for future work. Maintains a pool of over 100 translators.

Tru Lingua Language Systems, Inc., 2081 Business Center Drive, Irvine, CA 92626 Phone: (949)955-1151 Fax: (949)955-1153 e-mail: Trulingua@aol.com Contact: Diana Knapstein
Founded 1984. Accepts resumes. Translates mainly Spanish, French, German, Dutch, Portuguese and Japanese. Mostly technical, medical and lega. Prospective translators should be ATA certified, ATA members, and possess wide experience. Maintains a pool of over 350 translators.

Trustforte Language Services, 271 Madison Ave., 3rd Fl., New York, NY 10016 Phone: (212)481-4980 Fax: (212)481-4972 e-mail: aschroeder@trustforte.com Web site: www.trustfortelanguages.com Contact: Jackie Cordero
Founded 1992. Member: ATA. Accepts resumes. Works in most languages. Provides translators and interpreters to a variety of fields, from business to entertainment.

turkishtranslation.com, MSR Consulting Ltd., 33 N. High St., Clinton, CT 06143 Phone: (860)669-2777 Fax: (909)363-9150 e-mail: info@turkishtranslation.com Web site: www.turkishtranslation.com Contact: Asiye Yucel Member: ATA

-U-

Uniscape, Inc., 1292 Hammerwood Ave., Sunnyvale, CA 94089 Phone: (408)743-3500 Fax: (408)743-3600 Web site: www.uniscape.com Contact: Seda P. Mansour Member: ATA

United International Services, Inc., 12701 W. Warren, Dearborn, MI 48126 Phone: (313)846-6903 Fax: (313)846-4278 Contact: Faye Awada Member: ATA

United Nations Translators & Interpreters, Inc., 1515 E. Livingston St., Orlando, FL 32803 Phone: (407)894-6020 Fax: (407)894-6693 e-mail: unti@unti.com Web site: www.unti.com Contact: Fiona Como
Founded 1991. Member: ATA. Accepts resumes. Translates mainly Spanish, Creole, French, German, Italian, Farsi, Italian, Portuguese and Vietnamese. Mostly legal, medical, technical and INS documents. Uses about 50 translators.

Universal Dialog, 4909 Murphy Canyon Rd., Ste. 301, San Diego, CA 92123 Phone: (858)503-0010 Fax: (858)503-1935 e-mail: email@universaldialog.com Web site: www.universaldialog.com Contact: Alexandra Briskin Member: ATA

University Language Center, Inc., 1313 Fifth St. SE, Ste. 201, Minneapolis, MN 55414 Phone:(612)379-3574 Fax:(612)379-3832 e-mail: translation@ulanguage.com Web site: ulanguage.com Contact: Therese Shafranski, Translation Department Manager
Founded 1986. Member: ATA. Accepts resumes. Translates Spanish, French, German, Italian, Portuguese, Russian, Chinese, Japanese and Hmong, as well as Turkish, Indonesian, Italian and all Southeast Asian languages. Emphasis in all technical areas. The company handles all phases of production from translation to camera-ready art, including cultural assessment of the source documents. Maintains a pool of 250 translators.

U.S. Translation Company, 3701 Harrison Blvd., Ogden UT 84403 Phone: (801)393-5300 Fax: (801) 393-5500 e-mail: info@ustranslation.com Web site: www.ustranslation.com Contact: David Utrilla Member: ATA

-V-

Vanguard Academy, 6925 Turtlewood Drive, Houston, TX 77072 Phone: (281)530-9895 Fax: (281)575-0301 e-mail: vanguardacademy@hotmail.com Contact: Wendy Wang Member: ATA

Veduccio, Levine, Coleman, Sampson & Partners, 29 Winchester St., Boston, MA Phone: (617)574-0040 Fax: (617)574-0041 e-mail: Contact@veduccio.com Web site: www.veduccio.com Contact: Russell Veduccio Member: ATA

Ventwi Technology Partners, 400-1 Totten Pond Rd., Waltham, MA 02451 Phone: (781)890-7007 Fax: (781)890-4433 e-mail: mklinger@ventwipartners.com Web site: www.ventwipartners.com Contact: Michael L. Klinger
Founded: 1993. Member: ATA, NETA, STC. Accepts resumes. Translates mainly Japanese, French, Italian, German, Spanish, Korean, Chinese, Portuguese, Hebrew and Italian. Mostly software, medical and pharmaceutical. Has a pool of 500 translators.

Vice-Versa Translations, 2707 N. Surrey, Carrollton, TX 75006   Phone: (972)418-6969
e-mail: gqs@earthlink.net   Contact: Emilio Santiago   Member: ATA

Vital International Programs, Inc., 2300 W. Big Beaver Rd., Ste. 17, Troy, MI 38084   Phone: (248)649-2905
Fax: (248)649- 2962 e-mail: vitalinter@aol.com   Web site: www.vitalinternational.com   Contact: Member:
ATA

Voices for Health, Inc., 894 Fuller NE, #2, Grand Rapids, MI 49503 Phone: (616)458-8388 Fax: (616)458- 8322
e-mail: info@voicesforhealth.com   Web site: www.voicesforhealth.com Contact: Scott Van Til, Translations;
Iness Quillen, Interpretation.
Founded 1997. Member: ATA. Accepts resumes. Translates mainly Spanish, Vietnamese, Chinese and Italian. Mostly healthcare
and social services. Uses hundreds of linguists.

Vormbrock Translations, Inc., 10415 Jockey Club Drive, Houston, TX 77065   Phone: (281)894-9722   Fax:
(281)890-0062   e-mail: VTITrans@pdq.net   Web site: www.vormbrock.com Member: ATA

-W-

WKI International Communications, 27 W. 20th St., Ste. 402, New York, NY 10011   Phone: (212)255-6100
Fax: (212)255-8461   e-mail: smwoodruff@wkiintl.com   Web site: www.wkiintl.com Contact: Susan Woodruff
Member: ATA

Welocalize.com, 241 E. 4th St., Ste. 207, Frederick, MD 21701 Phone: (301)668-0330   Fax: (301)668-0335
e-mail: info@welocalize.com   Web site: www.welocalize.com Contact: E. Smith Yewell   Member: ATA

Wizards Of The Coast, Inc., P.O. Box 707, Renton, WA 98057 Fax: (425)204-5806
Web site: www.wizards.com   Contact: David Serra   Member: ATA

Word for Word, Inc., 325 W. Chickasaw Rd., Virginia Beach, VA 23462   Phone: (757)557-0131
Fax: (757)557-0186   e-mail: wrd4wrd@exis.net   Contact: Curtis Hovey   Member: ATA
WORDNET, Inc., 282 Central St., Ste. 2, P.O. Box 976, Acton, MA 01720   Phone: (978)264-0600 Fax:(978)263-
3839
e-mail: wordnet@wordnet.com Web site: www.wordnet.com   Contact: lee Chadeayne
Founded 1985. Member: ATA, German-American Business Council. Uses freelance translators and interpreters. Accepts
unsolicited resumes. Resumes are reviews and applicants are sent out forms to fill out, and are periodically tested and evaluated.
Main languages translated are French, Spanish, German, Italian, Chinese, Japanese, and Korean. Main areas are technical,
medical, machinery, legal, and business/marketing. The company specializes in translation, typesetting and printing, preparing
brochures, catalogs, manuals, legal agreements and Web pages.They help companies get started in the international marketplace.
Maintains a pool of some 2000 translators.

Worldwide Translations, Inc., 1 Warren Way, Amherst, NH 03031 Phone: (800)293-0412 Fax:(603)672-5574
e-mail: wwtranslate@cs.com Web site: www.wwtranslations.com   Contact: Jared Tardie
Founded 1994. Member: ATA, RAPS, FDLI, DIA, NAJIT. Accepts resumes. Translates mainly French, Italian, German,
Spanish, Dutch, Portuguese, Greek, Swedish, Japanese and Chinese. Emphasis on Medical, Machinery Manufacture and
Computer Products translation. Prospective translators should be native-speaking ATA members with 3+ years technical
translation experience and references. Resumes are responded to by telephone when work becomes available. The company is
expert in the CE Mark and Medical Device areas and specializes in the translation of instructional manuals. They hold their
translators to a high standard of accuracy. Maintains a pool of over 100 translators.

The Write Stuff, 11000 Lake City Way, NE, Seattle, WA 98125 Phone: (206)548-1111 Fax: (206)548-9116
e-mail: translations@writestuff.com   Web site: www.writestuff.com   Contact: Susan Hedding Member: ATA

Wudang Research Association, 8229 Perry St., Overland Park, KS 66204   Phone: (913)385-1975
e-mail: tmorgan@wudang.com   Web site: www.wudang.com   Contact: Theresa M. Morgan   Member: ATA

APPENDIX F: COMPUTERS, TRANSLATION, AND THE INTERNET

Digital technology as it relates to translation and to almost anything else in today's world is in a constant state of change. In the nearly three years since this handbook was last revised, computers have become more dominant in the translation craft. More work is now being transmitted electronically by e-mail attachment rather than by fax. The Internet has become a routine tool for translators – from work search to word search. And a growing number of translators has become involved in the translation of such computer-based material as websites, a process now generally referred to as localization. All this has resulted in this newly revised and expanded chapter that looks at all the above developments and how they benefit or fail to benefit translators.

Once you have read this chapter you will be glad to find out that one thing has not changed, which should come as no surprise: translation continues to be a human, rather than a machine function. Computers are no closer now to replacing human translation than they were three years ago, or at any other time in the past. Notwithstanding the great benefits translators are deriving from the digital revolution, computers continue to be the tools, rather than the decision-makers of the translation process.

Computers and Related Equipment

As was mentioned before, only a few years ago a translator would use a pen or a typewriter to translate. In 1980, for example, the ultimate text-producing tool in the world was the IBM Selectric electric typewriter, which we thought we would proudly bequeath to our children and grandchildren. All of this changed forever with the birth of the word processor, and more specifically, the PC, or Personal Computer, which is getting better every year, as if it were a magical tool with boundless possibilities. Certainly the PC has changed the lives of translators, increasing their productivity and profitability three- and fourfold, and enabling them to receive and transmit work, look for answers to linguistic questions, communicate around the world, and take advantage of computer-assisted tools (see below) that in certain cases can save a great deal of time and effort.

Bare Minimum Hardware and the Wish List

The electronic age offers a great deal more than the word-processor. There is the fax, modem, optical scanner, e-mail, various types of translation software such as translation memory, and last but not least, the Internet. No doubt, it all seems quite overwhelming. Which is the best tool? How much should I spend? How much do I need?

Perhaps the best way to start is by asking two questions: What is the bare minimum a translator needs to get started, and, if money were no object, what would be my wish list of electronic equipment?

The first thing you need to get is a good, current personal computer. This is a must. The question is whether to get a desktop PC, or a portable notebook? The desktop PC is bigger, heavier, has a larger, easier-to-read screen, and an easier-to-use keyboard. The notebook, on the other hand, only weighs a few pounds, can fit in your briefcase, can be used anywhere (it has a rechargeable battery that gives you several hours of use), and, like a toothbrush, becomes a truly personal item. This book is being revised on a three-year-old IBM ThinkPad notebook. Though thin (1.8 inches) and flimsy-looking, it is a real powerhouse. The base price was $1,699.00. For $99.98 I upgraded the memory from 32MB RAM (see glossary in the back of the book) to 64MB. For $225.98 I got a second battery for more cordless computing hours while traveling. For $237.98 I got a 3-year warrantee for parts and service. It has a 266MHz Intel Pentium II processor, 3.2GB of hard drive space (upgradable to 6.4GB), a 56K modem, a 3.5 inch disk drive, and a CD-ROM drive which at the moment hosts a disk containing the entire Encyclopedia Britannica. The color monitor, a 12-inch SVGA, has good, sharp resolution. It operates on Microsoft Windows® 98. I use it mainly for word-processing, for e-mail, to surf the net, occasionally for graphics, and sometimes to hear music. At the moment it has some 25 programs, including WordPerfect 6.0 for Windows, MS Word, Lotus Notes, as well as my Internet provider, to mention only a few.

To me as a translator and a writer, this notebook is the best of all possible worlds. On the other hand, many translators prefer a desktop PC for all sorts of reasons, not all of which are known to me. Since I have access to both, it's hard for me to judge. My suggestion to you is to check around and try both, and make your own decision. But again, a translator without a computer in this day and age is like a painter without brushes. One more thing: The standard computer for translators is the IBM or IBM-compatible. The Macintosh, favored by graphics people, is not nearly as widely used in our circles, so we will concentrate here on the former.

The above configuration of my notebook computer, which one can also get in a desktop PC (except for the batteries), is quite close to what a translator would consider a "wish list" configur-ation. Keep in mind that there is a vast difference between storing text and storing graphics on a hard drive. One hundred pages of text take less disk space that one or two pages of graphics. If your translation work entails extensive graphics, you need a bigger hard drive and a faster computer, and the cost can go up 50%-100%. Most translators, however, do not have such a need. Instead, they can store data on their hard drive, and when it gets too crowded, they transfer files to a disk.

The other item that's a must is a printer. Although you can deliver text on disk or by e-mail, there are many good reasons why you need a printer. First, there is still a widespread requirement for hard copy. Second, you may want to print drafts to check your translation, and third, you need a printer for correspondence, for printing your resume, and certainly for printing an invoice. We recommend the Hewlett Packard family of printers, particularly the LaserJets. Depending on the volume, you can start with a smaller model and go up to the HP 4+ or a newer model, which is a bit faster and better.

The next item that's a must is the facsimile machine, popularly known as the fax. These days information travels very fast, and a sure way to get translation assignments is via the fax. Once you have translated a document, the fastest way to send it back is as an e-mail attachment. In other words, the basic translator tools today are the computer, the printer, the fax and the modem.

Another item you may want to look into is the optical scanner, starting with a recent model of the HP ScanJet family.
Be sure to get it with the OCR, or Optical Character Reader. This optional piece of equipment provides two valuable functions—you can scan text from a page into a disk, which can be a great timesaving shortcut, and you can scan graphics, such as tables and photographs, into your text file.

What about the cost? You can easily spend around $5,000 on the above four items, if you go directly to the top of the line. But you don't have to start at the top of the line. You can start a couple of notches below the top, and still be able to give yourself a decent start.

You could, if you really want to watch your pennies, take advantage of the fact that computers are changing so fast, and look in the paper for a year or two old second-hand computer, but not older. You should be able to find a good one for $400-$800. You can do the same with the printer, by getting a second-hand one for about $100, or a new one for about $300-$400. A good modem (at least a 28.8 or higher) can be found for around $100, although you could spend $300-$400. A plain paper fax machine (thermal paper is out) can be found for around $200-$400, or you could start out by using a local service, like Kinko's. In short, you could get started with the basic equipment for as little as $600-$700 if you had to, and go on from there. As you prosper, you can start upgrading.

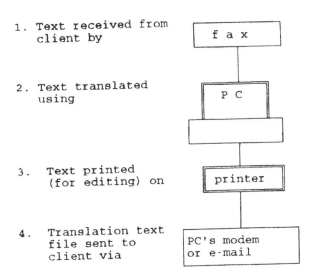

1. Text received from
   client by

2. Text translated
   using

3. Text printed
   (for editing) on

4. Translation text
   file sent to
   client via

Other Useful Kinds of Software

You can use your word-processing software for doing record-keeping and invoicing as well, but if your operation becomes more involved you may want to consider a database program, such as Excel, for record-keeping (and also for other databases, such as glossaries), and some basic invoicing program, which only runs $20-$30.

A typical translation process and the required hardware

To protect your computer against computer viruses—the dreaded new computer age affliction—you may want to get a program such as Norton AntiVirus. To be able to retrieve lost text, you need the Norton Utilities program. Both are excellent safety measures. Another safety measure is the constant backing up of all your files. This can be done on the hard drive or on an external medium such as floppy disk or CD disk. Computers are great when they work, but when they fail they can cause you serious losses, which you cannot afford.

For word-processing, translators uses mainly Microsoft Word, but also WordPerfect, the old favorite.

Foreign Language Software

English-language word-processing is the most advanced in the world. Great strides have been made in programs for other languages, but there is still a long way to go. Some languages, such as Russian, Chinese, Japanese, Italian and Hebrew are simply too complex in either their script or their noun and verb forms or both to lend themselves to, say, spell-check as readily as English. So don't expect to "cruise" as easily in those languages as you do in English. However, if you translate text from English into almost any other language, you are expected these days to deliver the text on electronic media, which means getting involved in word-processing in that language (see Appendix 3, Foreign Language Software Sources).

As a translator from English into a foreign language, you need software that accommodates not only your target-language, but also the source-language, namely, English. Sometimes you'll need to include English text in the body of your Chinese or Italian text. Also, you have to make sure your foreign language software is compatible with English-language software, so that it can interface with your client's equipment. Therefore, we are focusing here on American-made foreign language software, rather than foreign-made.

Foreign Language Software Sources

In recent years the leading source for European languages software was WordPerfect. Its language modules covered a large variety of languages, and there were frequent upgrades. The WordPerfect foreign language modules are still used by many translators, but the trend is shifting to the localized products of Microsoft. These products use the Unicode system which makes Microsoft's English word processing compatible with its foreign versions, enabling the user to use English and foreign word processing in the same document with relative ease. Microsoft's foreign language word processing is now part of its package of English word processing, which eliminates the high cost only a few years ago of buying foreign language modules separately.

Machine Translation Vs. Human Translation

Machine Translation, or MT, is the term used to describe trans-lation performed by a computer software program, as an alter-native to human translation (HT), performed by a human translator. Machine Translation belongs in the area of artificial intel-ligence. Artificial intelligence is the branch of computer science that deals with using computers to simulate human thinking. It looks to create programs that can solve problems *creatively,* rather than merely respond to commands. In other words, to operate just like the human brain.

In the late 1950s people in organizations such as the U.S. Air Force believed that computers would soon be programmed to accept human language input and translate it into English or into any other language. During the following 50 years, millions of dollars were spent by the Air Force and by other U.S. Government bodies and by big business in the hope of having computers take over the human function of translation. So far, the results have been quite limited, for two main reasons: (a) while computers have a seemingly unlimited capacity for processing data, they are a long way from having the capacity to think creatively like human beings; and (b) human language is not merely a collection of signs and symbols that can be easily programmed, manipulated, and computerized. This is true of human language used not only in poetry and philosophy, but also in technical subjects, in which language expresses thought processes far more complicated than merely "one plus one equals two."

Many people today maintain that computers will soon replace translators. Most of those people are not translation experts. In fact, hardly any of them are. Some point to the fact that computers have already replaced typists and secretaries and reduced the work force of many companies. All this reminds me of a remark by George Bernard Shaw, according to which a monkey could write *Hamlet* if it managed to hit all the right keys on the typewriter. Very few translators can lay claim to creating literary works on the order of *Hamlet*, but lumping translators with typists and office support staff is missing the whole point of translation. As long as language continues to communicate more than the immediate literal meaning of words, as long as there are shades of meaning that keep changing all the time, as long as people have to make value judgments about the meaning and intent of a text, one will continue to need human translators to get the job done.

In recent years several companies in the U.S. and around the world have produced software designed to translate from one language into another. This software varies from a very basic word finder for the tourist, to complex programs for translating technical and scientific data. Some of the latter range in price from as low as $250 to as high as $250,000, and have been sold to governments and international organizations. One important lesson, however, has been learned by both the makers of those programs and their consumers. Machine translation does not replace human translation. At best, the former can achieve around 60 percent accuracy, when the goal is as close to 100 percent as possible. Consequently, the expectations regarding MT have been modified, and it is now recognized that to achieve full accuracy such translations must be post-edited by a human translator.

All of the above notwithstanding, Machine Translation does have its uses. Certain limited language environments do allow for machine translation. One example is the Canadian weather bureau, which transmits weather reports in both English and French. The number of words involved in the daily weather report is very limited, and can be easily programmed into a computer for translation from one language into another. Another example is official forms which contain simple basic questions. An organization such as NATO can have forms put out in ten different languages and set up a program to automatically translate each form into those languages. A third example is the Caterpillar company in Illinois that sells its agricultural machinery around the world and maintains operation manuals in various languages. This company has invested millions in its in-house translation software which allows it to update and modify its technical literature in a cost-effective way. In all of the above examples the software was customized for one particular work environment where repetition is the common denominator.

Another use of machine translation is for processing a large body of a foreign language text to find out what the gist of it is, rather than to achieve a fully accurate translation, in order to decide whether on not to select parts of it for accurate (viz., human) translation. This process is only partially reliable.

Translators for the most part are not fond of post-editing machine translation. Often the pay is not adequate, and the work can be harder and more time consuming than translating directly from the original. This certainly applies to freelancers, but also to in-house translators who are on a salary.

At the present time the ones who benefit the most from machine translation are not those who buy such services, but rather the companies who develop and manufacture the software and the translators who work on those machine translation projects either as developers of the programs or editors of the machine-translated text. In other words, machine translation has not made translation cheaper for the average consumer of trans-lation services, and therefore does not pose a real threat to translators.

Example of machine translation from Russian into English:

Raw machine translation: A contemporary airport is the involved complex of engineer constructions and techniques, for arrangement of which the territory, measured sometimes is required by thousands of hectares (for example the Moscow Airport Domodedovo, Kennedy's New York airport).

Text edited by humans: The modern airport is an elaborate complex of engineering structures and technical devices requiring a large territory, which, in some places, measures thousands of hectares (for instance, Domodedovo Airport in Moscow or Kennedy Airport in New York).

Translation Memory

One computer tool commonly used today in the area of computer-assisted-translation (CAT) is called translation memory. Here sentences and other parts of translated texts are stored and can be used again when the same or similar translation is required. This tool is best applied to major projects, such as automotive operation manuals that are updated or modified on a regular basis, whereby most of the text remains the same while certain sentences and/or paragraphs are changed.

While this tool has its practical uses, it has been hyped beyond its actual application and has been promoted as a universal aid for translators in nearly all types of translation. Here one should be careful not to invest in this kind of software unless one has a clear ongoing use for it. This applies both to individual translators and to translation companies, since in both cases only a small percentage of the work done is of the above-described kind.

Furthermore, as in the case of machine translation and localization (see below), here too the tools are far from able to accomplish their stated goals, and are still being improved upon. Translation memory is certainly not human memory, and while it does work part of the time, human memory remains irreplaceable.

Localization

Localization is defined as "the process of creating or adapting a product to a specific locale, i.e., to the language, cultural context, conventions and market requirements of a specific target market. With a properly localized product a user can interact with this product using his or her own language and cultural conventions. It also means that all user-visible text strings and all user documentation (printed and electronic) use the language and cultural conventions of the user. Finally, the properly localized product meets all regulatory and other requirements of the user's country or region."

Clearly, this definition takes us out of the strict realm of translation into the domain of computer programming and international business. It alludes primarily to the localization of websites (as well as software) in other languages and cultures. Two other terms often used in conjunction with localization are internationalization and globalization. The first refers to the preparation of computer text to be used in localization in such a way that it meets the requirements of the target language and culture. Globalization generally refers to both processes together, namely, internationalization and localization.

With the fast proliferation of websites and the rapid growth of many kinds of computer software, a growing number of translation companies have ventured into the field of localization, and more than a few computer hardware- and software-producing companies (including giants like IBM and Microsoft) have turned to the field of translation as a function of localization.

Thus, localization has been presenting translators with new opportunities and some difficult questions. On the one hand, there is a huge volume of text these days in website and software development that necessitates multilingual translation. On the other hand, for a translator to become involved in localization a specialized knowledge of computers is usually required, since website and software localization requires not only language translation but also adaptation of computer commands to the requirements of the target language. Hence, a translator may want to carefully consider how far he or she may wish to become involved in technical computer work that requires skills and training beyond the scope of actual translation work.

It should be mentioned that localization in the sense of translating a text and adapting it to another culture existed long before the computer age. Thus, for example, an American advertisement company in the pre-computer era that planned an international ad campaign for a company such as Coca Cola, had to study the cultures of other countries and customize the ads not only in terms of the target language, but also the cultural conventions, preferences, taboos etc. of the target country. Furthermore, the act of translating itself is in a sense a form of localization, since language does not exist separately from its culture.

Website and software localization has been around now for several years. It relies heavily not only on human translation but also on machine and machine-assisted translation tools, such as translation software and translation memory. Given the limitations of these tools, the often unrealistic expectations of the marketplace and the eagerness to process a large volume of material in record time, localization has been experiencing many problems, and the goals its pursuers have set for themselves are yet to be realized. One should keep all of this in mind before getting involved in this area of translation.

The Uses of the Internet for Translators

The translation field has become increasingly "wired," witnessing a proliferation of sites relating to professional activities, job-hunting, commercial products, and online reference materials for translators. It is not an exaggeration to say that translators do themselves (and potentially their clients) quite a disservice by ignoring the virtual translation community.

This section will introduce you to a selection of highly-regarded and well-maintained sites of use to translators. It assumes basic Web literacy. Of course, the Internet's ever-changing nature guarantees that certain websites will decline or disappear, while new ones will emerge by the time this book becomes available. So please be aware that you will probably have to do some updating of the following information on your own.

Where We Are on the Web

First, let us invite you to Schreiber Publishing's website. Our address: **schreiberpublishing.com**. It first went online in March 1996. Its objective is to provide reference literature, training materials, and useful information for translators. We fully intend to keep expanding it, and we hope all translators will benefit from it.

Professional Activities

Translators wishing to learn about the state of their profession will benefit from a visit to the American Translators Association's site, **www.atanet.org**. I discuss the ATA in greater detail in the chapter on Translators' Organizations; its Website includes information on the Association's formal activities such as conferences, publications and accreditation procedures. Even if you are not an ATA member, the site is useful because it can guide you to other translation-related sites. Another major website of interest to translators is the site of the
international umbrella organization of the world's translator associations, the International Federation of Translators, found on **www.fit-ift.org**.

Aquarius, at **www.aquarius.net.** Claims to be "the world's language network." This commercial website lists translation agencies seeking translators and interpreters who, in turn, can post resumes to make their services known. It also links to other translation sites.

Networking with Other Translators

An extremely popular program on the Internet for translators has been the *Language Forum* of Compuserve, popularly known as FLEFO (Foreign Language Education Forum). You have to subscribe to this forum to be able to participate. You enter FLEFO in the keyword box and you find yourself in a virtual forum full of translators from around the world, who post messages and get answers to almost any question a translator may ask, from the cost of a dictionary, to the meaning of a word, to a social get-together. FLEFO can also link you to translation web- sites.

Another online forum for translators is the newsgroup: subscribers post messages and receive answers (say, to a specialized translation query). A newsgroup for translators is sci.lang. translation.

Reference Materials

The Translator's Home Companion at **www.rahul.net/lai/ companion.html**, provides Links to glossaries, dictionaries, translation publications, and other translators.

The Human Languages Page at **www.june29.com/IDP** provides links to other translation-related sites, including some listed here.

Language Today, an online publication (also available in print; see Bibliography appendix) covering language technology, translation and interpreting: **logos.it/language_today**

Online Dictionary Services

Eurodicautom at **www.europa.eu.int/eurodicautom** is a very useful service, Eurodicautom handles European languages such as Spanish, Portuguese, French, German, Italian, English, Danish and Dutch. Includes many specialized dictionaries in non-technical, legal and technical areas. Terms are both translated and defined.

Online Dictionaries at **www.yourdictionary.com** covers a far greater range of languages than the above entry. It provides links to dictionaries and translations in many specializations.

Glossaries

There are many mediocre glossaries out there in cyberspace, so use caution with this type of online resource. Here are some better ones:

www.refer.fr/termisti/liste.htm

www.yahoo.com/references/dictionaries

U.S. Government agencies provide some very useful glossaries. For example:

www.epa.gov (for environmental terminology).

Finding Cultural Information

A quick way to access cultural and historical information on other countries is via The Electronic Embassy at **www.embassy.org.** This service provides links to embassy and/or United Nations home pages of many nations. Most countries' pages include links to cultural resources such as online newspapers, libraries, and so on. You may have to do some digging to find the information you're after, but if it exists online, you will probably find it by starting here. Also the foreign ministries of various countries are a good source for all sorts of information related to that particular country.

Shopping for Dictionaries

A prime source for dictionaries is i.b.d. Ltd.'s website is:
www.ibdltd.com.
Another site under construction is: **www.schoenhofs.com**.
Major virtual bookstores also have good selections of dictionaries (see box). Examples:
www.barnesandnoble.com
www.amazon.com
www.borders.com
You may also wish to consult these websites of major dictionary publishers:
Elsevier at **www.elsevier.com**
Routledge at **www.routledge.com**
McGraw-Hill at **www.mcgraw-hill.com**

Machine Translation

If you want to experience some machine translation, try these two sites:
www.babelfish.com/Languages/English/EnglishMachine.shtml
http://babelfish.altavista.com

Order Form

Fax order to 443-920-3450,
or **e-mail** to SchreiberPublishing@comcast.net,
or **mail** to: **Schreiber Publishing**, PO Box 4193 Rockville, MD 20849 USA
or **call** toll free 1-800-296-1961 (in Maryland 301-725-3906)
or visit our website: **www.SchreiberLanguage.com**

_____ copies of *The Translator's Handbook* 8th Revised Ed. $25.95 $ _____

_____ copies of *American English Compendium* 2nd Revised Ed. List price: $24.95 You pay: $22.46 $ _____

_____ copies of *Spanish Business Dictionary* 3rd Edition. $24.95 $ _____

_____ copies of *Multicultural Spanish Dictionary, 2nd Ed* $24.95 $ _____

_____ copies of *Translator Self-Training* $69.00 <u>Circle language(s):</u>

     Spanish French German Russian Japanese Chinese Portuguese Italian Arabic Hebrew $ _____

_____ copies of *Translator Self-Training - Spanish Medical* $69.00 _ $ _____

_____ copies of *Translator Self-Training - Spanish Legal* $69.00 $ _____

sub-total $ _____

Maryland residents add 6% sales tax to sub-total $ _____

In the U.S. add $4.50 for shipping/handling per single copy and $2.00 for each additional book.
Overseas add US$9 for one book, and $5 for each additional book (for books priced under $50),
or $18 per book priced over $50 $ _____

Order total $ _____

Please charge my   Visa,   MasterCard;   Check or money order enclosed.

Name _____ Phone _____ E-mail _____
_____

Address_____ City _____ State____ Zip _____

Card No. _____ _____ _____ _____   Exp. date (month) ____ (year) ___